ENTREPRENEURS
WHO CHANGED HISTORY

ENTREPRENEURS
WHO CHANGED HISTORY

DK

SENIOR EDITOR: Victoria Heyworth-Dunne
SENIOR ART EDITOR: Stephen Bere
LEAD ILLUSTRATOR: Phil Gamble
EDITORS: Anna Cheifetz, Hannah Dolan, Joanna Edwards, Kathryn Hill, Helen Ridge, Alison Sturgeon
US EDITOR: Jennette ElNaggar
DESIGNER: Daksheeta Pattni
EDITORIAL ASSISTANT: Maisie Peppitt
SENIOR PICTURE RESEARCHER: Surya Sankash Sarangi
JACKET DESIGNERS: Priyanka Bansal, Surabhi Wadhwa-Gandhi
JACKET DESIGN DEVELOPMENT MANAGER: Sophia MTT
PRODUCTION EDITORS: Robert Dunn, Jacqueline Street-Elkayam
SENIOR PRODUCTION CONTROLLER: Rachel Ng
MANAGING EDITOR: Gareth Jones
SENIOR MANAGING ART EDITOR: Lee Griffiths
ASSOCIATE PUBLISHING DIRECTOR: Liz Wheeler
ART DIRECTOR: Karen Self
DESIGN DIRECTOR: Philip Ormerod
PUBLISHING DIRECTOR: Jonathan Metcalf
CONTRIBUTORS: Philippa Anderson, Jacob Field, Tim Harris, Ben Hubbard, Yuka Maeno, Robert Snedden

First American Edition, 2020
Published in the United States by DK Publishing
1450 Broadway, Suite 801, New York, NY 10018

Copyright © 2020 Dorling Kindersley Limited
DK, a Division of Penguin Random House LLC
20 21 22 23 24 10 9 8 7 6 5 4 3 2 1
001-316475-Sep/2020

A catalog record for this book is available from the Library of Congress.
ISBN 978-1-4654-9993-6

Printed and bound in Malaysia

For the curious
www.dk.com

CONTENTS

Entrepreneurs are individuals who dare to pursue their vision to create new businesses, products, or services, often at great personal risk. Their innovations not only drive progress and create opportunities, but they also make an indelible and lasting impact on our society.

New ideas have always been a fundamental component of economic growth and development. Without entrepreneurs, many great leaps forward would not have taken place. A foundation of the modern world, entrepreneurship is one of the chief means of increasing levels of production, alongside investment capital, labor, and natural resources.

However, despite entrepreneurs' overwhelmingly positive contribution to both society and the wider economy, their new enterprises are not always welcomed. Entrepreneurs often go against the grain, challenging the economic status quo in seeking to take advantage of an opportunity in the market, to introduce a bold new technology, or simply to follow a hunch. These individuals are risk-takers and prepared to jeopardize their reputations for a vision that may call for a substantial leap of faith. Ambitious, creative, resilient, and determined, entrepreneurs are prepared to overcome any obstacle in their commitment to an idea, often at great personal sacrifice. Failure can come at a heavy cost; equally, success can deliver huge financial and personal reward, as well as an enduring legacy.

The wheels of change

Examples of entrepreneurship can be found throughout history, although little is known about the lives of the economic innovators of the ancient world. The pioneers of the later medieval and early modern period are better documented.

At the time when the first roots of capitalism were beginning to emerge in Europe and eventually in North America, individuals turned from traditional ways of running businesses to experiment with new ideas. This led to developments such as international banking and Johannes Gutenberg's printing press.

By the early 19th century, the Industrial Revolution had transformed the world. Rates of economic growth and production soared as manufacturing was automated, made possible by inventions such as the steam engine. Modernization of transportation accelerated globalization, allowing entrepreneurs to build businesses across countries and even continents, and permitting industrialists like Andrew Carnegie and Cornelius Vanderbilt to amass huge fortunes.

As the 19th century progressed, innovation gathered pace. Thomas Edison spread electric power and light across the world. Meanwhile, the automobile was invented and assembly-line production allowed it to be manufactured for a mass market.

The first half of the 20th century saw entrepreneurs overcome the challenges of two world wars and the Great Depression. Visionaries like Coco Chanel, Walt Disney, and Clarence Saunders created empires in fashion, cinematic entertainment, and supermarket retail, respectively.

The potential opportunities—and risks—for entrepreneurs multiplied in the decades after World War II. The economy became increasingly globalized as modes of transportation and communication sped up. Oprah Winfrey and Richard Branson built business empires that covered a range of economic sectors, while pioneers like Bill Gates and Steve Jobs made computing technology a lynchpin of daily life.

Entrepreneurial impact
By the 1990s, the internet had emerged as a revolutionary force in the economy, forever altering traditional methods of doing business. Through seizing the opportunities that the digital economy has to offer, today's entrepreneurs, like

> ## "Many of life's failures are people who did not realize how close they were to success when they gave up."
>
> **Thomas Edison**, 1877

Jack Ma and Mark Zuckerberg, have the potential to capture the attention of billions of consumers, as well as gather information about—and potentially influence—their tastes and preferences.

Meanwhile, social entrepreneurship is growing, with the power to fix social problems in the long term by creating new institutions, such as Muhammad Yunus's concept of "microcredit" to help struggling entrepreneurs. This sector is likely to continue to expand in the wake of the COVID-19 pandemic and the ensuing global economic crisis, as people must apply innovative thinking to keep their businesses afloat.

Ultimately, however, entrepreneurs must still bring something novel to the marketplace to capture the attention and imagination of the consumer. Often, the best entrepreneurs are those who emerge during the most challenging of times and the most unstable of economies.

1

TRADE AND EXPLORATION

1360–1780

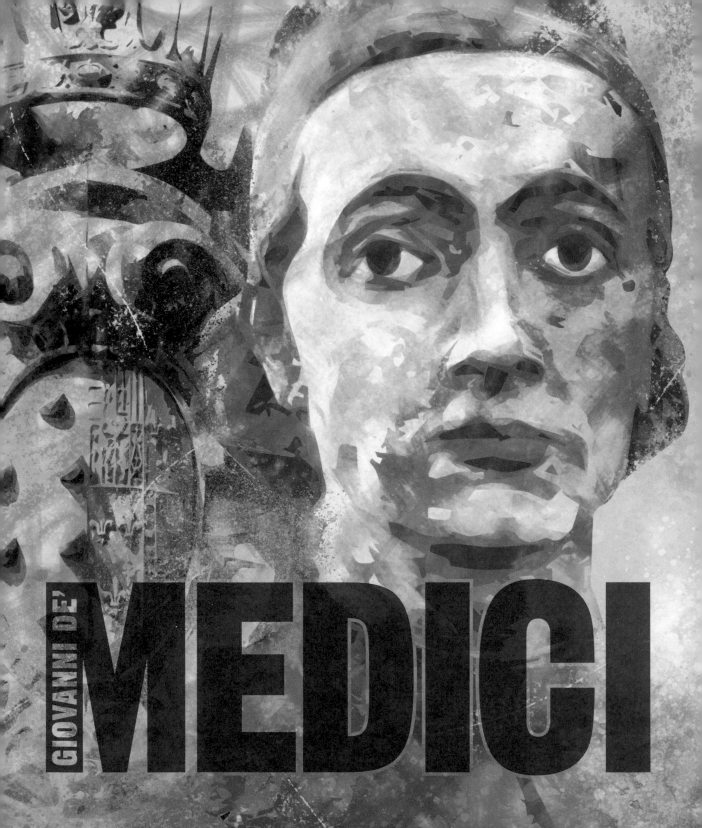

In founding the Medici Bank, the largest financial institution in 15th-century Europe, Giovanni de' Medici established the power base for the House of Medici. The family acquired vast wealth and political influence, becoming hereditary rulers of Florence and great patrons of the arts, architecture, and the sciences.

The Medici originated from the Mugello region of northern Tuscany, Italy. By the 14th century, many of the family had moved to Florence, where they were involved in its burgeoning banking sector. However, they were by no means the wealthiest family in a city that was becoming the greatest financial center in Europe. Giovanni di Bicci de' Medici was born around 1360. His father was not particularly successful, and when he died of plague in 1363, his estate amounted to only six florins to divide among his five sons.

The Medici Bank

Giovanni started his career in 1382 as an apprentice to his kinsman Vieri di Cambio de' Medici, who owned a bank in Florence. Giovanni was sent to work at its branch in Rome, servicing the needs of the bishops and cardinals who attended the papal court. He was so successful that he became its manager after three years, then a junior partner, and eventually took over from Vieri altogether by using his dowry to buy Vieri's stake. In 1393, Giovanni established the Rome branch of the bank as his own independent firm, taking on Benedetto di Lippaccio de' Bardi, a member from another

> " He died **exceedingly rich** in money, but still **more** in **good fame** and the **best wishes of mankind.**"

Niccolò Machiavelli, 1526

MILESTONES

BEGINS CAREER
Apprenticed to banker Vieri di Cambio de' Medici in 1382 and moves to work at his bank's Rome branch.

FOUNDS MEDICI BANK
In 1397, moves bank's head office, now in his control, from Rome to Florence as an independent firm.

COURTS INFLUENCE
Backs papal candidate Baldassarre Cossa in 1410, initiating a profitable relationship with papacy.

ENSURES STABILITY
Formally retires from banking business in 1420, handing over control to his sons Cosimo and Lorenzo.

> **"**I have not only **maintained** my reputation but **increased** my influence.**"**
>
> **Giovanni de' Medici**, 1429

GIOVANNI DE' MEDICI

COSIMO DE' MEDICI

LORENZO DE' MEDICI

Giovanni de' Medici's sons Cosimo and Lorenzo followed their father into the family banking business, helping secure the Medicis as the most powerful family in Europe, with unrivaled political, economic, and cultural influence.

THE HOUSE OF MEDICI

RECEIVED JUST 1⅕ FLORINS IN HIS FATHER'S WILL

WORTH **180,000 FLORINS** ON HIS DEATH

powerful Florentine banking family, as his partner. Four years later, he moved the bank's head office to Florence, effectively founding the Medici Bank.

The Rome branch continued to operate and was soon joined by new "banks" in Naples and Venice. Giovanni adopted a cautious business strategy and prioritized consolidation over rapid expansion. In addition to his banking business, he purchased properties in Florence, farmland in Tuscany, mines, and two woolen cloth workshops.

Politics and power

Giovanni was popular with the citizens of Florence and tried to avoid political intrigue. He reluctantly served as a member of the civic government in 1402, 1408, and 1411, and took up the prestigious office of *gonfaloniere* (titular head of Florence's government) only once, in 1421.

In 1420, Pope Martin V appointed the Medici Bank to act as papal bankers, which was crucial to the growing prosperity and power of the Medici family. That same year, Giovanni formally withdrew from the banking business. While his sons Cosimo and Lorenzo began to take on the signing of contracts, he continued to act as an advisor, ensuring a smooth transition. Giovanni urged his sons to remain aloof from civic

politics, advising them to become involved only if absolutely necessary. A modest man, Giovanni was made Count of Monteverde by Martin V in 1422, but he did not use the title, preferring to remain a citizen.

Medici's legacy

Giovanni contributed significantly to the improvement of Florence with several charitable projects, including a hospital for orphans. At the time of his death in 1429, Giovanni's careful succession plans ensured that the Medici Bank carried on its business without disruption and would, under the stewardship of his more able son Cosimo, continue to expand throughout Italy and beyond.

AMADEO P. **GIANNINI**

Founder of the Bank of Italy, and later the Bank of America, Amadeo P. Giannini built a banking empire that served ordinary people through local branches and fueled economic growth in the US.

Born in California to Italian immigrant parents, Giannini (1870–1949) founded the Bank of Italy in San Francisco in 1904, seeking out new customers among the city's working class. The bank flourished, and from 1909, Giannini was able to purchase other Californian banks. By 1918, the Bank of Italy had branches statewide. Giannini's bank continued to expand and, in 1930, changed its name to the Bank of America. By the time he died in 1949, it had more than 500 branches.

Johannes Gutenberg ushered in an age of mass literacy and learning in the 15th century through his invention of a printing press that used metal movable type. This revolutionary innovation marked the democratization of knowledge, enabling information to be disseminated more quickly and cheaply to a broader readership.

The son of a merchant, Johannes Gutenberg was born in the German city of Mainz around 1400 and trained as a goldsmith. By 1430, his family had fallen foul of disputes between commercial factions in Mainz and relocated to Strasbourg. Here, Gutenberg began to develop a range of money-making enterprises. One of these, which he attempted to keep secret, was a printing press. By 1448, he had returned to Mainz, where he borrowed money to fund his work.

Printing had been developed in China by the 3rd century CE, but reproducing texts remained expensive and time-consuming. Even by the 15th century in Europe, copies were still largely produced by hand. Gutenberg's press, which he finished in around 1450, would revolutionize the printing process. Its design, based on a winepress, applied an even pressure to paper or vellum, making the finished product more legible. Gutenberg combined this innovation with metal movable type. Early Asian printers had used wooden or clay blocks,

"exceedingly clean and correct in their script, and without error."

Aeneas Silvius Piccolomini, the future Pope Pius II, on the Gutenberg Bible, 1454

Examining a proof sheet that has just come off the press, Johannes Gutenberg is depicted in his workshop in this artist's impression.

JOHANNES GUTENBERG

1400–1468

GUTENBERG'S FIRST BIBLE COMPRISED 50,200 SHEETS OF PAPER

THE **GUTENBERG** PRESS PRINTED 3,600 PAGES PER DAY

BY 1500 THE **GUTENBERG** PRESS HAD PRINTED OVER 20 MILLION VOLUMES

which had the characters carved onto them. Gutenberg's cheaper and more durable type involved pouring a molten alloy (made of lead, tin, and antimony) onto brass letter molds. The letter blocks could then be arranged into the desired order for printing. He also developed a thick, oil-based ink that would stick to the metal blocks and transfer cleanly onto the paper.

First books

Scaling up his printing technology for commercial production required a large amount of capital, and Gutenberg borrowed heavily from a local financier, Johann Fust.

By 1455, the Gutenberg Press had been used to print a series of short documents, as well as a copy of the Bible in Latin.

Ironically, in the same year, Gutenberg faced financial ruin. Fust, tired of waiting for a return on his investment, sued Gutenberg for the repayment of his loan. The court ordered Gutenberg to repay him by handing over most of his printing equipment. Fust, assisted by his son-in-law Peter Schöffer, a calligrapher and printer who had worked for Gutenberg, continued to use the press, printing copies of the Bible as well as a Book of Psalms, which appeared in 1457.

Despite losing some assets in the settlement, Gutenberg continued to operate a printing workshop and may have printed a Breton-French-Latin dictionary from these premises. His activities appear to have declined, however, possibly as a result of failing eyesight. After a dispute over the control of Mainz erupted into violence in 1462, Gutenberg was forced to flee, moving to the nearby town of Eltville.

Gutenberg's method of printing spread throughout Germany. Despite this, he was not wealthy. In 1465, the Archbishop of Mainz granted him an annual pension in recognition of his achievements; he died three years later.

The Gutenberg Press signified the dawn of a new age of mass communication, but its most immediate impact proved to be spiritual. For the first time, Holy Scripture and other religious texts could be rapidly reproduced and read by the general public, helping to inspire the Protestant Reformation that swept across Europe during the 16th century.

CHARLES W. **HULL**

By inventing 3D printing, Colorado-born Charles ("Chuck") Hull has produced possibly one of the most revolutionary technologies of the last half century, with applications in all industries.

While working for a company that coated furniture with plastic using ultraviolet light, Hull (1939–) had the idea of layering the plastic to produce three-dimensional objects. In 1983, Hull began experimenting with computer-controlled ultraviolet light and using it to harden liquid resin into a desired shape. He called this process stereolithography. He patented his invention in 1986 and cofounded 3D Systems that same year. In 1987, 3D Systems created the first commercial 3D printer.

"The invention of **Gutenberg is** the **greatest event** that **history has recorded."**

Mark Twain, 1900

Movable type was first used in Korea in the 14th century, but Gutenberg's pioneering method of hand-molding metal blocks meant that letters could be produced quickly and in large quantities.

Jakob Fugger played a pivotal role in his family's domination of European banking and commerce during the 15th and 16th centuries. A successful financier and one of the first to lend money in exchange for shares in profits, he wielded more influence and power than some monarchs. He aptly came to be known as "Jakob the Rich."

The 10th of 11 children, Jakob Fugger was born in Augsburg, Germany, where his family had established themselves as successful textile merchants. As a young man, Fugger went to work in Venice and learned bookkeeping. He remained in Italy for seven years, then moved to Innsbruck to take charge of the Austrian wing of the family business. Fugger quickly proved his business acumen by negotiating a lucrative deal with the Habsburgs, an influential royal dynasty in central Europe. He advanced them long-term loans in exchange for a share of the profits from their copper and silver mines in the Tyrol region of the Alps.

These credit arrangements enabled the Fugger family to expand their own mining interests into Silesia (now Poland) and Neusohl (present-day Slovakia). They soon established a copper monopoly in these areas, generating huge profits by distributing the metal across Europe. Following the death of his elder brother Ulrich in 1510, Jakob became head of the Fugger family's business operations. A shrewd and hardworking leader, he launched the Fuggers into a variety of new business ventures, including trading spices, purchasing land, and moneylending; they loaned huge sums to crowned heads across Europe.

By the time Fugger died in 1525, his family were the most powerful financiers in Europe. Having had no children of his own, Fugger bestowed the family business on his nephew Anton, under whose equally enterprising leadership it reached peak levels of wealth in the mid-16th century.

"Second to none in the acquisition of extraordinary wealth, in liberality, in purity of life ..."

Jakob Fugger's epitaph, composed by himself, 1525

JAKOB
FUGGER

1459–1525

An ambitious financial reformer, Scottish economist John Law persuaded the French government to establish a central bank that issued paper money in place of gold and silver. While his scheme ended in chaos, his banking innovations have endured.

MILESTONES

BECOMES A FUGITIVE
After killing an adversary in a duel, flees to Amsterdam in 1694 and begins to study banking operations.

PUBLISHES PROPOSAL
His 1705 book urges reform in banking, including a central bank, paper money, and new credit systems.

ESTABLISHES BANK
Sets up the first French central bank in 1716, which issues millions of livres' worth of bank notes.

BOOM TO BUST
Central bank collapses in 1720 after issuing millions of shares, devaluing the livre and fueling inflation.

John Law spent his early years working for his family, who were bankers and goldsmiths, in Edinburgh. Moving to London, ostensibly to study, he spent much of his time womanizing and gambling. Law's life changed in 1694, when he killed an opponent in a duel. Sentenced to death, he fled to Amsterdam, where he became increasingly interested in finance. After a decade, Law returned to Edinburgh (where he was safe from rearrest), and in 1705 he published *Money and Trade Considered*, a book proposing that national banking systems should use paper money backed by land value, not precious metals.

First national bank
Settling in France, Law found its economy stagnant and national debt high. The regent was open to Law's reforms, so in 1716, Law founded the Banque Générale Privée in Paris, later nationalized as the Banque Royale. The bank was tied to the Mississippi Company, which Law had set up to exploit trade in France's colonies. Public demand for its shares was frenzied, but the "Mississippi Bubble" burst in 1720, leading to financial panic and the collapse of the Banque Royale. Blamed for the disaster, Law left Paris. He died in poverty in Italy.

JOHN LAW

One of the founding figures of the French insurance industry, Charles-Xavier Thomas de Colmar designed and manufactured the world's first commercially successful mechanical calculator.

Charles-Xavier Thomas (he later added "de Colmar") conceived the idea of a calculating device while he was Inspector of Supplies for the French Army, a position requiring constant repetitive calculations. After returning to civilian life, in 1819 he cofounded an insurance company—an industry that was entirely dependent on arithmetic. The following year, he patented the arithmometer, a machine that could add, subtract, multiply, and divide. Small-scale manufacture began in 1822 and was stepped up in 1851. Until 1878, it was the only mechanical calculator in commercial production. It improved the efficiency and profitability of de Colmar's insurance business, and sales to banks, other insurance companies, and government agencies in France and elsewhere made him a wealthy man. De Colmar invested the profits in creating better models of his machine; production continued until 1914, 44 years after his death.

"**The machine** from Thomas de Colmar ... **gives results** right away, **without fumbling....**"

Professor Louis-Benjamin Francoeur, 1822

MILESTONES

GAINS PATENT
Is awarded a five-year patent for the first model of his arithmometer calculating device in 1820.

GAINS RECOGNITION
In 1821, is decorated with the Chevalier of the Legion of Honour for his invention.

BEGINS PRODUCTION
Arithmometers start being made in Paris in 1822; a radically improved model is launched in 1851.

IMPROVES DESIGN
A third model goes into production in 1858 with simplified multiplication and division operations.

CHARLES-XAVIER THOMAS DE
COLMAR

BENJAMIN
FRANKLIN

Rising from humble origins, Benjamin Franklin became one of the most famous figures in colonial North America. Often remembered for his political and scientific activities, he was also an incredibly successful entrepreneur, whose print and publishing businesses made him one of the wealthiest individuals of his day.

The 15th of 17 children of a Boston candlemaker, Benjamin Franklin started working for his father at age 10. Franklin had received only two years of formal schooling and spent much of his meager salary on books to educate himself. His career in publishing began at the age of 12, when he was apprenticed to his brother, who was a printer. In 1723, Franklin moved to Philadelphia, continuing to work in print, then traveled to London, living there from 1724 to 1726. Finally resettled in Philadelphia, he briefly worked as a merchant's clerk before returning to printing.

Franklin had raised enough capital by 1728 to open his own printing business with his friend Hugh Meredith, whom he bought out two years later. Franklin was never short of work. He secured the contract to print paper money for the Pennsylvania Colony, as well as for Delaware, New Jersey, and Maryland. In 1729, he purchased a newspaper, the *Pennsylvania Gazette*, which he often contributed to. It was hugely popular and was produced until 1800.

Franchise system
Ever the innovator, Franklin established the first franchise system in American history. He made partnerships across the colonies from 1731. He would rent a shop and purchase printing equipment for his franchisee; in return, he would receive one-third of their profits for six years, after which they could buy the equipment from him. Franklin's most profitable

MILESTONES

STARTS BUSINESS
Aged 22, sets up a print business in 1728 with new equipment imported specially from England.

PUBLISHES ALMANACK
Starts printing *Poor Richard's Almanack* in 1732. It sells up to 10,000 copies a year for 26 years.

LEAVES PRINT
Retires from his printing business in 1748 to concentrate on politics and science.

GIVES BACK
Helps found the Academy for Education of Youth and Philadelphia City Hospital in 1751.

"Gain may be temporary and uncertain, but expense is constant and certain."

Benjamin Franklin, 1757

"Waste neither time nor money, but make the best use of both."

Benjamin Franklin, 1758

Benjamin Franklin is shown as a young man operating an 18th-century printing press in this artist's visualization of his workshop in Philadelphia.

enterprise was *Poor Richard's Almanack*, which first appeared in 1732. It contained meteorological and astronomical information, a calendar, and even witty advice penned by Franklin himself.

By 1748, Franklin was wealthy enough to retire from active involvement in his business, and he took on his foreman David Hall, who oversaw day-to-day operations, as his partner. Franklin had become increasingly involved in politics and held many public positions. He also conducted scientific research, winning renown for his experiments with electricity. Among his many inventions

were the lightning rod, a flexible catheter, swimming fins, bifocals, a musical instrument (the "glass armonica"), and a new type of heating stove.

In 1757, Franklin returned to London, where he remained for much of the next 18 years. During this time, he became an admired and respected figure in London society; however, growing discord between the British government and the American colonies forced him to return home in 1775. Originally a British royalist, he became a proponent of American independence, helping establish the US and draft the guiding principles of the new country. Franklin was the only Founding Father to have signed all three documents releasing the US from British rule: the Declaration of Independence, the US Constitution, and the Treaty of Paris. Franklin also served as a diplomat in Europe, going to France in 1776 and forging an alliance that was instrumental to American success in the Revolutionary War. On returning home in 1785, he served as President of Pennsylvania.

Financial legacy

At his death in 1790, Franklin left $4,400 (at the time) to the cities of Boston and Philadelphia, on the proviso that they place the money in a trust to provide small loans to help local entrepreneurs. The cities were permitted to take full control over the bequest only after 200 years. By 1990, the trust funds had grown very favorably. Philadelphia put this money toward scholarships and the Franklin Institute (a science museum), while Boston funded the Benjamin Franklin Institute of Technology.

CARL **BERTELSMANN**

German publisher Carl Bertelsmann successfully founded one of the world's largest media conglomerates.

In 1835, Bertelsmann (1791–1850) established his eponymous publishing company, focusing on religious works and hymn books. Taken over on his death by his son, and later by his grandson-in-law, the company expanded into novels, histories, and school books and bought rival publishing houses. By the mid-20th century, it was a global mass media conglomerate, incorporating music, radio and television broadcasting, and print.

FILED ZERO

PATENTS FOR HIS INVENTIONS

AT DEATH, HIS ESTATE WAS WORTH $43.5 MILLION

HAS APPEARED ON THE $100 BILL SINCE 1928

ELIZA LUCAS

PINCKNEY

In the 18th century, agriculturalist Eliza Lucas Pinckney became the first person in colonial America to successfully grow the tropical cash crop indigo. She went on to process it into a high-quality blue dye at a time when the world's textile industry was burgeoning. Exports of the dye brought prosperity to South Carolina.

Eliza Lucas Pinckney was born in Antigua in the West Indies, where her father was a British Army officer. She developed an interest in botany when her parents sent her to school in England. In 1738, 16-year-old Pinckney moved with her family to South Carolina, then a British colony, where they owned three plantations. Her mother soon died, and her father was forced to return to Antigua on military matters a year later. As the eldest child of four, Pinckney took charge of managing the Wappoo Plantation, where the family lived, and its workforce of 20 enslaved people, and oversaw the other plantations: two grew rice, and the third produced tar and wood.

Pinckney regularly corresponded with her father, who would send her seeds from the Caribbean, allowing her to experiment with new crops, such as fig, ginger, alfalfa, cotton, and indigo, in a bid to supplement the income from their plantations. In 1744, Pinckney successfully cultivated indigo plants and was soon using them to produce high-quality dye. She exported large amounts of the dye to England for use in the textile industry. Sharing her knowledge with other planters, Pinckney initiated the "Indigo Bonanza" in 1745, when the crop was grown across South Carolina; by the start of the American Revolution in 1765, indigo made up one-third of the colony's exports.

MILESTONES

MOVES TO S. CAROLINA
Migrates to the Wappoo Plantation in South Carolina, then a British colony, in 1738.

GROWS INDIGO
Experiments with indigo from 1739 to 1744 to keep the family's plantations out of debt.

SILK SIDELINE
Marries lawyer and planter Charles Pinckney in 1744. Experiments with silk culture on his plantation.

SHARES SKILLS
Starts South Carolina's "Indigo Bonanza" in 1745 by sharing her knowledge of growing indigo.

TAKES CHARGE
Manages the family's extensive plantations once again when her husband dies of malaria in 1758.

"I make no doubt indigo will prove a very valuable commodity."

Eliza Lucas Pinckney, 1741

DIRECTORY

Entrepreneurs of the ancient, medieval, and early modern eras helped lay the foundations of modern capitalism and global trade through their risky, sometimes daring, activities. Although not always successful, these pioneers paved the way for others in fields such as finance and international commerce.

PASION
(c. 430–370 BCE)

Believed to originate from Syria, Pasion was sold at an Athens slave market in 440 BCE to two bankers from Piraeus, the Greek port city that serviced Athens. A canny operator, Pasion rose to run their money-changing operation and was eventually granted his freedom, gaining the status of foreign resident. Pasion inherited his former masters' business and later became involved in the armaments trade. He was made a citizen of Athens after he donated 1,000 shields and a ship to its armed forces. He diversified into property, further growing his fortune, and became one of the wealthiest men in Athens.

IBN AL-SAL'US
(d. 1294)

Born into an Arab family in Palestine, Ibn al-Sal'us was raised in Damascus in Syria. He became a successful and respected merchant and an important local official. After gaining the attention of the Mamluk sultans—rulers of Egypt, part of Arabia, and the Levant—in 1290, he became *wazir* (chief advisor) to Sultan al-Ashraf Khalil and helped lead many successful Mamluk campaigns in Palestine and Armenia. Yet Ibn al-Sal'us clashed with other Mamluk officials, and when al-Ashraf Khalil was assassinated in 1293, Ibn al-Sal'us fell out of favor. The following year, he was arrested on charges of financial crime and died after being tortured.

GIOVANNI VILLANI
(c. 1276–1348)

Born in Florence, Giovanni Villani was an Italian banker and chronicler of history. In 1300, he joined the Peruzzi banking firm and spent the next seven years traveling Europe as an agent for the Peruzzis. In 1308, he returned to Florence and became active in civic politics. That year, he began the *New Chronicles*, a groundbreaking 12-book work on the history of Florence. He fell victim to the bubonic plague or Black Death.

RICHARD WHITTINGTON
(c. 1354–1423)

Popularly known as "Dick," Richard Whittington was the inspiration for the famed English folktale about an orphan who makes his fortune in London. The real Whittington was from a prominent gentry family in Gloucestershire, but, as a younger son, he would not have inherited his father's estate. He moved to London to work as a mercer, dealing in high-end cloth, often made overseas. Extremely successful, he diversified into money-lending and civic politics and served three times as Lord Mayor of London. He gave much of his fortune to good works and public buildings.

KATERINA LEMMEL
(1466–1533)

Born into a merchant family in the German city of Nuremberg, Katerina Imhoff married businessman Michael Lemmel in 1484. She was a successful entrepreneur in her own right, investing in property, metal manufacture, and wine-making. Widowed in 1516, she became a nun at the monastery Maria Mai. By managing her investments, she funded the monastery, but in 1525 she was forced to flee during an uprising. The nuns returned to find it plundered. Lemmel was never able to restore the damage and died eight years later.

ROSE LOK
(1526–1613)

The daughter of a wealthy London merchant and civic official, Rose Lok and her family were key supporters of the Protestant Reformation. One of 19 children, Lok worked as a "silkwoman," processing the textile into finished goods and selling it to wealthy customers, including members of the royal court. In 1543, Lok married a

Protestant merchant and shipowner. When the Catholic Mary I took the English throne in 1553, Lok sought refuge in Antwerp, Belgium. Returning from exile after Mary died in 1558, Lok remarried (her first husband had died) and wrote a memoir of the events of her early life. She died aged 84.

ISAAC LE MAIRE
(c. 1558–1624)

Belgian-born Isaac Le Maire was a grocer in Antwerp but fled in 1585 when the Spanish invaded. He resettled in Amsterdam as an overseas trader. When the Vereenigde Oostindische Compagnie (VOC, or Dutch East India Company) formed in 1602, Le Maire became its largest shareholder and governor until quarrels forced him to leave in 1605. He was involved in several enterprises that challenged the VOC. One of these, the Australian Company, found a new route from the Atlantic to the Pacific via South America in 1615, but Le Maire gained little financial benefit from the discovery.

LUZON SUKEZAEMON
(b. 1565)

Luzon Sukezaemon was born in the Japanese port city of Sakai. His original first name was Naya, but he changed it around 1593 after a trading voyage to Luzon, the largest island in the Philippines. Sukezaemon traded in the island's pottery, which was highly valued in Japan. With profits from his trading activities, he built a luxurious mansion for himself. Sukezaemon's extravagance stoked the jealousy of a local samurai lord, who confiscated his property. In response, Sukezaemon donated his residence to a local temple and fled to Cambodia, where he continued to work as a merchant.

LOUIS DE GEER
(1587–1652)

Born in Belgium, Louis De Geer moved to the Netherlands and trained as a coppersmith, then went into business as a metal manufacturer and banker. The Thirty Years' War (1618–1648) created a demand for metal to make weapons, and De Geer forged close links with the Swedish Crown. He won a monopoly on trading copper and iron in Sweden and built up its metalworking industry. De Geer was made a lord in Sweden and was key in founding the Swedish Africa Company, which was active in the slave trade from 1648 to 1663.

JOHAN PALMSTRUCH
(1611–1671)

Johan Wittmacher was born in the Latvian city of Riga and moved to Sweden in 1647. There he started a bank, was ennobled, and given the Swedish surname Palmstruch. His bank—Stockholms Banco—used cash deposits to finance loans and was the first bank in Europe to issue paper money that could be exchanged for gold or silver. When, in 1668, the value of the notes outstripped the bank's assets, it collapsed, and Palmstruch was sentenced to death. This punishment was later reduced to imprisonment.

WILLIAM PATERSON
(1658–1719)

A Scottish native, William Paterson worked in Bristol, the Bahamas, and Europe before settling in London as a wealthy overseas trader. In 1692, he proposed the founding of a bank from which the government could borrow; this formed the basis of the Bank of England and was incorporated in 1694.

A founding director, Paterson left in 1695 after clashing with colleagues. He promoted the founding of a Scottish colony in Panama, but his expedition in 1698 ended in failure. He was a strong supporter of the successful union of England and Scotland in 1707.

MARY KATHERINE GODDARD
(1738–1816)

Born in Connecticut, Mary Katherine Goddard assisted her brother in the publication of newspapers in Baltimore, Providence, and Philadelphia. In 1774, she became editor and publisher of the *Maryland Journal* and ran a printing press and bookstore. In 1775, she was appointed postmaster of Baltimore, the first woman in US history to hold such a position. In support of the revolution against British rule, in 1777, her press produced the second copy of the Declaration of Independence (and the first to include the signers' names). She was later removed from her higher posts but ran her bookstore until 1810.

MAYER AMSCHEL ROTHSCHILD
(1744–1812)

The son of a German-Jewish family from Frankfurt, Mayer Amschel Rothschild was apprenticed to a bank before going into business. He dealt in rare coins and luxury goods, before diversifying into banking services. One of his earliest clients was William IX of Hesse-Kassel, a wealthy local ruler whose fortune Rothschild adroitly managed. With business in Frankfurt booming, Rothschild decided to expand—his sons established a branch of their bank in London in 1804 and another in Paris in 1811. Although Rothschild died the following year, he had already established the foundation of an international banking empire.

2

INDUSTRY AND INNOVATION

1780–1890

One of England's first industrialists, metalwork manufacturer Matthew Boulton transformed factory production methods using steam power, in collaboration with engineer James Watt.

Matthew Boulton joined his father's business, which produced metal buckles and trinkets, on leaving school in 1743. Inventive and intensely ambitious, Boulton took over and expanded the company on his father's death, opening Britain's first large-scale factory—the Soho Manufactory—in 1765. Boulton's desire to improve the factory's power supply (its water wheel was efficient only when the river was in full flow) stoked his interest in the work of James Watt, a Scottish engineer who had invented a new steam-powered engine. By 1775, the pair had joined forces, with Boulton championing Watt's engine designs and supplying them to other industries, including the Royal Mint, for whom he also struck millions of coins under license at his steam-powered plant.

MILESTONES

ESTABLISHES FACTORY
In 1762, starts construction of the Soho Manufactory, which covers 13 acres of land near Birmingham, UK.

IMPROVES POWER
Meets James Watt, whose new steam engine can supply greater, more efficient power, in 1768.

LOBBIES PARLIAMENT
Successfully persuades Parliament in 1775 to extend Watt's patent for an additional 17 years.

JOINS SOCIETY
Is elected a fellow of the Royal Society, London, with James Watt, in 1785.

"**I sell here, Sir,** what all the world desires to have: **POWER.**"

Matthew Boulton, 1776

MATTHEW BOULTON

James Watt was a Scottish scientific instrument maker and engineer whose improvements to the steam engine made it the principal power source of the Industrial Revolution.

Born to a shipbuilder in 1736, Watt initially trained as a maker of scientific instruments. Around 1764, he became interested in steam engines when he was asked to repair an early model designed by Thomas Newcomen. Watt realized he could refine its design to make it more powerful, while also burning less fuel. With the industrialist Matthew Boulton as his partner and backer, Watt was able to start manufacturing his new engines in 1775, and they were soon adopted in mines, factories, and mills. Continuing his experiments with thermodynamics, Watt made further modifications to his engine. By 1790, he had registered three new patents, earned over £70,000 in royalties, and become a member of the Royal Society.

MILESTONES

MAKES INSTRUMENTS
Establishes workshop at Glasgow University in 1757, creating scientific instruments.

STEAM BREAKTHROUGH
Improves efficiency of Newcomen steam engine in around 1764 by adding a separate condenser.

FORMS PARTNERSHIP
Establishes Boulton & Watt with Matthew Boulton in 1775 to commercialize his new steam engine designs.

KEEPS INNOVATING
Continues research work, despite retiring in 1800, patenting several more important inventions.

"I am a great **friend to experiment** ... I cannot **trust** to **theory.**"

James Watt, 1794

JAMES
WATT

POWERS THE PRODUCTION OF COTTON, FLOUR, IRON, PAPER, COINAGE, TEXTILES, BEER ...

BOULTON & WATT ENGINES USED **75% LESS FUEL** THAN OLDER **MODELS**

SUPPLIED ALMOST ONE THIRD OF STEAM ENGINES USED **WORLDWIDE 1775–1800**

STRUCK 90,000,000 COINS FOR THE **EAST INDIA COMPANY IN 1808**

The steam engines produced by Boulton & Watt were at the forefront of the Industrial Revolution. Improving existing early designs and replacing traditional methods of energy such as water and horse power, the engines provided a more efficient and effective method of powering the new machinery that was transforming factories, mills, mines, agriculture, and transportation.

Early engines

The first steam engine had been designed by Thomas Savery in 1698 and improved by Thomas Newcomen in 1711. Used primarily for pumping water, they were powered by heating, cooling, and reheating steam, making them very inefficient. While repairing a Newcomen engine at Glasgow University in 1764, Watt realized that he could radically increase the engine's efficiency by adding a separate condensing chamber.

Instead of repeatedly heating and cooling a single working cylinder, Watt's engine used two chambers: the working cylinder received steam from a boiler and remained hot, while the second chamber was kept cool, so that steam entering from the hot cylinder condensed into water. This water then flowed back into the boiler to be used again.

Boulton & Watt's steam engine had the advantage that it could be located anywhere—unlike traditional power sources such as water wheels.

The problem for Watt was how to make this innovation a commercial product. In 1768, he entered into partnership with physician and inventor John Roebuck, patenting his design in 1769. However, three years later, Roebuck was declared bankrupt, and his share in Watt's design passed to Matthew Boulton.

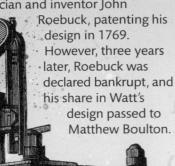

GEORGE **STEPHENSON**

Dubbed the "Father of Railways," George Stephenson built the first commercial steam locomotive, developed the world's first passenger rail network, and devised "standard gauge" track.

A self-taught engineer, Stephenson (1781–1848) graduated from repairing steam engines in mines to developing a locomotive engine in 1814. In 1823, he set up a factory in Newcastle to produce the world's first commercial locomotives, including the award-winning "Rocket." Quickly enlisted by railway companies as their chief engineer, he oversaw the construction of much of Britain's early passenger network, linking new industrial centers such as Manchester and Birmingham.

The metal manufacturer was interested in an efficient steam engine as his factory was struggling with the erratic power supply provided by a water wheel.

Perfect partnership

Watt relocated to Birmingham in 1774 to develop his engine designs. The Boulton-Watt partnership was an immediate success; though opposites in many ways, the men were drawn together through mutual admiration. Boulton was a businessman who hired the best designers and craftspeople to develop items highly desirable in both Britain and Europe, while Watt was a dedicated engineer who thrived on fixing faults

"I can **think** of **nothing** else, **but this machine.**"

James Watt, 1765

> **"It will coin faster** with greater ease, with **fewer persons, less expense,** and **more beautiful** than any coining **machine** ever made."**

Matthew Boulton, 1789

with existing machines and making them market leaders. At Boulton's factory, Watt had abundant resources and some of the best ironworkers in England to build his new steam engines. He was also free to research other innovations.

Boulton successfully extended the patent on Watt's steam engine design and started manufacturing copies for tin and copper mines in Cornwall, which until then had relied on the inefficient Newcomen engine to pump out water.

Power revolution

Capitalizing on this early success, Boulton urged Watt to build a steam engine that could produce a rotary action, rather than the up-and-down movement used to pump water. In 1781, Watt launched his rotary "sun-and-planet" gear, followed by a double-acting engine (in which pistons pushed and pulled), a "parallel motion" design, as well as a centrifugal governor to control engine speed. Watt's engine design was finalized in 1790, with the addition of a pressure gauge. There was a flood of

orders for the engine from flour, cotton, paper, and iron mills, which all wanted the new technology. By 1800, Boulton & Watt had supplied around 450 of the 1,500 steam engines that were in operation around the world, with each machine able to power an entire factory.

New opportunities

Eager to find new applications for steam power, Boulton founded the Soho Mint in 1788 with the aim of overhauling Britain's coinage, much of which was counterfeit. His new minting machines could press coins of uniform size, shape, and weight, with lettered rims. In 1797, the Royal Mint commissioned him to produce 45 million new penny and two-penny pieces. Boulton's lettering technique is still used on British £1 and £2 coins today.

In 1800, Boulton and Watt both retired, and their company passed to their sons. Through their development and sale of the Watt engine, they had fueled the Industrial Revolution and launched the modern age of factory production.

James Watt and his business partner Matthew Boulton produced their steam engines at the Soho Manufactory, Birmingham, UK, from 1775 to 1800. ▶

A 19th-century shipping and railroad magnate, Cornelius Vanderbilt was a ruthless, shrewd, and competitive businessman. Able to offer reliable services and cheap fares without compromising on comfort, he undercut his rivals and broke down steamship monopolies. He embraced new transportation technologies, later moving from water to rail.

Cornelius Vanderbilt was born on May 27, 1794, in Staten Island, New York. His parents were poor and his father worked as a ferryman. From him, Vanderbilt learned a plain-spoken, blunt approach to dealing with people, while his mother taught him the benefits of frugality and hard work.

At the age of 11, Vanderbilt left school and went to work with his father, who ferried passengers between Staten Island and Manhattan. In 1810, he spotted his first business opportunity: convincing his parents to loan him $100, he bought a sailing boat and started his own ferry business. His parents did this on the condition that Vanderbilt gave them part of his profits until the loan was paid off.

Vanderbilt's ferry business was an almost overnight success. Within a year, he was able to pay back his parents' loan as well as an additional $1,000 as their share of the profits. Vanderbilt learned that by undercutting the competition and marketing his ferry business aggressively, he could quickly create a large customer base. He would repeat this strategy for almost every subsequent business venture.

Steamship success

Over the next two years, Vanderbilt amassed a whole fleet of ships and had a working capital of several thousand dollars. During the War of 1812—a three-year conflict between the United States and Britain—the US government awarded Vanderbilt a contract to supply ships to the Eastern Seaboard. Vanderbilt was

Vanderbilt earned much of his fortune in the steamboat industry in New York and New Jersey. By the time of his death, his family was one of the wealthiest in the whole of the United States.

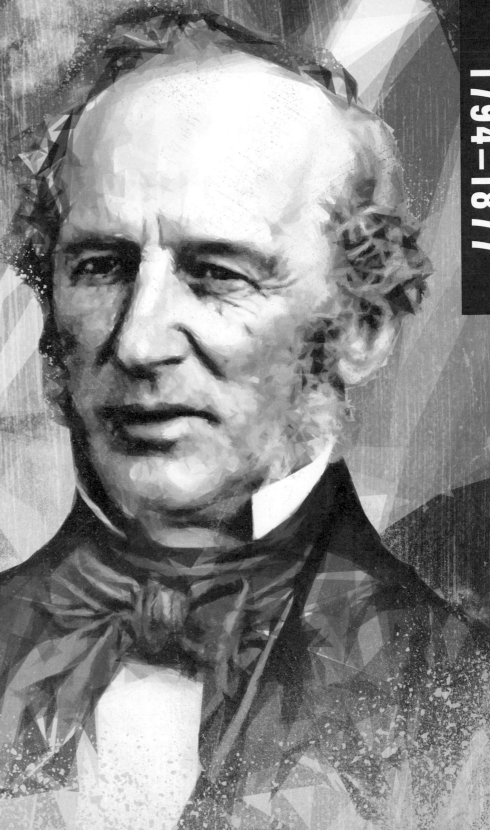

CORNELIUS

VANDERBILT

1794–1877

"There is **no** friendship in **trade**."

Cornelius Vanderbilt, 1857

known as the "Commodore" because of his shipping success, a nickname in which he took great pride.

Vanderbilt was drawn to business figures he could learn from. One such man was Thomas Gibbons, who employed Vanderbilt to run his steamship business in 1818. Gibbons was embroiled in a legal battle to break a competitor's monopoly of a steamboat route between New York and New Jersey. Gibbons won the case and did his best to bankrupt his rival by undercutting him with his own steamships.

Across the ocean
Learning from his experience with Gibbons, Vanderbilt then set about undercutting rival steamship businesses and breaking their monopolies until they were forced to buy him out. Already a millionaire, Vanderbilt took advantage of the California Gold Rush of 1849 by expanding his shipping business to include oceangoing steamships that took prospectors and other customers from New York City and New Orleans to San Francisco via Nicaragua. During the US

Vanderbilt bought multiple railroad lines between New York and Chicago. He was famously involved in a financial battle between financier Jim Fisk (right) and his associates Daniel Drew and Jay Gould for control of the Erie Railroad Company.

Civil War (1861–1865) Vanderbilt sold or leased all his ships, at the time making him the richest man in the US.

After retiring from shipping, in 1864 Vanderbilt decided to go into the railroad business by buying up most of the stock in the New York and Harlem Railroads. He

STAKES 1870

continued to buy up other railroads and eventually controlled every line from New York to Chicago.

By standardizing rail timetables and fares, Vanderbilt helped revolutionize rail travel in the US. He ordered the building of the Grand Central Depot (now Station) in New York. The railroad terminal's construction created thousands of jobs at a time when the US was in the midst of a financial crisis. In 1870, he consolidated two lines to form the New York Central and Hudson River Railroad.

University legacy

Despite his enormous personal wealth, Vanderbilt had no interest in giving his money to charity. However, he was persuaded by his second wife to donate $1 million (then the largest charitable gift in US history) toward the building of a university in Nashville, Tennessee, which would become the Vanderbilt University. He died on January 4, 1877, aged 82.

J. P. **MORGAN**

Financier, banker, and industrialist John Pierpoint Morgan **initiated the formation of several multinational companies.**

After first working as an accountant, Morgan (1837–1913) founded J.P. Morgan in 1895. It became one of the largest banks in the world. Morgan then became a railroad magnate in 1902 and merged several companies to form the largest US corporations, including the US Steel Corporation and General Electric. He later influenced multiple banks and insurance firms by sitting on their boards.

GAVE HIS **BEST STEAMSHIP** TO UNIONISTS DURING THE **US CIVIL WAR**

WENT INTO RAILROAD BUSINESS AGED **70** IN 1864

LEFT AN **ESTATE** OF ALMOST **$100 MILLION**

American P. T. Barnum was a promoter, philanthropist, publisher, and popularizer of the three-ring circus, the human freak show, and the public museum. A showman, entrepreneur, and reputed hoaxer, Barnum is best remembered for his traveling spectacle "The Greatest Show on Earth," which transformed popular entertainment.

MILESTONES

CREATES MUSEUM
Opens Barnum's American Museum in 1842. It has over 30 million visitors but burns down in 1865.

PROMOTES CULTURE
Organizes sellout US tour for soprano Jenny Lind in 1850, bringing vast profits and respectability.

FACES BANKRUPTCY
Loses money in effort to develop city of Bridgeport in 1850s. Tours Europe to revive his fortunes.

CIRCUS SUCCESS
Joins James A. Bailey to create Barnum & Bailey in 1881—the first circus to have three ground rings.

Born in Bethel, Connecticut, in 1810, Phineas Taylor Barnum began his entrepreneurial career at age 12 by selling homemade cherry rum at town gatherings. By his 20s, Barnum had made enough money to found his own newspaper, the *Herald of Freedom*, but his talent for promotion soon drew him to showmanship. He began to bring human freak shows and related curiosities to a mass audience. This included "renting" an elderly black woman named Joyce Heth, whom Barnum presented as the "161-year-old nurse to George Washington."

In 1841, Barnum bought New York's American Museum, reopening it with theatrical acts, exotic animals, and unusual displays such as the "Feejee Mermaid" (purported to have a human head and a fish's body) and "General Tom Thumb," a 25-in (63-cm) boy. Eager to garner respectability as a promoter and quash rumors that his exhibits were hoaxes, Barnum risked his fortune to set up a US tour for Swedish soprano Jenny Lind. Although she was almost unknown in the US, Barnum's marketing campaign ensured seats were filled for the nine months of her tour. In 1870, at age 60, Barnum agreed to collaborate on a new enterprise: "The Greatest Show on Earth." A traveling circus, it successfully toured the US, with Barnum building the show a permanent home in New York—called the Hippodrome (later known as Madison Square Garden)—in 1874. Ever enterprising, Barnum amalgamated his circus with James A. Bailey's renowned "Great London Show" in 1881; it continued to tour even after Barnum's death in 1891.

> "Whatever you do, do it **with all your might.**"

P.T. Barnum, 1880

Barnum's circus venture included attractions such as Jumbo the Elephant, whose skeleton remained a popular attraction after his death in 1885.

P. T. BARNUM

1810–1891

BIDDY

MASON

After being freed from slavery, Biddy Mason was employed as a midwife and nurse, using skills she had acquired while enslaved. She saved enough money to buy land in Los Angeles and became a successful property entrepreneur. One of the city's wealthiest women, she spent her fortune on supporting her local community.

Bridget, nicknamed "Biddy," Mason was born into slavery in Mississippi in 1818. In 1836, she was given to plantation owner Robert Smith. He converted to Mormonism in 1847 and decided to move his family and slaves from Mississippi to Utah, where the church was establishing a community. Biddy, who by now had three daughters, accompanied him on the trip. The Smiths moved again four years later to a Mormon missionary outpost, settling in San Bernardino, California, along with Biddy and her family. Smith was aware that slavery was illegal in California but kept Biddy and her family enslaved. In 1856, helped by friends who were formerly enslaved, Biddy successfully petitioned a local judge to free her and Smith's other slaves; she took the surname Mason from the middle name of the city's mayor.

Mason and her daughters then moved to Los Angeles. While enslaved, Mason had worked as a midwife and nurse and had an extensive knowledge of herbal medicine; she could now use these skills to work for herself. Mason's medical expertise was in high demand, and she saved the money she earned from her work. She saw the importance of owning land and property so invested in several plots in downtown Los Angeles. Through a series of skillful property transactions, Mason amassed a large fortune. A generous philanthropist, she funded many charities and was a founding member of the First African Methodist Episcopal Church, the oldest African American church in Los Angeles.

MILESTONES

CONTESTS STATUS
Is granted freedom from slavery in January 1856 by California district judge Benjamin Hayes.

SAVES INCOME
Becomes well known for her nursing skills between 1856 and 1866; saves her earnings of $2.50 a day.

STARTS TO INVEST
Spends $250 on property in 1866, becoming one of the first black women to own land in Los Angeles.

PROPERTY MOGUL
Is one of LA's richest women by the 1880s, as her downtown plots rapidly increase in value.

FUNDS PHILANTHROPY
Accumulates $300,000 by 1891, much of which is spent on helping local people and her family.

"If you hold your hand closed, **nothing good can come in.**"

Biddy Mason

LYDIA PINKHAM

American Lydia Pinkham was best known for her "women's tonic," which went from a home-brewed remedy to being manufactured in a commercial laboratory as part of her highly successful business.

Born Lydia Estes in Lynn, Massachusetts, Pinkham grew up in a Quaker family. She married Isaac Pinkham in 1843 and, while raising their family, made many home remedies containing herbs and roots, which she shared with her neighbors. These would form the basis of her later fortune. In 1873, after a financial crisis ruined her husband, Pinkham decided to sell her tonics commercially. Her "vegetable compound," which had an alcohol content of around 18 percent, went on sale in 1875. Although its medical efficacy was never proven and skeptics questioned it, the tonic became incredibly popular as a treatment for menstrual discomfort and menopausal problems. Pinkham was a shrewd marketer—she used a portrait of herself prominently in advertisements, and she personally replied to women who contacted her for advice. She also wrote a "facts-of-life" manual for women, which she distributed free of charge.

> "Her face, as used in her advertisements, was her fortune."
>
> *Editor of the New Haven Register,* 1883

MILESTONES

BUSINESS BEGINS
Starts remedy business in 1873, when a global depression leaves her family in financial crisis.

MASS MARKETING
"Lydia E. Pinkham's Vegetable Compound" tonic is patented in 1876 and sold across the US.

DISPENSES ADVICE
Sets up Department of Advice in 1880s, with an all-female staff to respond to letters.

When dry goods salesman Levi Strauss acquired a patent for using metal rivets to reinforce the pockets of work trousers, he helped create one of the world's most iconic brands of blue denim jeans.

From Buttenheim, Germany, Levi Strauss (born Loeb Strauss) emigrated to the US at the age of 18 to join his brothers in their New York wholesale business. In 1853, in response to the Gold Rush, he moved west to San Francisco to set up a branch of the family enterprise under his own name: Levi Strauss & Co. He sold dry goods supplied by his brothers, including textiles such as denim, canvas for tents, bedding, and clothes.

His business thrived, and within a few years, he had sent more than $4 million back to New York. In 1873, Strauss and Jacob Davis—a tailor who was one of his customers—took out a patent on a new style of work trousers that were strengthened by metal rivets: the now ubiquitous blue denim jeans. By the 1880s, the durable, riveted jeans were bestsellers, and Strauss opened his own factory to make them. Strauss was a great philanthropist, supporting orphanages, setting up university scholarships, and providing funds to build a new railroad from San Francisco to the San Joaquin Valley.

This early advertisement for Levis Strauss jeans with copper rivets was aimed at laborers such as miners, farmworkers, and cowboys.

~the miner
farmer mechanic and cattle raiser
all over the west
prefer

cut full
honestly made

Levi Strauss & Co's.
copper riveted Overalls
the most persistently advertised – the best selling brand. it will pay you to handle them

"I don't believe that **a man** who once forms the **habit of being busy** can **retire** and be **contented.**"

Levi Strauss, 1895

LEVI STRAUSS

MILESTONES

GOES WEST
Travels to California via Panama in 1853, to profit from the influx of miners attracted by the Gold Rush.

GRANTED PATENT
Together with tailor Jacob Davis, receives a patent for using metal rivets on the seams of jeans in 1873.

PHILANTHROPIC WORK
Among other projects, helps to fund 28 scholarships at the University of California, Berkeley, in 1897.

West African Mbanaso Okwaraozurumba, who came to be known as Jaja of Opobo, was sold into slavery at the age of 12. He went from paddling trade canoes to becoming the head of one of the royal houses of the Bonny Empire, eventually establishing himself as king of the city-state of Opobo—an international trading hub for palm oil products.

Jaja's slavers took him to Bonny, a kingdom in southern Nigeria that was organized into "canoe houses." Each canoe house was a separate trading unit run by a wealthy merchant. Jaja was sold to one canoe house then given as a gift to Chief Alali of the Anna Pepple Royal House. Jaja started paddling trade canoes, traveling to the markets of this river region where he met local businesspeople and European palm oil traders. Jaja worked directly for the chief but also began to develop his own trade in palm oil on the side and eventually earned enough to buy his freedom. When the chief of the Anna Pepple Royal House died, the ambitious Jaja took his place. An astute businessman, Jaja incorporated other canoe houses in the area and increased his number of British trade contacts. Following a dispute with another canoe house, Jaja established the city-state of Opobo in 1869. Subsequently, by continuing to take over other canoe houses and controlling the British merchants' trade routes, Jaja made Opobo the most prosperous city-state in the area, with a monopoly on the palm oil trade.

Enemies and exile

Jaja's financial position was further strengthened when he began to export palm oil directly to Great Britain rather than through British traders—though this went against British imperial interests. At the Berlin Conference of 1884—a meeting of European powers to decide which nations would control trade in the African colonies—Britain claimed Opobo as its own. The British accused Jaja of trading illegally and exiled him in 1887 to the Caribbean island of St. Vincent. They allowed him to return three years later, but he died en route. Many people believed that he was poisoned.

"In a **short time** [Jaja] will **either** be **shot** or he will **beat down** all his **rivals**."

Sir Richard Burton, British consul, 1867

Queen Victoria welcomed Jaja to Buckingham Palace in 1887. He was invited to London for trade negotiations before being arrested.

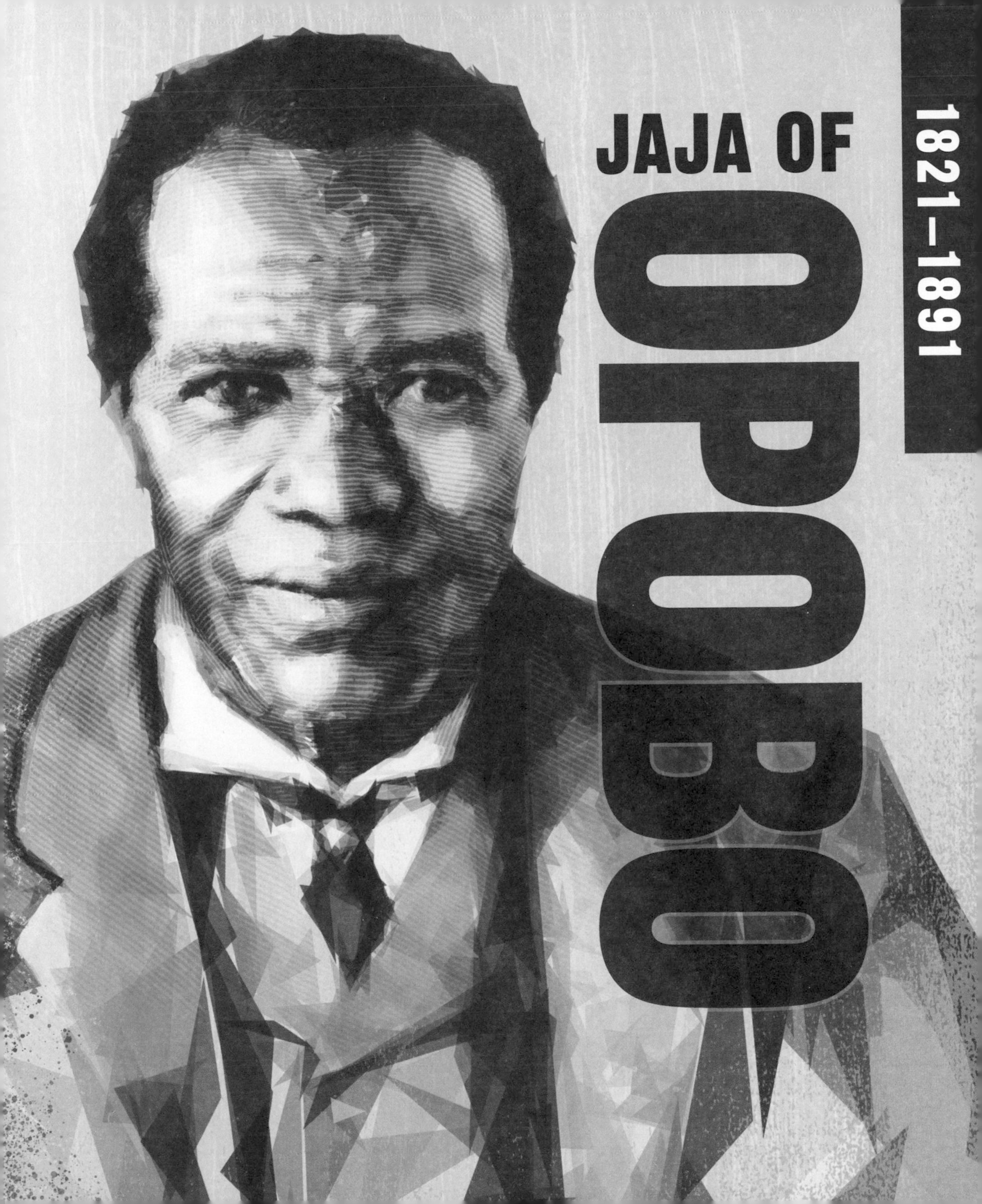

JAJA OF **OPOBO**

1821–1891

German businessman Friedrich Bayer (formerly Beyer) began his career as an apprentice selling natural dyes to the textile industry. After teaching himself how to produce artificial dyes, he founded his own company. This would go on to become Bayer AG, one of the largest manufacturers of chemicals and pharmaceuticals in the world.

While an apprentice working for Wesenfeld & Co. in Wuppertal, Germany, 14-year-old Friedrich Bayer became familiar with the workings of the dyeing trade and went on to be a successful salesperson. In 1848, at the age of 23, he founded his own dye company and established a distribution network across Europe.

Until the mid-19th century, dyes were derived from plants, minerals, and animals. From the 1850s, companies could manufacture artificial dyes in a wider range of colors by combining chemical extracts from coal tar with other compounds. Bayer decided to start producing artificial dyes and, with a friend, dyer Johann Friedrich Weskott, he experimented with new chemical combinations and produced dyes of far better quality than his competitors. In 1863, the two men established the company that would later become Bayer AG. They initially employed just 12 workers, but the company grew rapidly, and by 1880, that number had increased to 300. Bayer died in 1880, at a time when the company was supplying dyes and chemicals to textile companies worldwide. He did not live to see the company's most famous product—the painkilling drug aspirin, a pharmaceutical spin-off from the dye industry first distributed in 1899.

"During my **years** as an **apprentice ...** I **learned** I would **rather** have my **own company** than **work** for **someone else.**"

Friedrich Bayer

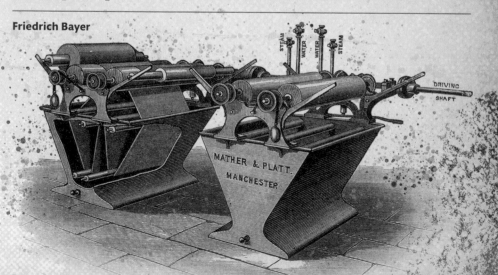

Early dyeing jiggers used by Friedrich Bayer & Co. passed fabrics through rollers to dip them in and out of large vats of dye.

FRIEDRICH
BAYER

1825–1880

ANDREW

CARNEGIE

Scottish-born Andrew Carnegie spearheaded the expansion of the US steel industry, adopting innovative processes and vertical integration to improve efficiency. He became one of the wealthiest Americans of his time and a leading philanthropist who encouraged other rich business leaders to give away their wealth.

Andrew Carnegie was determined to escape the poverty that forced his parents to emigrate from Dunfermline to the US when he was 13. In the US, his father still struggled to support the family, and Carnegie soon had to earn his own money. He started as a bobbin boy in a Pennsylvania cotton factory and, despite the 12-hour day, found time to learn to read and write. By the age of 14, he had become a messenger in the Pittsburgh telegraph office and was quickly promoted to the role of telegrapher. An avid reader, he was eager to further his own education and took advantage of the generosity of a local citizen, Colonel Anderson, who opened his library to working boys. Carnegie was so grateful for this opportunity to better himself that he "resolved, if ever wealth came to me, [to see to it] that other poor boys might receive opportunities similar to those for which we were indebted to the noble man."

In 1853, Carnegie was spotted by Thomas Scott of the Pennsylvania Railroad Company, who took him on as his private secretary and personal telegrapher. Working in this fast-growing business taught Carnegie vital management lessons, and within 10 years he had risen to become railroad superintendent. Scott

"Virtue is its own and the only ... great reward."

Andrew Carnegie, 1902

MILESTONES

MANUFACTURES STEEL
Founds Edgar Thomson Steel Works in 1872; uses new Bessemer process to revolutionize production.

IMPROVES EFFICIENCY
Buys coke fields, ships, and railroads in the 1890s, using vertical integration to control production.

MAKES MILLIONS
In 1901, aged 66, sells company to United States Steel Corporation for $480 million and retires.

PHILANTHROPIC ACTS
Between 1901–1919, donates almost 90% of his fortune to educational and social projects.

Carnegie's "Lucy" furnace, built in 1870, produced 100 tons (91 tonnes) of iron in one day in 1874, breaking an iron-making record.

SAID LIFE SHOULD BE LIVED IN **3 STAGES:** GETTING **EDUCATED** MAKING **MONEY** GIVING **MONEY AWAY**

DIED HAVING GIVEN

$350

MILLION TO CHARITY

helped Carnegie begin investing in burgeoning industrial concerns, including ironworks, railroads, and oil. Noting the increased interest in steel, demand for which grew during the US Civil War, Carnegie traveled to the UK to meet steelmakers. He foresaw iron and steel as essential to the industrialization of the US and, in 1865, left the railroad business to manage the Keystone Bridge Company and focus on these concerns. In 1872, aged 37, he set up Edgar Thomson Steel Works, which would evolve into The Carnegie Steel Company. Carnegie's success lay in finding and adopting any innovations that would reduce the cost of large-scale steel production. After observing the Bessemer process in the UK, he pioneered its use in the US. By the 1890s, he had introduced the more efficient open-hearth furnace to American steelmaking, and the US outstripped the UK's steel output for the first time. In pursuit of efficiencies, Carnegie developed the concept of vertical integration—controlling every aspect of the steelmaking process. He purchased coke fields to access raw materials, as well as railroads and steamships to transport goods. When the business was sold for around $480 million (more than $14 billion today) in

GEORGE **PEABODY**

Born in Massachusetts, George Peabody was an American financier who pioneered international credit and became renowned for his extensive philanthropic initiatives in the US and the UK.

Peabody (1795–1869) left school at the age of 11 and was soon trading in wool, linen, and dry goods. He moved into merchant banking and first visited the UK in 1827, relocating to London 10 years later. He became the most noted American banker in the city and helped establish US international credit. His joint business Peabody, Morgan & Co. would go on to become J.P. Morgan. He gave away more than half his fortune, setting up libraries, schools, and housing associations for the poor.

1901, Carnegie devoted himself to philanthropic activities, which reached across the US and English-speaking world.

Legacy of philanthropy

Carnegie believed that the rich were trustees of wealth and should use it to promote others' happiness and welfare. He wrote often on social issues, stating in his article, "The Gospel of Wealth", that, "A man who dies thus rich dies disgraced". Carnegie never forgot the kindness of Colonel Anderson and was true to his promise, spending more than $55 million on building 2,509 libraries in the US and elsewhere. He established colleges, schools, institutions, and trusts that continue to benefit people today, including the Carnegie Endowment for International Peace, the Carnegie Trust for the Universities of Scotland, and the Carnegie Museums of Pittsburgh.

Carnegie's Keystone Bridge Company was contracted to erect the superstructure of Eads Bridge in St. Louis. Made from steel and wrought iron in 1874, it still stands today.

KEYSTONE BRIDGE COMPANY

DIRECTORY

Industrialization began in the mid-18th century and later swept the world. Entrepreneurs formed companies with truly international outlooks, and mass production allowed more products to be sold to wider markets than ever before. For driven individuals, success could be far-reaching.

REBECCA LUKENS
(1794–1854)

The highly educated daughter of a Pennsylvanian iron manufacturer, Rebecca Webb Pennock married Dr. Charles Lukens in 1813. She urged him to invest in the iron business, and they leased a local ironworks, borrowing heavily to convert it to manufacture boiler plates for steam-powered ships. After her husband and her son died in 1825, Lukens took sole control. Battling recession, debts, and flooding, Lukens expanded the business and by 1847 had built the preeminent manufacturer of boiler plates in the US.

EBERHARD ANHEUSER
(1806–1880)

Born in Germany, Eberhard Anheuser emigrated to the US in 1843. He settled in St. Louis and set up a successful soap and candle manufacturing company. Anheuser invested in a local business, the Bavarian Brewing Company, and when it almost went bankrupt in 1860, he bought out its other creditors and began running it himself, changing its name to E. Anheuser & Co. The following year, his daughter married Adolphus Busch, a German immigrant who later became Anheuser's business partner in his brewing business. In 1879, the company was renamed Anheuser-Busch and is now one of the largest beer producers in the US.

CYRUS MCCORMICK
(1809–1884)

A farmer's son from Virginia, Cyrus McCormick was the first person to build a mechanical reaper—a machine enabling farmers to efficiently harvest crops. He developed a prototype of his machine in 1831, winning a patent three years later. He commercially marketed the device in the 1840s and built a Chicago factory to target farmers in the Midwest. Even after the patent's expiry, his business still thrived, due to his innovative production and marketing techniques. By the time McCormick died, his company was known globally, and in 1902, it merged to form the International Harvester Company.

SAMUEL COLT
(1814–1862)

On a sea voyage in 1830, the American-born Samuel Colt made a model of a revolving cylinder mechanism that would allow a handgun to be fired six times without reloading. Colt patented his invention in 1835 and began to manufacture his "revolver" and other firearms. Early failures forced Colt to close his factory in 1842, but he reopened it in 1847 after receiving an order for 1,000 pistols. In 1855, Colt opened a cutting-edge factory that mass-produced firearms. By 1862, his company was one of the world's most successful firearms manufacturers.

HENRI NESTLÉ
(1814–1890)

Born in Frankfurt, Germany, Henri Nestlé was apprenticed to a pharmacist before moving to Switzerland. He carried out research in various fields, but the invention that made his fortune was "farine lactée." This infant formula blended powdered milk with a flour from which the acid and starch had been removed, as infants found these hard to digest. By 1869, it was on sale across Europe and in the US. In 1874, Nestlé sold his business, which is now the largest food company in the world.

THOMAS ADAMS
(1818–1905)

US-born Thomas Adams is known for having first launched chewing gum as a mass-market product. He discovered the potential of a natural gum called *chicle* while experimenting on it as a cheaper alternative to rubber tires. The tire experiments failed, yet Adams realized *chicle* could create a superior chewing gum to that made of spruce resin or sweetened paraffin. He began selling it in 1869, won a patent in 1871, and, by adding flavors, made it the most popular chewing gum in the US.

ELIZABETH HOBBS KECKLEY
(1818–1907)

Elizabeth Hobbs Keckley was born into slavery in Virginia. Taught to sew by her seamstress mother, she made dresses for white women and freed black women, some of whom helped her buy her freedom and would become her initial client base. After moving to Washington, she set up a dressmaking business of 20 seamstresses. There, her talents caught the notice of the first lady, Mary Todd Lincoln, to whom she became both personal designer and friend. Keckley also founded a charity to support freed slaves and wounded black soldiers and published a book.

CHARLES T. HINDE
(1832–1915)

Working on the riverboats of the Mississippi River, Ohio-born Charles T. Hinde became a steamboat captain then set up a shipping business. After seeing the commercial potential of railroad travel, in 1870 Hinde sold his interests in water transportation to become an agent for railroad companies. In 1879, he moved to California, working in property and hotel development. He also invested in mines and shipping and worked on charitable causes.

GOTTLIEB DAIMLER
(1834–1900)

In 1872, German engineer Gottlieb Daimler worked for Nikolaus Otto, the developer of a petroleum-powered internal-combustion engine. After clashing with Otto, Daimler was sacked in 1880 and went into business with a former colleague. They developed the first motorcycle in 1885 by adding a gasoline engine to a bicycle and then built an automobile. In 1890, they founded Daimler Motors Corporation and sold automobiles commercially.

PERSIS FOSTER EAMES ALBEE
(1836–1914)

The American wife of a New Hampshire politician, Persis Foster Eames Albee worked as an agent for David H. McConnell, a New York book dealer. In 1886, McConnell began selling cosmetics instead of books, and Albee became his key salesperson. She traveled house-to-house, directly marketing their products to female customers. Albee's great innovation was to recruit and train hundreds of other women as "depot agents," giving them the opportunity to gain financial independence by selling products. She helped develop new cosmetics and ran her own shop. The company was later renamed Avon, and Albee is known as the first "Avon Lady."

JAMES J. HILL
(1838–1916)

James J. Hill had an impoverished childhood in Ontario, Canada. In his late teens, he migrated to Minnesota, the center of river transportation in the US and worked in shipping. In 1870, he set up a business arranging steamboat transportation for freight, particularly coal. Hill then entered the railroad business, heading a consortium that bought the bankrupt St. Paul and Pacific Railroad. Under Hill's leadership, it prospered and expanded. He purchased other regional railroads and in 1890 amalgamated them into the Great Northern Railway, which eventually ran from coast to coast.

ADOLPHUS BUSCH
(1839–1913)

The youngest of 21 children, Adolphus Busch emigrated to the US from his native Germany in 1857. He settled in St. Louis and set up a company supplying brewers. In 1865, he went into business with a local brewer, Eberhard Anheuser, and was made a partner in 1873. He encouraged the use of refrigeration and developed a way to pasteurize the beer so it could be distributed nationally. Busch also helped develop the beer Budweiser, which became a global brand. The company was renamed Anheuser-Busch in 1879, and after Anheuser died the following year, Busch became its president. Under his leadership, it became the largest brewer in the US, with factories, facilities, and distribution hubs across the country.

GEORGE CADBURY
(1839–1922)

In 1861, English brothers George and Richard Cadbury took over their father's chocolate and cocoa manufacturing business. They made the company profitable and in 1879 moved the factory from Birmingham to a rural site they named Bournville. They ensured superior working conditions, giving employees access to their own social security program. In 1893, George purchased land to build a model village for Bournville employees, with decent, affordable housing. He campaigned for social reform, among other charitable works. After Richard died in 1899, George became chairman of Cadbury's, which continued to thrive under his leadership.

3

POWER
AND
MONOPOLY

1870–1940

JAMSETJI
TATA

Indian entrepreneur, industrialist, and philanthropist Jamsetji Tata was the founder of the Tata Group, which later became the biggest conglomerate in India. At the height of British rule in India, Tata set out to prove his country could compete with its colonial masters in the manufacturing of—and trade in—textiles, iron, and steel.

Jamsetji Nusserwanji Tata was born in South Gujarat, 1839. He graduated from college in Bombay (now Mumbai) and in 1858 joined his father's export firm—which traded in cotton, opium, and tea—helping set up branches in China, Japan, Europe, and the US. In 1868, he founded his own company; this was the start of what would become the Tata Group.

Convinced that he could make inroads into the British dominance of the textile industry by producing high-quality cotton in his own country, Tata acquired a cotton mill in 1869. Two years later, he visited Lancashire, England, to make an extensive study of its cotton manufacturing processes and trade. When he returned home, Tata set up the Central India Spinning, Weaving, and Manufacturing Company in 1874, establishing the Empress Mills in Nagpur, close to rail links, cotton fields, and fuel sources. Tata's mills would become major contributors to India's global textile trade for the next century.

For the rest of his life, Tata pursued three goals: to set up an iron and steel company, to generate hydroelectric power, and to create a world-class scientific institution. He began organizing India's first large-scale ironworks in 1901, which became the Tata Iron and Steel Company in 1907, and planned the Bombay hydroelectric power plants that would form the Tata Power Company in 1906. In all his projects, he was known for implementing unprecedented welfare policies to benefit and protect his factory workers.

MILESTONES

BECOMES A TRADER
Starts work at his father's export trading company in 1858, aged 20, helping to establish it overseas.

COTTON MANUFACTURE
Notes the huge potential of the cotton industry while in China in the 1860s; buys a mill in 1869.

BOOSTS EDUCATION
Establishes the J.N. Tata Endowment in 1892, a fund to encourage Indian students into higher education.

BUILDS LUXURY HOTEL
Oversees work on the Taj Mahal Hotel in 1903. It is the first building in Bombay to use electricity.

"With honest and straightforward business principles ... [and] attention to details ... there is a **scope for success."**

Jamsetji Tata

American industrialist John D. Rockefeller made a fortune from refining oil—his Standard Oil Company became one of the largest and most successful businesses in history. It gained such a monopoly that it led to the passing of antitrust laws at the end of the 19th century.

ROCKEFELLER
JOHN D.

MILESTONES

LEARNS BOOKKEEPING
Is apprenticed at a shipping company in 1855, aged 16, after taking a short business course.

STARTS BUSINESS
Sets up his own commission merchant business in 1859, grossing $450,000 in the first year.

MOVES INTO OIL
Constructs first oil refinery in Cleveland in 1863; buys out his business partners in 1865, gaining total control.

DOMINATES US OIL
His Standard Oil Company refines about 90 percent of all the oil in the US by 1882.

The California entity of Rockefeller's Standard Oil Company produced its own monthly magazine to explain its business operations and plans to shareholders, employees, and the general public.

Born in New York in 1839, John Davison Rockefeller was a hard worker from the start, with a single-minded focus on wealth. Some attribute this to his troubled upbringing; his father was a traveling salesman, swindler, and bigamist, and the family lived in poverty. From a young age, Rockefeller started making money from various ventures and secured his first office job, aged 16, as an assistant bookkeeper at a produce shipping company. Within four years, he had started his own business with a partner, Maurice Clark, and set up as a merchant selling hay, meats, grains, and other goods on a commission basis.

Oil rush

Productive oil wells had been established in Pennsylvania in the early 1860s, and Rockefeller saw his opportunity to become a part of the booming oil business, providing a cheaper fuel than whale oil for lighting: kerosene. He built his first oil refinery in Cleveland in 1863, the largest in the area. By 1870, he had formed the Standard Oil Company and soon began to buy out his more cautious business partners and competitors at greatly discounted rates in a bid to create an oil monopoly. No blood was spilled in what Rockefeller's opponents called the "Cleveland Massacre," but in 1872, by which time the company controlled nearly all the refineries in Cleveland, Rockefeller

STANDARD OIL BULLETIN

PUBLISHED MONTHLY BY THE STANDARD OIL COMPANY (CALIFORNIA) 1925
FEBRUARY

1839-1937

Standard Oil was a monopoly, and although Rockefeller dismantled the Trust, it essentially continued as a web of different companies, with Rockefeller expanding into the iron ore industry, including transportation, and acquiring more oil businesses. In 1909, spotting a loophole in the law in New Jersey, Rockefeller and his son, who was now involved in the business, recreated the Trust as a single holding company.

Business split

The exposure of Rockefeller's ruthless business practices by a tenacious journalist named Ida Tarbell eventually led to the breakup of Standard Oil. In 1911, the press was full of the story as the massive corporation was split into 34 separate companies. Rockefeller was already considering retirement and the dispersal of some of his fortune. He was a devout Baptist and, around the turn of the century, had begun to focus his attention on philanthropy. He founded major US institutions, including the Rockefeller Institute for Medical Research in 1901 (now Rockefeller University), and the Rockefeller Foundation in 1913. By the time of his death, aged 98, in 1937, Rockefeller had given away more than $500 million.

Employees are seen here filling barrels with engine oil for shipment at the Standard Oil Company's refinery in New York.

was able to negotiate very favorable transportation rates for his oil with the railroad companies, allowing him to keep his oil prices lower than his competitors.

Rockefeller went on to buy up oil pipelines, oil terminals, and competing refineries in other cities. He set up the Standard Oil Trust, with himself as head, and dominated the oil industry across the US, with a near monopoly by 1882. Some admired his business skills, but many disliked how he undercut, or bought out, smaller oil companies and regarded him as a robber baron.

The Standard Oil Trust soon became a target for journalists and politicians. The US Congress ruled, with the Sherman Antitrust Act in 1890, that

"It is a **religious duty** to get all the money you can, fairly and honestly; to **keep all you can,** and **to give away all you can."**

John D. Rockefeller, 1928

AS A BOY, ASPIRED TO EARN **$100,000** | **CONTROLLED 90%** OF US **REFINERIES** AND **PIPELINES** BY 1880 | STILL **ONE** OF THE **RICHEST** MEN **EVER** TO HAVE LIVED

"WHO IS THE POOREST MAN IN THE WORLD? … THE POOREST MAN I KNOW OF IS THE MAN WHO HAS NOTHING BUT MONEY; NOTHING ELSE IN THE WORLD UPON WHICH TO DEVOTE HIS AMBITION AND THOUGHT."

John D. Rockefeller
Address to Fifth Avenue Baptist Church, 1897

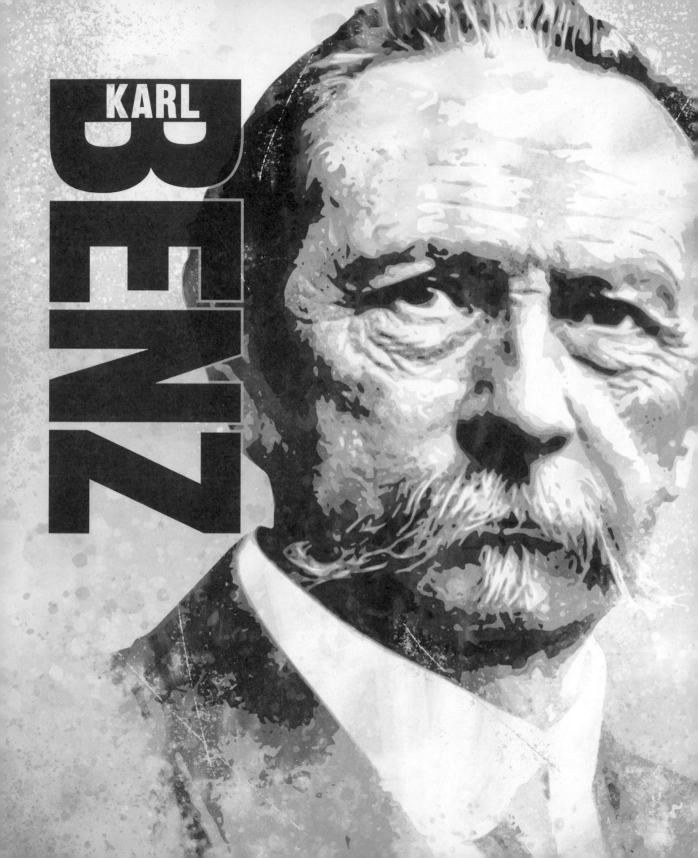

Engineer Karl Benz's vision was to design a mode of transportation for the general public that required neither horses nor rails. In developing the "horseless carriage," the first practical automobile powered by an internal combustion engine, he revolutionized the way in which people were able to travel.

Karl Friedrich Benz was born in Karlsruhe, Germany, and was just two years old when his father, a train driver, died. As a boy, Benz fixed watches and clocks to help his mother financially. At school, he excelled at his studies and went on to take a degree in mechanical engineering at Karlsruhe University. While there, he studied the steam train and began to formulate his ideas about a self-propelled engine that would run on something other than steam and could travel freely without rails. After graduating from college at the age of 19, Benz worked in various companies as a mechanical engineer, but he spent every spare moment on his engine design.

Building his vision

In 1871, Benz set up a workshop in Mannheim with a partner, August Ritter, but the business ran into difficulties, and Benz's tools were confiscated by bailiffs. Benz's future wife, Bertha Ringer, paid off his debts, and when they married in 1872, Bertha used her dowry to invest in her new husband's workshop.

Benz set to work on his engine design, devising and patenting an electric coil ignition system, a speed regulation system, spark plugs, a radiator, a carburetor, a clutch, and a gear-changing mechanism in the process. Finally, in 1883, he found backers for his "horseless

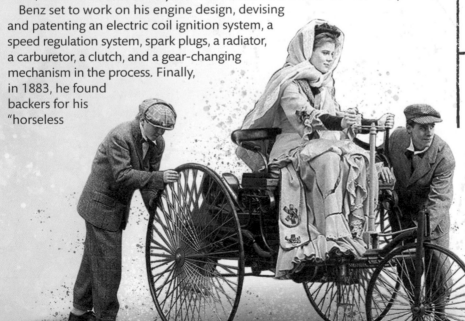

MILESTONES

CHANGES PATH
Focuses on locksmithing as a student, before switching to mechanical engineering in 1860.

BUILDS BRIDGES
Works at a bridge-building company in 1868, before a brief stint in Vienna at an iron construction company.

CREATES FIRST CAR
Takes the first orders for his Benz Motorwagen in 1888, making it the first automobile for the public.

BREAKS RECORD
Introduces a racing car, the Blitzen Benz, in 1909. Sets a land-speed record of 140 mph (226.1 km/hr).

Karl Benz's wife, Bertha, had complete faith in her husband's vision for a "horseless carriage." It was only with Bertha's help that Benz was able to accomplish his dream.

69

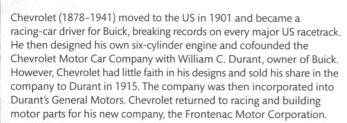

LOUIS-JOSEPH **CHEVROLET**

Born in Switzerland, Louis-Joseph Chevrolet was a racing-car driver, automobile designer, and cofounder of the Chevrolet Motor Car Company.

Chevrolet (1878–1941) moved to the US in 1901 and became a racing-car driver for Buick, breaking records on every major US racetrack. He then designed his own six-cylinder engine and cofounded the Chevrolet Motor Car Company with William C. Durant, owner of Buick. However, Chevrolet had little faith in his designs and sold his share in the company to Durant in 1915. The company was then incorporated into Durant's General Motors. Chevrolet returned to racing and building motor parts for his new company, the Frontenac Motor Corporation.

carriage": bicycle manufacturers Max Rose and Friedrich Esslinger. Together, the three men set up a new company, Benz & Co., and Benz built the first automobile, which he dubbed the "Motorwagen." In 1886, he successfully patented his design as the first "gas-fueled automobile."

Marketing the Motorwagen

Bertha Benz played a major role in bringing her husband's invention to the public's attention, and she also helped enhance its design. In a bid to generate publicity for the Motorwagen while proving its reliability, she and her two teenage sons went for a 75-mile (120 km) "joyride" from Mannheim to Pforzheim in the Motorwagen in 1888. Leaving in the morning, they completed the trip by nightfall. It was the ultimate road test and publicity stunt.

Bertha had to make regular stops to refuel the gas tank at apothecary shops that sold the gas solvent ligroin. She also visited a cobbler's to improve Benz's brake design, nailing leather strips to the wooden brake blocks to create the world's first brake pads. When she reached Pforzheim, Bertha sent a telegram to her husband to tell him about the trip.

The outing was a marketing success. Many people saw the Motorwagen drive past and news about it spread quickly. Orders for the automobile poured in to Benz & Co., and Benz expanded his

Benz's Motorwagen turned heads in the cities of Europe when it took to the streets. Sales of the automobile soared following its appearance at the Paris World's Fair in 1889.

"Only one person remained with me in the **small ship of life** when it seemed **destined to sink.** That was **my wife."**

Karl Benz, 1925

factory facilities to cope. An improved Motorwagen design was launched at the 1889 Paris World's Fair to great acclaim, and over the next decade the number of Benz & Co. employees grew from 50 to 430.

By the end of the century, Benz & Co. was the leading producer of automobiles in Europe, and Benz had patented further engine designs. He retired from the company in 1903 but remained on the board of directors. In 1926, Benz & Co. merged with its competitor, Daimler, to form the Daimler-Benz corporation. Karl Benz died in 1929, followed by Bertha in 1944. However, his many innovations continued to influence the automotive industry.

THE MOTORWAGEN HAD ONLY **2 GEARS**

BUILT **25** MOTORWAGEN MODELS BETWEEN **1886** AND **1893**

BENZ & CO. PRODUCED **572** AUTOMOBILES **IN 1899**

A prolific American inventor, Thomas Edison held a record number of patents and understood that having an idea was not enough—it had to be commercially viable. He set up the world's first research facility to develop and manufacture groundbreaking inventions and initiated the birth of the electricity industry, changing society forever.

MILESTONES

FILES PATENT
Gets the first of his 1,093 successful US patents in 1868, at age 21. Later holds patents worldwide.

INVENTIONS HUB
Sets up the world's first industrial research facility for invention in New Jersey in 1876.

RECORDS PRESIDENT
Captures the voice of US President Rutherford Birchard Hayes on his phonograph in 1877.

MAKES A MOVIE
Projects moving pictures using his Kinetograph, a cine camera, for the first time in 1896.

Born in Ohio, Thomas Alva Edison was the youngest of seven children. Finding it difficult to concentrate at school because of hearing difficulties, he was educated at home by his mother, a former teacher. With her encouragement, Edison developed into an avid reader who loved learning and experimentation.

At the age of 12, Edison started selling newspapers and confectionery on the Grand Trunk railroad line. This brought him into contact with the new technology of telegraphy, which was used to communicate daily news to the station office. Setting up a printing press in a baggage car, Edison started his first enterprise: turning these bulletins into a newspaper, which he sold alongside his other papers.

Communications industry

In 1863, Edison was taught to operate a telegraph by the father of a child he had saved from being struck by a train. Substituting for men who were fighting in the American Civil War, he spent the next five years moving from city to city as a telegrapher. Edison became increasingly interested in communications technology and electricity and began experimenting with improving the process of telegraphy.

Moving to New York in 1869, aged 22, Edison set up an electrical engineering company with two partners and developed a telegraph that could print changing stock prices on a ticker tape. Selling nearly 5,000 of these stock tickers between 1871 and 1874, he saved enough money to set up a small laboratory in Newark,

Edison demonstrates his cine camera alongside George Eastman (left) in 1928. Eastman invented Kodacolor film, which was used in Edison's camera to create the first films made for cinema.

"Genius is **1 percent inspiration** and **99 percent perspiration.**"

Thomas Edison, 1901

THOMAS EDISON

1847–1931

INVENTED THE LIGHT BULB

PHONOGRAPH

FIRST COMMERCIAL LAMP

Many of Edison's most important innovations came to fruition at his "inventions factory" in Menlo Park, New Jersey. The facility used scientific research to explore ideas, with a view to creating practical products for the mass market.

New Jersey. Here, he focused on improving telegraphy equipment, developing receivers, automatic printers, and the quadruplex, which could transmit two signals in different directions through the same wire. Rivalry between the leading telegraph companies created such demand for his inventions that Edison was soon able to expand his business.

In 1876, he built a new research facility, which he described as his "invention factory," in Menlo Park, New Jersey. With

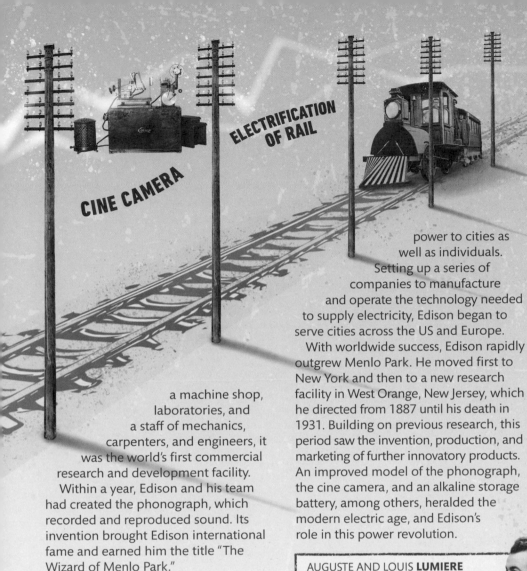

CINE CAMERA

ELECTRIFICATION OF RAIL

a machine shop, laboratories, and a staff of mechanics, carpenters, and engineers, it was the world's first commercial research and development facility. Within a year, Edison and his team had created the phonograph, which recorded and reproduced sound. Its invention brought Edison international fame and earned him the title "The Wizard of Menlo Park."

Power and light

Wanting to explore the potential of electricity, Edison formed The Edison Electric Light Company in 1878. By October 1879, he had created the first successful incandescent light bulb, lasting 13.5 hours and in May 1880 gave visitors a ride on the first electric railroad at Menlo Park. With mass production of electric lamps using his bulbs underway, Edison began to develop an electrical system that could provide economic light and power to cities as well as individuals. Setting up a series of companies to manufacture and operate the technology needed to supply electricity, Edison began to serve cities across the US and Europe.

With worldwide success, Edison rapidly outgrew Menlo Park. He moved first to New York and then to a new research facility in West Orange, New Jersey, which he directed from 1887 until his death in 1931. Building on previous research, this period saw the invention, production, and marketing of further innovatory products. An improved model of the phonograph, the cine camera, and an alkaline storage battery, among others, heralded the modern electric age, and Edison's role in this power revolution.

AUGUSTE AND LOUIS **LUMIERE**

The Lumière brothers, Auguste and Louis, advanced cinema photography and formed an innovative photographic company.

Auguste (1862–1954) and Louis (1864–1948) helped their father in his small photographic plate business as teenagers. In 1881, Louis invented a new "dry plate" process for developing film. After seeing Edison's cine camera, which could show images to only one viewer, the brothers developed their Cinématographe device, which could project film onto a screen. Lumière and Sons went on to become one of the world's leading photographic companies, making numerous films, including the first newsreels and documentaries.

HENRY FORD

An industrialist, mechanical engineer, and business magnate, Henry Ford is best known for creating the Model T Ford, the first affordable automobile for the masses. Ford's innovations revolutionized the way people traveled and brought mass production and consequently mass consumption to the US and the world.

The son of Irish immigrant farmers, Henry Ford was born in Michigan in 1863. He became obsessed with mechanics after receiving a watch for his 12th birthday and resolved to become a mechanical engineer and build automobiles after seeing an early steam road engine.

At 16, Ford began work as an apprentice engineer in a machine workshop in Detroit. He later took on a succession of jobs that allowed him to improve his mechanical and engineering knowledge, while continuing to experiment in his spare time. One of his earliest inventions was a tractor built from a steam engine motor and the body of an old mowing machine. Ford became convinced that gas-powered engines could replace traditional horse power and transform both farm machinery and everyday travel.

Gasoline power

In 1896, while employed by the Edison Illuminating Company in Detroit, Ford developed a gas-powered automobile mounted on four bicycle wheels called the "Quadricycle." His efforts attracted the attention of lumber baron William H. Murphy, who in 1899 set Ford up in his own business—the Detroit Automobile Company. The venture was a failure; the cars were made from low-quality parts and cost too much to buy while Ford exasperated his workers and backers by procrastinating over designs.

MILESTONES

EARLY EXPERIMENTS
Invents the gas-fueled Quadricycle in 1896, after years of testing gas- and steam-powered engines.

FAILED BUSINESS
Establishes the Detroit Automobile Company, 1899, which closes just two years later.

MODEL T ARRIVES
Founds the Ford Motor Company, 1903. Produces the first affordable car, Model T, five years later.

VAST NEW FACTORY
Builds Ford Motors' River Rouge Plant, the largest integrated factory in the world, in Detroit, 1928.

FAMILY CONTROL
In 1943, at the age of 79, resumes presidency of Ford after the death of his only son, Edsel.

Henry Ford and his son, Edsel, drove out in the 15 millionth Model T car in 1927. Ford famously remarked that "Any customer can have a car painted any color that he wants so long as it is black."

produce luxury cars, which took too much time and money, Ford aimed to "build a car for the great multitude"— one that was spacious, reliable, and affordable. His first design, the Model A, was an instant hit.

Affordable road travel

Ford's persistence paid dividends: between 1903 and 1908, the Ford Motor Company manufactured nine different cars. None, however, surpassed the Model T: a four-cylinder, left-hand drive car that was simple to drive, easy to repair, and affordable at $850.

The Model T Ford made car travel a possibility for ordinary people, for whom it had always been too expensive, and by 1927, the company had sold more than 15 million of them. The car's success fostered a rapid period of modernization and urbanization in the US, encouraging a boom in highways, service

Ford's assembly line technique for car manufacture allowed his company to move into plane, tank, and engine production during World War II, which reinvigorated company profits.

When his preference for designing racing cars over a marketable vehicle brought him into conflict with the company board, Ford quit, vowing to work only for himself from then on.

In 1903, he founded the Ford Motor Company with $28,000 in cash put up by new shareholders who deemed him worthy of the risk. Rather than

> "**Failure** is simply the **opportunity** to **begin again** ... more **intelligently.**"

Henry Ford, 1927

stations, automobile clubs, and building in suburban areas, as previously remote and rural locations became more easily accessible.

Manufacturing revolution

Ford's mission to reduce costs led to a radical manufacturing innovation: mass production. At first, Ford's workers built each car from the bottom-up before moving on to the next one, but in 1913, he introduced the moving assembly line: each worker stood beside a moving conveyor belt and constructed one part before the conveyor belt took it on to the next worker, who would assemble another part until the car was complete. This new method reduced production time from 12 hours and 8 minutes to 1 hour and 33 minutes per car and caused a worldwide revolution in factory processes. Profits were passed on to the consumer in the form of affordable cars, and, in 1914, Ford increased his workers' pay to $5 (double the industry average) and reduced their working day from nine hours to eight. Now workers had more time and the means to be consumers themselves. Through innovative car production, Ford had improved manufacturing systems, democratized travel, and fueled the rise of a middle class eager to spend their wages on a wave of new products.

When Ford died at age 83 in 1947, his holdings went to the Ford Foundation, which became the wealthiest private foundation in the world.

THERE WERE **10,000** JOB APPLICATIONS TO FORD IN **1914**

BY 1927, A **MODEL T** WAS PRODUCED EVERY **24** SECONDS

MADE MORE THAN **8,000** B-24 LIBERATOR BOMBERS **DURING WWII**

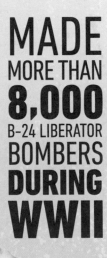

"WE BELIEVED THAT WHEN A MAN BOUGHT ONE OF OUR CARS, WE SHOULD KEEP IT RUNNING FOR HIM AS LONG AS WE COULD AND AT THE LOWEST UPKEEP COST. THAT WAS THE ORIGIN OF FORD SERVICE."

Henry Ford
Ford News, June 1, 1927

◀ *Henry Ford joins farmers* about to harvest wheat, riding one of his own gas-powered tractors, Michigan,1944.

MADAM C. J. WALKER

African American businesswoman, activist, and philanthropist Madam C. J. Walker built an empire selling her hair products to black women against a backdrop of early 20th-century racial inequality. She also provided work opportunities for thousands of women of color while supporting many African American causes.

Sarah Breedlove (she later took the name Walker after marrying her second husband) was born in Louisiana in 1867, but she moved to Missouri in 1889 following the death of her first husband. A single parent, she found work in a laundry. In the late 1890s, she began to suffer hair loss and sought products to help the condition. One such treatment was made by entrepreneur Annie Turnbo Malone. Seeing an opportunity, Breedlove began selling Malone's products door-to-door and then created her own formula using petroleum jelly and sulfur.

Breedlove moved to Colorado in 1905 with her daughter and married Charles Joseph Walker a year later. Restyling herself as Madam C. J. Walker, she established a successful line of hair-care products designed for black women and developed methods of application and grooming. Recruiting black women through connections with local churches (where she would personally demonstrate her products), she built a network of door-to-door sales agents and set up a mail-order service. Walker gradually expanded her business into the Caribbean and Central America, and her business model gave thousands of black women the opportunity to work for themselves. Among Walker's philanthropic activities was a donation of $1,000 toward the building of a YMCA in Indianapolis and in 1919, the year she died, a gift of $5,000 to an anti-lynching fund set up by the Advancement of Colored People.

MILESTONES

MAKES HAIR PRODUCT
Sells Annie Malone hair products in 1904, then designs her own, causing controversy with Malone.

LAUNCHES COMPANY
In 1905, moves to Denver, remarries, and markets Madam C. J. Walker's Wonderful Hair Grower.

SETS UP COLLEGE
Briefly relocates to Pittsburgh and establishes Lelia College of Beauty Culture in 1908.

POLITICAL ACTIVISM
Speaks against lynching at a 1917 White House visit; supports rights of black soldiers in World War I.

> "Don't sit down and wait for the opportunities to come. **Get up and make them.**"

Madam C. J. Walker, 1914

Madam C. J. Walker's face appeared on the lid of her bestselling product, Wonderful Hair Grower.

Melitta Bentz invented the coffee filter in 1908 and set up a business to sell it. Now known as the Melitta Group, the company remains a leading coffee brand worldwide.

A German housewife, Amalie Auguste Melitta Bentz invented the first coffee filter in her kitchen in Dresden using a brass pot in which she had punched holes and a piece of blotting paper she had ripped out of her son Willy's school notebook. Acquiring a patent for her invention, Bentz set up her business, M. Bentz, with her husband Hugo and their two sons in Dresden in 1908. The following year, Bentz's porcelain pour-over coffee makers and paper filters were a huge success at the Leipzig Trade Fair, and her company flourished. Passionate about providing good working conditions at her factory and treating her employees fairly, Bentz introduced a five-day working week, a Christmas bonus, and 15 days of vacation a year. She and her husband retired in 1932.

MELITTA BENTZ

"My mother, who had an excellent taste in coffee, was often **irritated by the coffee grounds** in her cup.**"**

Horst Bentz, son, 1949

MILESTONES

AWARDED PATENT	WINS MEDALS	CREATES BRANDING	HELPS EMPLOYEES
Receives a patent for a paper coffee filter in 1908 from the Imperial Patent Office in Berlin.	In 1910, wins gold and silver medals at the International Hygiene Exhibition in Dresden.	Introduces distinctive red-and-green packaging in 1922, to protect the brand from imitators.	Establishes Melitta Aid in 1938, a social fund for employees of the company.

Tomáš Baťa was a hugely successful businessman who not only built his family business into an internationally recognized footwear company but also sought to look after his workers.

On April 3, 1876, Tomáš Baťa was born into a family of shoemakers in Zlín in what is now the Czech Republic. With his brother and sister, he set up a company in his hometown in 1894, with 10 employees. Facing financial setbacks, Baťa began making shoes using cheaper canvas instead of leather, known as Baťovka. This proved so popular that the company was soon employing 50 people. Further growth came when Baťa won a contract to supply military boots during World War I. As the business expanded, he built houses to accommodate his workers, as well as schools, a hospital, and even a Baťa cinema. The Baťa Shoe Company became the leading manufacturer of footwear in Czechoslovakia and began building factories in other parts of Europe, together with towns for its employees to live in. Tomáš Baťa served as mayor of Zlín from 1923 until his death in a plane crash in 1932. Today, the company he founded has 5,300 outlets spread over 70 countries and employs over 80,000 people.

"Don't tell me **it can't be done**—tell me you just **don't know how to do it.**"

Tomáš Baťa, and now the Baťa company motto

TOMÁŠ BAŤA

DIRECTORY

In the late 19th and early 20th centuries, entrepreneurs created many of the most powerful international companies and brands in economic history. Some gained monopolies over entire sectors, becoming so large and influential that governments had to pass laws to break them up.

ASA GRIGGS CANDLER
(1851–1929)

After working as a pharmacist, US businessman Asa Griggs Candler became a beverage manufacturer. He invested in Coca-Cola, which at the time was being sold as a tonic. Candler purchased the business in 1891 and incorporated it the following year. He increased production, established more factories, and expanded sales across the US and abroad. In 1899, he secured Coca-Cola's first licensing agreement with a local company, allowing them to produce and distribute the drink. This template was the foundation of Coca-Cola's rapid growth. In 1919, Candler sold the company for $25 million.

WILLIAM E. BOEING
(1881–1956)

The son of German and Austrian immigrants, William E. Boeing was born in Detroit. He was interested in aircraft and founded the Pacific Aero Products Company in 1916, which he renamed the Boeing Airplane Company in 1917. It initially made aircraft for US armed forces and civilian clients but diversified into airmail and air passenger services, creating a new company called United Aircraft and Transport in 1929. Boeing had to break this up in 1934 under anti-trust legislation, but the Boeing Company continued, focusing on aircraft manufacture, and became an international leader in its field.

GEORGE EASTMAN
(1854–1932)

Originally working in banking and insurance, New Yorker George Eastman founded a film processing company in 1880. He introduced the Kodak camera in 1888, a button-operated handheld device that contained a 100-exposure roll of film. Cameras were sent back to Eastman's company to develop, print, and reload the film. In 1892, the company was renamed Eastman Kodak, and it thrived. Eastman stepped down in 1925 to focus on charitable activities and gave away more than half of his fortune. Later, he suffered from intense spinal pain and took his own life.

MILTON SNAVELY HERSHEY
(1857–1945)

Born in Pennsylvania, Milton Snavely Hershey was apprenticed to a local confectioner. In 1876, he opened his own store, but it failed after six years, as did his sweet-making business in New York. In 1886, Hershey founded the Lancaster Caramel Company, which he sold for $1 million in 1900. Using this money, he built a chocolate factory, completed in 1905, and developed his own highly popular milk chocolate. The area around the factory grew into the company town of Hershey. Before his death, Hershey gave the bulk of his assets to a charitable foundation.

WILLIAM RANDOLPH HEARST
(1863–1951)

The son of a politician and gold-mine owner, William Randolph Hearst went into media. In 1887, he took over the failing *San Francisco Examiner* and made it profitable. He then bought the *New York Morning Journal* in 1895 and entered into a circulation war with the owner of the *New York World*, using attention-grabbing headlines, color magazines, and illustrations. Over two decades, Hearst acquired publications across the US and became involved in film and radio and book publications. The Great Depression forced him to break up his corporation, and by his death, his personal power had waned.

TSUDA UMEKO
(1864–1929)

The daughter of a politician and educator, Tsuda Umeko was born in Edo (now Tokyo). She studied in the US until she was 18, then taught in Japan. Returning to the US in 1889, she gained a degree from Bryn Mwr College. After graduating in 1892, she campaigned for higher education for Japanese women. She moved back to Japan and set up a scholarship to fund women studying abroad. In 1900, Tsuda founded Joshi Eigaku Juku (now Tsuda University)—a women's university in Tokyo.

RINALDO PIAGGIO
(1864–1938)

In 1884, Italian vehicle manufacturer Rinaldo Piaggio set up his eponymous company in his home city of Genoa. He initially outfitted ships before moving into manufacturing railroad cars and locomotives. During World War I, Piaggio diversified into aviation, hiring specialist engineers. In 1924, he bought a manufacturing plant in Tuscany that produced trams, trucks, and cable cars. By the time of Piaggio's death in 1938, the company was already exporting products across the world. His sons succeeded him as CEO.

HELENA RUBINSTEIN
(1872–1965)

Born into a Jewish family in Kraków, Austria-Hungary (now Poland) Helena Rubinstein emigrated to Australia in 1896. She opened a cosmetics shop in Melbourne, first importing stock from Europe before manufacturing her own products. Returning to Europe in 1908, she opened high-end beauty salons in London and Paris, then moved to New York in 1914. Although Rubinstein had established salons in cities across the US, her business moved toward researching, manufacturing, and distributing her cosmetic products, focusing on skin care. A philanthropist, she established the Helena Rubinstein Foundation in 1953 to coordinate her charitable endeavors.

BACH THAI BUOI
(1874–1932)

Born into poverty in Vietnam, Bach Thai Buoi learned about machinery and production in a municipal workshop, and later spent time in France, introducing Vietnamese products at the Bordeaux Fair. On his return, he helped supply sleepers to the Indo-China railroad, and went on to invest in coal mining. He saw the potential for developing Vietnam's waterways, and, by appealing to Vietnamese passengers' sense of nationalism, successfully saw off Chinese and French competition to run a waterway transport route between major Vietnamese cities, growing his fleet from three to 30 ships.

LUISA SPAGNOLI
(1877–1935)

Italian-born Luisa Spagnoli comanaged a grocery store before launching the confectionery company Perugina. She opened a factory in Perugia, her home city, in 1907, creating the company's most famous product the baci ("kiss") in 1922. The success of Perugina allowed Spagnoli to branch out into fashion. From 1928, she became the first person in Italy to breed angora rabbits, using their soft and silky wool to make high-quality, luxury knitwear products for her eponymous clothing company. After Spagnoli's death, her son took over the clothing business, expanding it into an international enterprise.

WILLIAM S. HARLEY
(1880–1943)

The son of English immigrants, William S. Harley was born in Milwaukee and worked in a bicycle factory at age 15.

He began making motorcycles with a friend, Arthur Davidson, by mounting gas engines on bicycles. In 1903, the pair started the Harley-Davidson Motor Company, which produced motorcycles. Harley also went to college, gaining a degree in mechanical engineering in 1907. With his eye for detail and his innovative designs, the company grew, providing motorcycles to the US armed forces during both world wars. Harley remained the company's chief engineer and treasurer until his death.

CONRAD HILTON SR.
(1887–1979)

Growing up in New Mexico, Conrad Hilton began his career in hospitality by converting part of his father's house into a small hotel, later partnering with him to run a general store. After serving in World War I, Hilton bought hotels across Texas and grew the business to expand across the US. In 1946, he formed the Hilton Hotels Corporation and after 1948 began to open hotels outside the US. He acted as president until 1966, when his son Barron Hilton took over.

DAVID SARNOFF
(1891–1971)

Born in Uzlyany, Russia (modern-day Belarus), David Sarnoff emigrated to the US in 1900, settling in New York. In 1906, he became a radio operator for American Marconi, where he excelled. In 1919, it was purchased and formed part of a new company, the Radio Corporation of America (RCA). Sarnoff was its commercial manager before becoming president in 1930. He was a visionary leader, instrumental in the development of radio and television, as well as helping found NBC, the US's oldest major broadcast network.

4

MANUFACTURING AND MASS PRODUCTION

1914–1960

Clarence Saunders revolutionized the way people shopped. He developed "self-service" grocery shopping in his Piggly Wiggly stores at a time when store assistants usually collected products for their customers. By introducing checkouts, clearly priced goods, and itemized receipts, he set the foundations for the supermarkets of today.

Born in 1881, Clarence Saunders grew up in a poor family in Virginia. They later moved to Tennessee, and, at the age of 14, Saunders worked part time in a grocery store. Having attended school for just two years, he educated himself by reading widely. From his late teens, Saunders worked in wholesale grocery companies in Clarkesville and Memphis. He observed how customers in stores lined up to present their shopping lists to an assistant, who then collected their groceries from behind a counter. He thought this method of shopping was inefficient and costly and decided to set up his own self-service grocery store.

Piggly Wiggly

Saunders opened his first Piggly Wiggly store in Memphis in 1916. By cutting the costs of using assistants, he was able to offer goods at cheaper prices. The store was an instant success. Within six years, there were more than 1,200 Piggly Wiggly outlets, half of which were franchises, making it one of the largest grocery chains in the US. In addition to self-service, Saunders introduced other innovative ideas that he patented, including a store layout that had aisles ending at a checkout, pricing on each item, and a printed receipt listing the goods bought.

Piggly Wiggly was listed on the New York Stock Exchange in 1922. However, due to the failure of some New York franchises, the share price started to fall a year later. Saunders took out large loans and bought a significant amount of

Saunders's Piggly Wiggly branches offered customers a completely new shopping experience, where they could pick up a wooden shopping basket, select products themselves, and take them to a cashier-operated checkout.

CLARENCE

SAUNDERS

1881-1953

FRANK WINFIELD **WOOLWORTH**

A visionary retailer, Frank Woolworth founded one of the largest store chains in the world and pioneered sales methods that are still used today.

As a youngster, Woolworth (1852–1919) experienced bad service in a store and was determined to set up a retail outlet where anyone could buy anything and receive good service. At 26, he opened "Woolworth's Great Five-Cent Store" in Utica, New York. He bought directly from manufacturers, sold at a fixed price of five cents, and displayed merchandise in self-service cases. As he expanded, the business became F. W. Woolworth Company. By the time of his death, Woolworth had more than 1,000 stores in the US alone.

Piggly Wiggly stock to bring the share price back up, though traders on the New York Stock Exchange viewed this as bad practice. Saunders was forced to declare himself bankrupt and lost control of his business.

Sole Owner
Saunders created a competing grocery chain in 1928. He named it Clarence Saunders, Sole Owner of My Name Stores, Inc., in a bid to reclaim his name and restore his reputation after the negative press following his Piggly Wiggly resignation. The public came

> ## "**Enthusiasm** must be in the **firm belief** in the **thing sold,** not an **enthusiasm limited** in the **desire** to **sell.**"
>
> **Clarence Saunders**

The Piggly Wiggly company had its own fleet of delivery trucks that collected supplies to fill the shelves of Saunders's grocery stores.

to refer to the chain as "Sole Owner." Hundreds of Sole Owner outlets quickly appeared across the US, bringing in millions of dollars in revenue. During the early 1920s, when Piggly Wiggly was thriving, Saunders had built an ostentatious pink marble mansion in Memphis called the Pink Palace. He had lost the Pink Palace when he became bankrupt, but with his new fortune from the Sole Owner shops, he built an estate called Woodland. He also bought a professional football team to promote his new grocery chain. He named the team the Clarence Saunders, Sole Owner of My Name Tigers.

In 1930, at the start of the Great Depression (1929–1939), Saunders lost his Sole Owner stores and his football team when he again filed for bankruptcy. Despite this second disappointment, Saunders refused to give up and, in the years that followed, developed two more ideas for retail outlets. The first was an automated grocery, Keedoozle, in 1937. It resembled a large-scale vending machine, with merchandise traveling on conveyor belts to checkout stations. Unfortunately, the automation often broke down and Keedoozle failed. Up until his death in 1953, Saunders worked on another pioneering shopping concept where customers could pick their own groceries, bag them, and then operate the checkout, reducing the need for store workers at cash registers. He named it Foodelectric, and although one outlet was planned, it never opened.

Saunders's drive to improve customer experience while reducing costs has influenced the way stores operate today.

SOLD $100 MILLION WORTH OF GROCERIES IN 1923

HAD 220 "SOLE OWNER" SHOPS IN 15 STATES BY 1927

BUILT AND LOST 2 FORTUNES

Born into poverty, Coco Chanel was a seamstress and bar singer before setting up a small hat store in Paris. Business savvy, with an innate sense of style and an independent spirit, Chanel grew her clothing brand into a fashion empire that survived two world wars and revolutionized womenswear with its perfect balance of elegance and comfort.

MILESTONES

FIRST BOUTIQUE
In 1910, with help from two wealthy lovers, opens her first store as a milliner in Paris, called Chanel Modes.

ENTERS COUTURE
Opens a couture house in Biarritz in 1915, attracting wealthy clients and cementing her success.

LAUNCHES PERFUME
In 1921, releases her first perfume, Chanel No. 5, which quickly becomes a global success.

STAGES RETURN
Reopens her couture house in 1954 and enjoys new success with her tweed suits, especially in the US.

The daughter of a laundrywoman and an itinerant salesman, Gabrielle Bonheur "Coco" Chanel was born in 1883 in a poorhouse in Saumur, France. Sent to a convent orphanage at 11, after the death of her mother, Chanel was taught to sew by the nuns and found work, aged 18, as a seamstress in the town of Moulins. Working as a cabaret singer to supplement her income, it was on the stage that she acquired the nickname "Coco." Chanel later concealed her impoverished beginnings, but her childhood instilled resourcefulness and a deep understanding of the value of money and social connections as a means to independence and freedom.

Social reinvention
In 1906, Chanel became one of the mistresses of racehorse owner Étienne Balsan, who moved her into his château in Compiègne. She began making the hats she wore to the races herself and convinced Balsan to help her open a small millinery in Paris. Balsan introduced her to wealthy polo player Arthur Capel in 1908. Chanel was associated with a number of rich men throughout her career, but she later stated that Capel was the only man she ever loved. Chanel ran her millinery in a ground floor

Chanel skillfully popularized her own style. Photographed in Paris in 1958, her simply cut suit and two-tone shoes reflect the classic look of her model.

"In order **to be irreplaceable,** one must always **be different.**"

Coco Chanel

94

COCO

CHANEL

1883–1971

designed less-structured, pared-down clothes out of jersey, a fabric commonly used for men's underwear. The demand for practical clothing increased during World War I, and Chanel's collection became an immediate success. Two years later, she opened her first couture house in Biarritz, and another in Paris in 1918.

Unconventional icon

By the 1920s, Chanel was a wealthy and independent businesswoman, renowned for her distinctive style and strong character. Her business flourished while she continued to flout convention. The "little black dress," launched in 1926, repurposed a color associated solely with postwar mourning to create an item that was aspirational, accessible, and practical. She also began to produce a range of makeup, jewelry, and perfumes, starting with the hugely popular No. 5 in 1921.

Chanel began an affair in 1923 with the Duke of Westminster, who often took her to Scotland. There, she was inspired to use tweed, another traditionally masculine fabric, which she transformed into elegant womenswear, including her iconic suits.

When France declared war on Germany in 1939, Chanel closed her business and moved in to the Ritz hotel in Paris with

apartment owned by Balsan, while living with Capel, who helped her establish her business. In 1913, Capel financed her boutique in the resort of Deauville. There, inspired by the simplicity of contemporary menswear, Chanel launched a sportswear line for women. Long, flowing skirts and corsets were the norm, but Chanel instead

> "Dress shabbily and they remember the dress; **dress impeccably** and **they remember the woman.**"

Coco Chanel

her lover Hans Günther von Dincklage, a German officer. After the war ended, Chanel reopened her fashion house, despite criticism over her links with von Dincklage. She disapproved of the trends that had emerged in her absence from the fashion world and was determined to come back with something innovative.

In 1954, at the age of 71, she launched a new collection. Reviving the popularity of her suit designs, it was praised for providing a fresh alternative to the structured style of the "New Look." Another fashion hit in 1955, the 2.55 quilted leather bag with a chain shoulder strap, cemented her return.

Throughout the 1960s, a celebrity clientele, including Jackie Kennedy and Grace Kelly, ensured further success. Chanel continued to work until her death in 1971 at the age of 88. She was buried in her favorite Chanel suit.

Chanel's rags-to-riches *story inspired her designs, which used the simple lines, limited palette, and practical fabrics of everyday workwear to produce haute couture.*

DESIGNED THE **FIRST** SUITS FOR **WOMEN**

HAD **5** BOUTIQUES ON ONE STREET IN 1935

LIVED IN THE **RITZ** HOTEL, PARIS, FOR **34** YEARS

"THERE IS NO TIME FOR CUT-AND-DRIED MONOTONY. THERE IS TIME FOR WORK. AND TIME FOR LOVE. THAT LEAVES NO OTHER TIME."

Coco Chanel

Chanel's use of costume jewelry, especially pearls, became part of her signature look, pictured here in 1936. ▶

The cofounder of Metro-Goldwyn-Mayer (MGM) studios, Louis B. Mayer was the most successful movie producer of the 1930s and '40s. Under his direction, MGM built the biggest stable of star actors, top directors, and acclaimed screenwriters in Hollywood, during what was considered to be the golden age of film.

MILESTONES

FIRST SUCCESS
Opens his first nickelodeon (a cinema charging 5 cents for admission) in 1907.

MAKES MOVIES
Establishes his own movie production company when he moves to California in 1918.

MGM MERGER
Joins forces with Marcus Loew in 1924 to form Metro-Goldwyn-Mayer (MGM) studios.

EARNS FORTUNE
In 1937, becomes the first person in the US to command a salary of more than $1 million.

HAS HUGE HIT
Acquires sole distribution rights in 1939 for *Gone with the Wind*, the most successful movie ever.

Louis Burt Mayer, born Lazar Meir, was the son of Ukrainian Jewish immigrants, who settled in New Brunswick, Canada. Mayer had a poor upbringing, and to support his family, he left school at 12 to work in his father's scrap metal business. At that time, an entertainment revolution was taking place in the US, and thousands of motion-picture theaters, known as nickelodeons, were opening. In 1907, Mayer, who had moved to New England, saved enough money to renovate a 600-seat theater in Haverhill, Massachusetts; when it reopened, it offered cheap tickets and a steady stream of new movies. In 1915, Mayer paid $25,000 for exclusive rights to show the epic *The Birth of a Nation* in New England, despite not having seen the movie himself. It was a gamble that paid off, earning him more than $100,000, and three years later, he owned the largest chain of cinemas in New England.

Making movies
Showing movies was not enough for Mayer—he wanted to make them as well, and now he had the finances to do so. He moved to Los Angeles in 1918 and set up a movie studio, producing a series of romantic tearjerkers with popular actress Anita Stewart. Although small, the company was dynamic and profitable, and in 1924 Mayer's talent caught the attention of Marcus Loew, owner of the film company Metro-Goldwyn. Loew asked Mayer to head up his West Coast studio, which he agreed to do, on the condition that "Mayer" was included in the company's

A cameraman and sound technician recorded the roar of MGM's trademark lion, Leo, for the MGM movie logo in 1928.

100

MAYER

"I want to make **beautiful pictures** about **beautiful people.**"

Louis B. Mayer, 1925

Mayer's movie-making formula of elaborate sets, gorgeous costumes, and noncontroversial story lines wowed audiences around the world and made the producer (left) the top earner in the US.

name. In 1925, Mayer became head of operations at the Metro-Goldwyn-Mayer (MGM) studio in Hollywood—a position that he held until 1951.

While Mayer took charge of spotting talent, setting budgets, and approving new productions, his colleague Irving Thalberg controlled the movie-production process. Mayer and Thalberg had already worked together and made a brilliant team. Mayer's vision was to create new stars, tie them to MGM on long contracts, and produce good-quality, feel-good movies that emphasized the virtues of family and patriotism. Mayer had a knack for discovering actors with raw talent. Greta Garbo, Joan Crawford, Rudolph Valentino, and Clark Gable were just some of the many stars he found and nurtured. He also managed and developed child actors, including Judy Garland and Mickey Rooney. However, Mayer was not liked by all the actors who worked for him. Some found his attempts to control their private lives overbearing, and there were also allegations of inappropriate behavior toward some female actors.

The golden age

By 1927, MGM had established itself as the most successful studio in Hollywood. In that same year, its rival Warner Bros. released the

GEORGE **EASTMAN**

New York native George Eastman was a pioneer of easy-to-use film cameras, an innovation that made photography much more accessible.

Eastman (1854–1932) felt that cameras were too cumbersome and expensive. In 1880, he invented a machine that made possible the production of flexible roll film. His Eastman Kodak Company, set up in 1888, produced the handheld Kodak camera, using 100-exposure roll films instead of a glass-plate negative for each exposure. Thomas Edison (see pp.72–75) also used these rolls in a cine camera that he was developing. The Eastman Kodak Brownie camera brought photography to the masses in 1900—it retailed at $1 and 150,000 were sold in the first year.

first "talking picture," *The Jazz Singer.* MGM responded with *Alias Jimmy Valentine* in 1928 and continued to release a stream of box-office hits.

Mayer relied heavily on the production talent of Thalberg. In 1936, Thalberg died, and many thought this would hit MGM's fortunes. In fact, the company continued to flourish. By 1939, two-thirds of Americans attended a cinema at least once a week, and the constant demand for new movies kept studios working around the clock. There were up to 18 movies in production at MGM at any one time.

When color movies emerged in 1939, MGM again took advantage. It was the sole distributor of *Gone with the Wind* and released the musical *The Wizard of Oz.* However, after World War II, Mayer's romantic and family-friendly story lines started to lose their appeal. Budget cuts also meant that Mayer was unable to produce movies of the quality he desired, leading to tensions within the company. Mayer left MGM in 1951, and his subsequent attempts to establish an independent studio were unsuccessful.

SIGNED JUDY GARLAND TO MGM WHEN SHE WAS 13 YEARS OLD

REMAINED HEAD OF MGM FOR 26 YEARS

Konosuke Matsushita was the founder of Panasonic Corporation, one of the world's major consumer electronics manufacturers. His impoverished childhood and lack of education informed many of his business strategies; Matsushita believed that companies should help society to end poverty and improve people's lives.

The youngest of eight children, Konosuke Matsushita was born in Wakayama, southern Japan, in 1894. Matsushita's family had been well off, but when he was four years old, his father made poor business decisions that led to the loss of their land and farm, and they were forced to move to the city. Aged nine, he was sent to Osaka to become an apprentice at a store selling *hibachi* (portable braziers for cooking and heating). He then took up another apprenticeship at a bicycle shop, where he learned to be a salesman.

Bright idea
At the age of 15, Matsushita took a job at the Osaka Electric Light Company and quickly became a skilled technician. While he was there, he worked on a design to improve an electrical socket and showed it to his manager, who rejected the idea. Matsushita was convinced that the product would be successful, and so in 1917, he left the company to start a new business. His wife, Mumeno, whom he had married in 1914, her brother, Toshio, and two former colleagues joined him.

The group had very little money, so all they could afford to get started were some manual tools and basic supplies. After weeks of research and analysis, Matsushita's socket was ready. Sales were poor, however, and before the end

A National Television Car
toured Japan in 1953, exhibiting Matsushita's company's new household appliances.

KONOSUKE

MATSUSHITA

1894–1989

PANASONIC 1953: "THE YEAR OF ELECTRIFICATION"

Known as the "Year of Electrification," 1953 heralded an age when demand for electrical products grew globally. Domestic appliances such as fans, televisions, and washing machines were mass-produced by Matsushita's company.

of the year, his two former coworkers had left the business. Matsushita's luck then turned when one company suddenly placed a large order. The surprise sale gave Matsushita enough money to officially establish his new company in 1918 as Matsushita Electric Housewares Manufacturing Works—known today as Panasonic. He built a factory and within four years had 50 people working there.

Affordable luxuries

At a time when electrical appliances were considered luxury items, Matsushita wanted to make them affordable for everyone. In 1927, he launched the "Super Iron," having set up a new division within his company to mass-produce it, thereby lowering production costs. This allowed him to sell it for just 3.2 yen, well below the 5 yen price tag of other irons on the market. The Super Iron was a hit, and by 1928, Matsushita had increased his number of employees to 300.

However, following the Wall Street Crash of 1929, the company suffered a rapid drop in sales and, as a result, had a lot of unsold stock. Matsushita's staff

> "After all, **business** is ultimately for the **betterment** of our **society.**"
>
> **Konosuke Matsushita**

feared their jobs would be cut, but he reassured them otherwise. Instead, he halved the factory's production by having his employees work half days and encouraged them to sell any remaining stock. Within months, his employees had sold off all overstock, the economy had started to recover, and Matsushita's factory resumed full-scale production.

Company mission

One of Matsushita's business strategies had been inspired by a religious gathering that he attended in 1932. He realized that while religion could guide people toward happiness and peace of mind, so too could business, by providing the "physical necessities required" for human contentment. As he later explained to his employees,

he felt it was up to the company to try to help make the world a better place and overcome poverty by supplying goods "as plentiful and inexpensive as tap water."

By 1933, Matsushita's company was manufacturing more than 200 products. It moved to a new head office and factory in Kadoma, northeast Osaka, where Panasonic

Matsushita created an innovative bicycle lamp in 1923. His existing lamp often went out when he cycled at night, but his improved battery-powered bullet-shaped lamp stayed bright for much longer than other lamps.

"Your **business** is not a **means** of **maintaining** your **livelihood** or an **obligation**, but **something** you want to **strive for.**"

Konosuke Matsushita

is still based today. In 1935, as international exports of his products grew, Matsushita set up a trading department called Matsushita Electric Trading Company. This was a forward-thinking decision at the time, as other manufacturers paid little attention to their sales overseas, and the company's exports increased further.

Postwar struggles

By 1945, Matsushita had lost 32 factories and offices as a result of World War II. When the Allied forces occupied Japan after the war, they issued new laws—

directives that aimed to break up family-led conglomerates—that threatened to shut down his company. In addition, because Matsushita's company had produced military equipment during the war, the Allied forces ordered him to step down as its president. Matsushita contested his situation more than 50 times. Finally, in 1947, with the support of a petition by the newly formed labor union, as well as retailers and affiliates, Matsushita was permitted to remain and his firm allowed to operate as before.

Western expansion

In 1951, Matsushita went to the US and saw that his company needed to keep up with Western technologies. To do this, he formed a partnership with the Dutch electronics company Philips. In 1959, he expanded his export business by forming Matsushita Electric Corporation of America. Despite stepping down as president in the early 1960s, Matsushita retained an active role in his company's operations until 1973. He spent much of his retirement writing about his business and social philosophies, sharing his beliefs that it was possible to develop "a road to peace and happiness through prosperity." He died aged 94.

WERNER VON **SIEMENS**

Born in Hanover, Germany, Werner von Siemens studied science and technology at the Prussian Military Academy's School of Artillery and Engineering. His invention of the improved pointer telegraph led him to set up the company now known as Siemens AG.

After building an improved pointer telegraph in 1847 (which used a needle to point to letters rather than Morse code), Siemens (1816–1892) established his company with fellow engineer Johann Georg Halske. The technology used in the telegraph laid the foundations for an enhanced generator that achieved high rotational speeds, a huge advancement in electrical engineering that eventually led the company to construct the world's first electric locomotive in 1879. Siemens was committed to retaining qualified employees and set up various social policies, including a pension program.

In a photograph from 1964, Matsushita is surrounded by Panasonic electrical products. ▶

MILESTONES

MAKES ALICE COMEDIES
Releases "Alice's Day at Sea," the first work to be distributed by The Walt Disney Studios, in 1924.

CREATES ICON
Screens Mickey Mouse film *Steamboat Willie* in 1928: the world's first cartoon with synchronized sound.

GAINS RECOGNITION
Releases the world's first full-color cartoon, *Flowers and Trees*, in 1932; it wins an Academy Award.

CREATES PERSPECTIVE
In 1937, invents the Multiplane Camera, which produces an illusion of depth in animated films.

SMALL-SCREEN DEBUT
Launches TV anthology *Disneyland* in 1954; it helps finance his new theme park in California.

A gifted storyteller and innovative animator, Walt Disney transformed the entertainment industry in the 20th century. He pioneered new technology, techniques, and formats in film and television and brought his iconic characters alive through his world-famous theme parks.

Born in 1901 in Chicago, Illinois, Walter Elias Disney was a keen artist as a child. In his 20s, he began experimenting with hand-drawn cel animation and set up his first studio in 1922. Despite the growing popularity of his cartoons, which he called "Laugh-O-grams," the studio ran into debt and was forced to close in 1923.

Deciding to try his luck as a director in Hollywood, Disney moved to California and won a contract for a series of cartoons called the *Alice Comedies*. The first to mix live action with animation, they marked the founding of The Walt Disney Studios. In 1928, the world's first "talking picture" was released. Quickly realizing the potential for animation that synchronized action and sound, Disney produced *Steamboat Willie*, starring Mickey Mouse. It was an immediate hit and established Disney's reputation for innovation. His talent for taking risks and pioneering new formats continued over the next three decades, with the introduction of color to cartoons, full-length animated films, and television programs. In 1955, he took his desire to both entertain and educate away from the screen and into real life, opening the Disneyland theme park—based on his characters—in California.

"I suppose my formula might be: dream, diversify, and never miss an angle."

Walt Disney, 1958

WALT DISNEY

1901–1966

MILESTONES

STARTS FRANCHISING
Founds McDonald's System, Inc., in 1955. Buys out McDonald brothers for $7.6 million in 1961.

CATERS TO DRIVERS
Opens first drive-through format in Arizona in 1975; they come to account for 70 percent of revenue.

BUSINESS CHIEF
Makes himself senior chairman of McDonald's to oversee his business with complete authority in 1977.

Known as "fast food's founding father," milkshake machine salesman Ray Kroc saw the franchise potential in a family-owned hamburger bar called McDonald's, transforming it into a global brand.

Raymond Albert Kroc worked in various jobs before becoming a salesman for the Multimixer, a blender that could mix five milkshakes simultaneously. In 1954, Kroc visited a hamburger bar in San Bernardino, California, run by Maurice and Richard McDonald, which used eight of his Multimixers. He was immediately struck by its assembly line system, which enabled super-quick delivery of beverages, hamburgers, and fries to customers.

Spotting a business opportunity, Kroc offered the McDonalds a deal: he would set up a chain of McDonald's and pay the brothers a fee. Kroc began selling single-restaurant franchises so that owners would be running their own McDonald's hamburger bar. Kroc's vision was to establish uniformity across every outlet. To do this, he set up a training program in which franchisees were taught how to run a McDonald's to the required standards of "Quality, Service, Cleanliness, and Value." These operational principles, along with the provision of familiar food and concentration of restaurants in suburban areas, attracted a new market: families. By 1961, Kroc had set up over 200 McDonald's outlets across the US, and by the time he died in 1984, there were 7,500 globally.

RAY KROC

The famous golden arches, part of the design of many McDonald's restaurants since 1953, were incorporated into the company's logo in 1962.

McDonald's
SPEEDEE SERVICE SYSTEM
15¢
HAMBURGERS
We have Sold OVER 1 MILLION

McDonald's

US billionaire Howard Hughes turned his eclectic interests into legendary business achievements, gaining renown as a movie producer, pioneering aircraft designer and manufacturer, and an aviator.

The son of a successful inventor, Howard Robard Hughes Jr. showed an aptitude for engineering as a child, building his own radio transmitter and motorized bicycle by the age of 12. In 1924, his father died, leaving him the family tool manufacturing business and a significant fortune. Hughes decided to move to Hollywood and invest his money in the movie industry. Over the next two decades, he produced a number of box-office hits, garnering both Oscar and Academy Award nominations.

Interested in aviation since childhood—he had taken his first flight aged 14—Hughes obtained his pilot's license in 1928 and founded the Hughes Aircraft Company in 1932. Designing and flying his own planes, he set a series of world and transcontinental speed records.

Hughes experienced mental health problems, including obsessive-compulsive disorder, and by the 1950s was increasingly reclusive. In 1953, he set up the Howard Hughes Medical Institute, one of the world's primary charities and a leader in medical research.

MILESTONES

RUNS FAMILY BUSINESS
Takes over the Hughes Tool Company in 1924, turning it into a multibillion dollar asset; sells it in 1972.

MAKES MOVIES
Sets up as a Hollywood filmmaker in 1926; has major success, but filming often overruns time and budget.

TAKES FLIGHT
Founds the Hughes Aircraft Company in 1932; in 1938, sets a world flight record of 91 hours 14 minutes.

An Indian businessman and aviation pioneer, J. R. D. Tata started India's first airline and founded many of the Tata companies that today form the Tata Group—India's largest conglomerate and a global success story. Socially conscious, Tata also did much to further India's medical, cultural, and scientific interests.

MILESTONES

DISCOVERS AVIATION
Falls in love with flying as a child in France watching Louis Bleriot; takes his first flight aged 15 in 1919.

JOINS FAMILY FIRM
Becomes an unpaid apprentice at Tata in 1925; is appointed to the company board in 1926.

TAKES TO THE SKIES
In 1932, Tata Air Services begins flying passengers and mail between Karachi, Mumbai, and Chennai.

GLOBAL EXPANSION
Diversifies Tata Group from 1938 into hotels, automobiles, steel production, tea, and IT.

Jehangir Ratanji Dadabhoy Tata was born in Paris to a French mother and an Indian father. He studied in France, Japan, and the UK, where he had hoped to attend Cambridge University to study engineering. In 1925, however, as a French citizen, he was drafted into the French Army for one year of mandatory service. Afterward, his hopes of returning to education ended when tradition compelled him to join the Tata family business in India, which his great-grandfather had started in 1868.

India and business were unfamiliar to him, but he fulfilled his obligation, starting in the company as an unpaid apprentice in December 1925 at the age of 21. Less than a year later, on the death of his father, Tata was appointed to the board of Tata Sons, the group's flagship company. By 1929, Tata had decided to surrender his French citizenship and fully embrace his life in India.

Leading with aviation
Tata had a keen interest in the fledgling aviation industry, having watched the early flights of famous aviator Louis Bleriot as a child in France. In 1929, he became one of the first Indians to be granted a commercial pilot's license, and three years later, he set up Tata Air Services. This courier service connected Karachi, Ahmadabad, Bombay (now Mumbai), and Madras (now Chennai), and Tata piloted the first flight from Karachi to Bombay. Rebranded as Tata Airlines, later Air India, the service was India's first domestic carrier and was run by Tata until 1977 despite being nationalized by Nehru's government in 1953.

The airline was his passion, but Tata also devoted energy to diversifying the family business. In 1938, despite being the youngest member of the Tata Sons board, he became group chairman. The Tata Group was already the largest industrial corporation in India at the time, but Tata drove a period of

"If you **want excellence,** you must **aim at perfection.**"

J. R. D. Tata, 1981

J. R. D.

TATA

1904–1993

further expansion. By the 1970s, he had added to the group a chemical production plant, the Tata Engineering and Locomotive Company (later renamed Tata Motors), software and technology services, a cosmetics firm, and a tea business.

New business style

Indian tradition expected family companies to be run by family members, but Tata broke with this practice. He turned the Tata Group into a business federation where entrepreneurial talent and expertise were encouraged across the conglomerate's various enterprises.

He also became famous for succeeding in business while maintaining high ethical standards. Corruption was rife in Indian commerce, but Tata was unusual in refusing to bribe politicians for contracts or connections. In addition, the welfare of his employees was extremely important to him. He encouraged a close relationship between workers and management and championed an

Tata piloted Tata Air Services' inaugural Puss Moth flight in 1932. In 1948, he was also on board the airline's first international flight, operating under the new name Air India.

eight-hour working day, free medical aid, a workers' pension fund, and an accident compensation program.

Tata was showered with honors in India, much to his bemusement, but despite his high public profile, he was said to be shy and self-effacing. He believed that casual charity was not the solution to India's struggle with poverty but that building the country's scientific and economic capacities was. To this end, he set up numerous institutions, including a hospital, two science institutes, and a national center for the performing arts.

He also held the view that India needed to stem its growing population and helped to start what became the International Institute of Population Studies. In his later years, he gave much of his wealth to start the J.R.D. Tata Trust for charitable purposes. In 1991, when he stepped down from Tata Sons aged 87, the group was generating more than $4 billion in annual revenue. He died two years later in Geneva.

OLIVE ANN **BEECH**

A pioneer in the American aerospace business, Olive Ann Beech was the cofounder, president, and chairwoman of the Beech Aircraft Corporation.

Born Olive Ann Mellor, Beech (1903–1993) was said to have been precocious from an early age. After attending business school, she worked as a secretary in a company making small aircraft and learned the details of aircraft design. There she met her future husband, aircraft engineer Walter Beech. The couple set up Beech Aircraft Company in 1932. When her husband died in 1950, Beech ran the business. She earned many awards and honorary appointments and is considered by many to be the First Lady of aviation, even though she never flew a plane.

"**Never** start with **diffidence. Always** start **with confidence.**"

J. R. D. Tata, 1982

DIRECTORY

The global economy continued to grow during the early to mid-20th century, despite two world wars and the Great Depression of the 1930s. This expansion helped establish mass production worldwide, and many entrepreneurs founded conglomerates involved across multiple sectors.

HENRY LUCE
(1898–1967)

Born in China to US missionaries, Henry Luce started his journalistic career in Chicago. In 1921, he worked at the *Baltimore News* with old friend Briton Hadden, with whom he formed Time, Inc., in 1922, along with another friend Robert Livingston Johnson. The next year, they published the first issue of *Time*, a weekly news magazine. In 1929, Luce founded business magazine *Fortune* before buying *Life* magazine in 1936, which he relaunched with a concentration on photojournalism. Luce remained editor in chief of all Time Inc.'s publications until 1964.

PIETRO FERRERO
(1898–1949)

A pastry chef and store owner from northern Italy, Pietro Ferrero founded his famed confectionery brand Ferrero, in 1946. After World War II, Italy had a chocolate shortage, so Ferrero invented *Giandujot*, a sweet paste made mostly from sugar and hazelnuts, with some cocoa added. Ferrero's invention was the basis of what became Nutella but was modified and developed by his son following Ferrero's death in 1949.

Nutella launched in 1964 and was the foundation for Ferrero's growth into one of the world's largest chocolate and confectionery companies.

JUAN TRIPPE
(1899–1981)

The son of a banker, Juan Trippe was a pilot during World War I. In 1922, he started a small air taxi service and three years later cofounded Colonial Air Transport, carrying passengers and mail. In 1927, it merged with two airlines to form Pan American Airways (Pan Am). With Trippe as president, Pan Am established routes across the globe and in the 1930s was the world's largest airline. In 1955, it pioneered the use of commercial jet aircraft. Trippe is now credited with having boosted the rapid growth of commercial aviation.

JOSEPH-ARMAND BOMBARDIER
(1907–1964)

Canadian-born Joseph-Armand Bombardier first worked as a garage owner. He invented the snowmobile, a vehicle for seven passengers with skis and tracks, and received a patent for it in 1937. He opened a factory in 1940 and during World War II produced military vehicles for the Allies. After the war, Bombardier's smaller recreational snowmobiles for one or two people became their most popular design. Since Bombardier's death, his company has diversified into railroad and aerospace manufacture, and in 2003 it sold its snowmobile division.

SIR LOUIS ODUMEGWU OJUKWU
(1908–1966)

Louis Odumegwu Ojukwu, born in southeastern Nigeria, started his transportation business in 1934, building up a vast fleet of trucks. He then diversified into food importation, property, textiles, and cement and became the richest person in the country. Just before Nigeria won independence from Britain in 1960, Ojukwu was knighted by Britain's Queen Elizabeth II. The following year, he became the founding president of the Nigerian Stock Exchange. Ojukwu was also active in politics and served in Nigeria's House of Representatives.

RICHARD A. HENSON
(1910–2002)

Born in Maryland, Richard A. Henson began work in commercial aviation in 1931 after earning a pilot's license. He flew passengers in his airplane and worked as a test pilot. In 1932, he began the Henson Flying Service and six years later set up a flight school. In 1962, he formed the Hagerstown Commuter airline, which flew from Maryland to Washington, DC. His business model of using small aircraft to connect small cities to larger ones became one of the main elements of the US's "spoke and hub" system of air travel. Henson expanded operations across the southeastern US, retiring in 1989 when US Air bought his business.

DAVID PACKARD
(1912–1996)

Originally from Colorado, David Packard attended Stanford University, where he met William R. Hewlett, his future business partner. In 1939, they established Hewlett-Packard, which manufactured electronic testing and measurement devices and later produced calculators, printers, and computers. It was incorporated in 1947, with Packard as president until 1964, when he became CEO and chairman of the board. Packard stepped down in 1968 but returned as chairman from 1972 to 1993. By this time, Hewlett-Packard had grown into one of the largest information technology and electronics companies in the world.

BROWNIE WISE
(1913–1992)

The groundbreaking US saleswoman Brownie Wise was born in Georgia. From 1942, she worked in a clothing store as a secretary and also sold home cleaning products by demonstrating them at parties. Wise then began to sell Tupperware—plastic food storage tubs. Its inventor, Earl Tupper, noted Wise's success, making her vice president in 1951. She recruited thousands of women as agents to sell Tupperware directly to consumers via home parties. Wise was innovative and successful, but

following clashes with Tupper, she lost her job. She tried to market cosmetics with home parties but had less success.

RUTH HANDLER
(1916–2002)

Born in the US to Polish-Jewish immigrants, Ruth Handler moved to Los Angeles with her husband in 1938 and made and sold plastic furniture. In 1945, they formed Mattel, a company selling picture frames and later, toys. Its most popular product, launched in 1959, was the Barbie doll, which Handler invented and named after her daughter. In 1970, Handler developed breast cancer and founded a company to make breast prostheses. Later investigated for fraud, she resigned from Mattel in 1975.

BETTE NESMITH GRAHAM
(1924–1980)

From the age of 19, Bette Nesmith Graham worked as a secretary, and by 1951 she was the executive secretary at a bank. A talented artist, Graham developed a water-based paint to correct typing mistakes. She called it "Mistake Out" and began to sell it in 1956. After losing her secretarial job, Graham focused on her new venture. She won a patent for the product, renamed "Liquid Paper," and by 1967 her business was worth more than $1 million. She sold it in 1979 to the Gillette Corporation.

LILLIAN VERNON
(1927–2015)

Originally from Leipzig, Lilli Menasche fled Germany at age 6 to avoid anti-Semitism. In 1937, she emigrated to the US, taking the name Lillian Vernon. In

1951, she sold monogrammed purses and belts by mail order, expanding into other products, mostly aimed at young women. The business was incorporated in 1965 with Vernon as CEO and in 1987 became the first female-founded company publicly traded on the American Stock Exchange. Vernon sold the business in 2003.

BERRY GORDY JR.
(b. 1929)

After dropping out of high school in 1950, African American Berry Gordy pursued a career in boxing before opening a record shop in Detroit, his hometown. He wrote and recorded music and, in 1959, founded the record label Tamla. A year later, he launched its sister label, Motown, which became the name of his umbrella corporation. Gordy signed many of the greatest musical performers of the day, such as Marvin Gaye and Diana Ross, and released many international hit records. In 1972, he moved Motown to Los Angeles, where it became involved in movie production. Gordy sold the company in 1988.

WALLACE MCCAIN
(1930–2011)

The son of a seed potato exporter, Wallace McCain was born in Canada. In 1956, he founded McCain Foods Limited with his brother. They opened a plant in their hometown and built the business steadily, capitalizing on public demand for convenience food, notably frozen chips. McCain expanded by opening plants abroad and offering a wide range of food and drink products. In 1994, McCain was forced out as co-CEO after a dispute with his brother. He then bought the failing Maple Leaf Foods, which he successfully revived.

5

ADVERTISING AND CONSUMERISM

1930–1980

ESTÉE LAUDER

Cosmetics pioneer Estée Lauder established her own beauty company in 1946, offering high-quality skin care products designed to make people look and feel beautiful. Through her creativity, innovative marketing strategies, and personalized service, she built one of the best-known global beauty brands.

Estée Lauder was born Josephine Esther Mentzer in New York in 1906, to Jewish immigrant parents. Her father, who was Czech, nicknamed her Esty; she later spelled it Estée because she thought the accent added sophistication.

Lauder learned about business at her father's hardware shop, but it was beauty that always fascinated her; she especially enjoyed watching her mother apply various creams as part of her skin care routine. Lauder's uncle, John Schotz, was a chemist, and he taught his niece to make batches of his own recipe skin cream. Lauder soon began marketing the product—she named it the Super-Rich All-Purpose Crème and sold it to hairdressing salons.

Beauty business
In 1930, Lauder married her first love, Joseph Lauter. He later changed his name to Lauder to correct a misspelling that had occurred when his father had moved to the US from Austria. Lauder's beauty creams soon became the family business; together the couple made a range of skin care products in the kitchen of a former restaurant.

With an innate instinct for what women wanted, Lauder paid attention to every detail of her products, from the color of the packaging to the name. She also believed that, to make a sale, her customers needed to see the results of her products on their own faces, and so she would visit New York hairdressing salons and perform makeovers on potential customers. Lauder had charm, humor, and style, and she was a brilliant self-publicist and

MILESTONES

ACTING AMBITION
Has dreams of becoming an actress but focuses fully on creating her beauty creams from 1942.

COFOUNDS COMPANY
Establishes Estée Lauder, Inc., in 1946 with her husband, offering four skin care products.

ADDED EXTRA
Offers the first "gift with purchase" in 1948, now a commonplace beauty marketing strategy.

EXPANDS BUSINESS
Takes out a loan to launch products internationally in 1960, first in London and then in Paris.

"I wanted to see my **name in lights,** but I was willing to settle for **my name on a jar.**"

Estée Lauder, 1985

product with a purchase. Saks Fifth Avenue sold out of her products within two days. In 1953, Lauder launched Youth-Dew, an aromatic bath oil that doubled as a perfume, which quickly became a hit with consumers.

When Lauder launched her business internationally in 1960, she added a personal touch once again. She traveled to Harrods in London and then to Galeries Lafayette in Paris, where, denied a meeting with the buyer, she spilled Youth-Dew on the store floor, prompting customers to ask about its intoxicating aroma. The ruse secured Lauder her own makeup counter.

THE FIRST DEPARTMENT STORE TO STOCK HER PRODUCTS SOLD OUT IN 2 DAYS

YOUTH-DEW BATH OIL DROVE UP ANNUAL SALES BY 400% BY 1958

marketer. She would tell her delighted customers to "telephone, telegraph, tell-a-woman" about the benefits of her products.

Breakthrough

Lauder and her husband formed Estée Lauder, Inc., in 1946 and offered four skin care products in its range: the original Super-Rich All-Purpose Crème, The Cleansing Oil, The Crème Pack, and The Skin Lotion. A turning point for the company came in 1948, when the New York department store Saks Fifth Avenue ordered $800 worth of Estée Lauder products. Lauder invited the store's biggest customers to see her new line, offering a free

Global brand

Lauder's business success soon made her one of the richest self-made women in the world. She moved

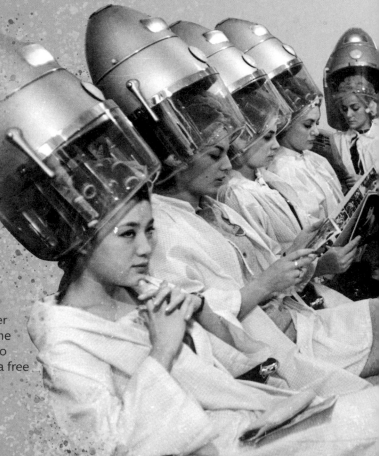

in elite social circles, mixing with royal figures and famous celebrities, which boosted the profile of her brand.

Expanding her products to include the men's fragrance and grooming line Aramis in 1964, Lauder then diversified again to form the beauty brand Clinique in 1968. She stepped back from running the business in 1973 and her eldest son, Leonard, took over. Lauder died in 2004. Today, her company is one of the world's leading producers of skin care, makeup, fragrances, and hair care products.

"I didn't get there by **wishing for it** or **hoping for it,** but by **working for it.**"

Estée Lauder, 1993

Lauder's business strategy was to sell her products by demonstrating their high quality. She personally gave her customers makeovers, first in New York hair salons and later in Saks Fifth Avenue.

"I'VE ALWAYS BELIEVED THAT IF YOU STICK TO A THOUGHT AND CAREFULLY AVOID DISTRACTION ALONG THE WAY, YOU CAN FULFILL A DREAM. MY WHOLE LIFE HAS BEEN ABOUT FULFILLING DREAMS. I KEPT MY EYE ON THE TARGET, WHATEVER THAT TARGET WAS."

Estée Lauder

Estée Lauder launches new fragrance "Knowing" with model Paulina Porizkova at the Lord & Taylor store, New York, in 1988. ▶

Born into a Korean landowning family in 1910, Lee Byung-chull started a small trading company that grew into the global Samsung Group. Eager to be a market leader in all sectors, he focused on innovation, successfully making the group's electronics division into the world's largest producer of consumer products and fueling industrial growth in South Korea.

MILESTONES

STARTS SAMSUNG
Sets up Samsung Trading Co. in Daegu in 1938, trading and exporting food such as dried fish and fruit.

KOREAN WAR YEARS
Relocates business from Seoul to Busan in 1950 and profits from supplying trucks to US forces.

POSTWAR GROWTH
With government support, expands business during the 1950s into chemicals, textiles, and insurance.

ELECTRONIC BOOM
Moves into electronics in the 1960s, manufacturing products such as fax machines and televisions.

Lee Byung-chull attended Waseda University in Tokyo, Japan, but did not complete his course. His first business venture, a rice mill, failed, but, undeterred, he set up a second, Samsung Trading Co., exporting foodstuffs from Korea to China, which proved successful. The start of the Korean War, between South and North, in 1950 forced him to move farther south to Busan, but it also created a new opportunity—supplying trucks to troops from the US, South Korea's ally.

After the war, Byung-chull concentrated on developing businesses that would reduce the needz for South Korea to import essentials such as food and textiles. Expansion was aided by protectionist government policies that aimed to boost domestic enterprises and promote postwar recovery. Convinced that technological innovation was the key to reviving economic prosperity, Byung-chull began adding new divisions to Samsung, including finance, insurance, and, in the 1960s, electronics.

The electronics sector proved particularly successful, with Samsung Electronics launching a popular black-and-white television, then moving into semiconductors, computer hardware, and telecommunications. The company is still one of the world's biggest producers of computer chips. Always focused on processes, quality, and growth, Byung-chull closely managed his businesses and believed in encouraging the potential of every employee. By the 1980s, he had added shipbuilding to Samsung's interests, establishing the group as a world-leading conglomerate. He died in 1987 having helped transform South Korea into a modern industrial nation and a technological powerhouse.

"In Korean, the word **Samsung** means **'three stars'** ... Lee Byung-chull's vision was for his company to become **powerful and everlasting like stars in the sky.**"

Samsung Global Newsroom

LEE BYUNG-CHULL

1910–1987

Enzo Ferrari's single-minded determination and obsession with car racing led him to become a legendary sports car producer. As an accomplished racing driver, engineer, racing team director, and manufacturer, he dominated competitions worldwide for decades, and his cars are still a mark of quality today.

Born in Modena, Italy, Enzo Anselmo Ferrari was the son of a metal fabricator who supplied parts to the Italian railways. In 1908, aged 10, Ferrari was taken by his father to see his first car race at the Circuito di Bologna, firing his ambition to become a racing driver. Ferrari survived service in the Italian Army during World War I, but nearly died in the 1918 postwar flu pandemic that swept Europe. Desperate to find work after recovering, he was rejected for a job at Fiat but found employment as a test driver for a small firm in Turin. A year later he moved to Milan, joining Costruzioni Meccaniche Nazionali, first as a test driver and then as a racing driver.

Alfa Romeo years

By 1920, Ferrari had garnered enough success to be offered a job at Alfa Romeo as a racing driver, winning his first Grand Prix in Ravenna for them in 1923. Allegedly, the family of legendary Italian fighter pilot Francesco Baracca, killed in action in 1918, were so impressed by Ferrari's courage in this race that they presented him with their son's squadron badge – a prancing horse on a shield. Ferrari adopted this famous symbol for his company, Scuderia Ferrari, set up in 1929 as a racing division of Alfa Romeo. In 1932 Ferrari retired from driving and turned his attention to directing the large racing team of over 40 drivers. However, by

Ferrari (left) and head mechanic Vittorio Bellentani (right) discuss the Lancia Ferrari D50 outside the Ferrari factory in 1956. The car featured unique side-mounted fuel tanks.

MILESTONES

SURVIVES PANDEMIC
Recovers from flu in 1918, which killed his father and brother in 1916; decides to become a racing driver.

JOINS ALFA ROMEO
Starts 19-year association with Alfa Romeo in 1920 as a racing driver; becomes the racing team director.

ESTABLISHES FERRARI
In 1939 sets up Auto Avio Costruzioni to produce his own Ferrari racing cars and to run his own team.

TOPS THE WORLD
Leads Ferrari team to its first world race win at recently formed Formula 1 Championships in 1952.

"No one remembers who took **second place."**

Enzo Ferrari, 1983

131

The founder of Fiat (Fabbrica Italiana Automobili Turino), Giovanni Agnelli used his engineering and entrepreneurial skills to become one of Italy's leading industrialists and businessmen.

After leaving a career in the military in 1893, Agnelli (1866–1945) was appointed mayor of his home town, Villar Perosa. Hearing of the newly invented horseless carriage, and sensing a business opportunity, he co-founded Fiat with eight other investors in 1899. By 1902, he had been appointed managing director and begun to establish Fiat as the largest and most profitable car manufacturer in Italy, renowned for its engineering. Agnelli remained head of Fiat until his death in 1945.

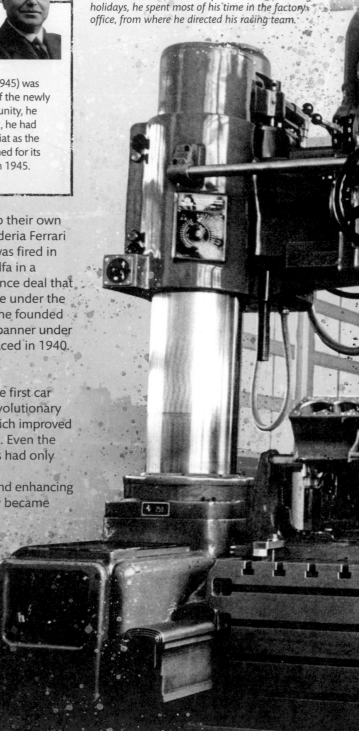

Ferrari opened his factory in Maranello, Italy, in 1943, where it is still in operation. Never taking holidays, he spent most of his time in the factory office, from where he directed his racing team.

PARTICIPATED IN 1ST FORMULA 1 WORLD CHAMPIONSHIP IN 1950

REJECTED AN $18 MILLION BUY-OUT OFFER FROM FORD IN 1963

WON 11 GRAND PRIX AS A DRIVER

1937, Alfa Romeo had set up their own racing department. The Scuderia Ferrari division closed and Ferrari was fired in 1939. Determined to beat Alfa in a Ferrari car, but with a severance deal that meant he could not compete under the Ferrari name for four years, he founded Auto Avio Costruzioni – the banner under which the first Ferrari cars raced in 1940.

Racing for business

In 1947, Ferrari produced the first car to bear his name, using a revolutionary 12-cylinder (V12) engine, which improved the car's speed and handling. Even the most advanced Alfa Romeos had only eight cylinders.

Fixated on winning races and enhancing performance, Ferrari quickly became known for his autocratic management style, and for encouraging intense competition among his drivers. His team soon found success on the track, winning its first major victory in the 24 Hour race of Le Mans in 1949. The next year,

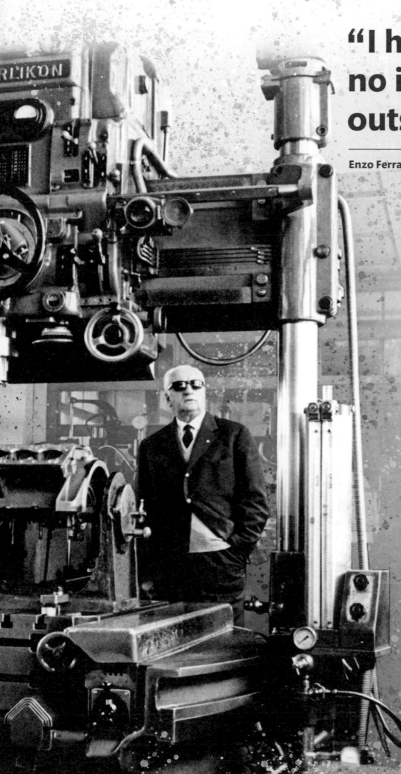

"I have in fact no interest in life outside racing cars."

Enzo Ferrari, 1963

Ferrari joined the newly established Formula 1 World Championship (it is the only team to have participated since its inception), gaining a first win at Silverstone, England, in 1951 and the world title in 1952.

Needing to fund his company's costly racing activities, Ferrari decided to start selling road cars. In 1954, he opened a dealership in Manhattan, New York, and was soon supplying top-of-the-range cars to a rich and famous clientele in the US and Europe. Ferrari's stroke of genius was to bring the best features of his competition cars – innovative engines, racing styling, and lightweight construction – to his commercial vehicles, making them some of the most desirable sports cars on the market. However, it was racing that continued to be Ferrari's passion – this "great mania to which one must sacrifice everything".

By the end of the 1960s, even Ferrari's competitive drive could not mitigate the rising costs of running a racing team, and he sold 50 per cent of his company to Fiat (later rising to 90 per cent), on the basis that he retained complete control of racing activities. Despite retiring as president in 1977, he maintained this control until his death, aged 90, in 1988.

Over the course of his lifetime, Ferrari's cars claimed 13 world championships and had over 4,000 major race wins.

MARY

KAY ASH

From an initial investment of just $5,000, groundbreaking businesswoman Mary Kay Ash built one of the largest cosmetics companies in the US: Mary Kay, Inc. Motivated by her own direct sales experience, her aim was to create a "dream company" that would help women enjoy greater financial independence.

For more than 20 years, Texan Mary Kay Ash hosted "home shows" for the company Stanley Home Products, encouraging people to buy its wares. She was such an inspirational seller that she was headhunted by a competitor in 1952; however, she later resigned from her new role after seeing several men she had trained receive promotions ahead of her.

Ash was determined not to let gender discrimination halt her career, and in 1963, she and her husband, George Hellenbeck, planned to start their own direct-selling business, Mary Kay Cosmetics. But a month before its launch, George died of a heart attack. Undeterred, and with the support of her 20-year-old son, Richard, Ash went ahead with the new company, investing her own savings into the business. Initially, her cosmetics were sold by a team of just nine salespeople, whom she referred to as beauty consultants.

Big business

Ash's company ethos was to treat her mostly female workforce with respect. She offered them flexible working hours and sales incentives: every year, the company's top five sellers received a pink Cadillac. Ash's consultants bought cosmetics from her at wholesale prices and sold them for a profit at home shows. If a consultant recruited another seller, they earned commission. Mary Kay Cosmetics made a profit in its first year and had sales of $1 million in its second year. By 1996, sales were more than $1 billion, and the company continued to grow even after Ash's death in 2001.

> **"**Every **achievement, big** or **small, begins** in your **mind."**

Mary Kay Ash, 1995

MILESTONES

FORMS BUSINESS
Launches her company, Mary Kay Cosmetics, in 1963, a month after her husband's death.

EXPANDS RAPIDLY
Builds a manufacturing plant in 1969 in Dallas, Texas, to keep up with demand for products.

GOES INTERNATIONAL
Establishes the first international subsidiary of Mary Kay Cosmetics in Australia in 1971.

FOUNDS CHARITY
Sets up The Mary Kay Foundation in 1996 to help women with cancer and victims of domestic abuse.

EXPANDS WORKFORCE
Company employs more than 1 million beauty consultants in more than 30 countries by 2003.

American businessman and entrepreneur Sam Walton founded the retailer Walmart, which became the biggest corporation in the world and the largest private employer. Walton changed the face of shopping with his ambitious goals for outstanding value and great customer service, and his principles still underpin the retail giant today.

Born in Oklahoma in 1918, Samuel Moore Walton grew up during the Great Depression. He earned his own money from a young age doing odd jobs, which included selling milk and delivering newspapers. Walton went on to the University of Missouri, where he funded his economics degree by continuing to deliver newspapers and working as a waiter. After graduating, having done casual work for years, he went into retail because he felt jaded and wanted a more satisfying job. He started as a trainee manager for J. C. Penney in Iowa, where he learned many of the management techniques he was to apply later in Walmart, including calling employees "associates" to make them feel like an intrinsic part of the company and having management walk the store floor.

First retail ventures
Walton's career was interrupted by US military service during World War II, although he did not serve because of a medical condition. When he finished in 1945, he opened his first store, a Ben Franklin franchise in Newport, Arkansas. He set himself a goal of making it the best, most profitable variety store in the state within five years. By 1962, he had 15 Ben Franklin franchises.

Walton's second Ben Franklin franchise in Bentonville, Arkansas, was the first store to carry his name. Set up in 1950, it is now the Walmart Museum.

WAL-MART

SAM WALTON

1918–1992

> # "The customer can fire everybody in the company simply by spending his money somewhere else."

Sam Walton, 1992

While still operating his Ben Franklin franchises, Walton explored possible partnerships to accelerate expansion but decided to strike out alone. In 1950, he opened Walton's Five-and-Dime, his first self-owned store, on the central square in Bentonville, Arkansas, which offered discounted products across all ranges.

Walton wanted to launch a chain of large stores that offered discounts on all items, located in small towns. He opened his first Walmart (derived from Walton Mart) in 1962 in Rogers, Arkansas, and within five years had 24 stores, ringing up sales of $12.7 million. Walmart went public in 1970. By 1972, there were 51 US stores with sales of more than

---

GEORGE **COLES**

Australian businessman and philanthropist Sir George James Coles founded the retail firm Coles Group, one of the nation's largest retailers. The company was sold for $22 billion in 2007.

In 1910, Coles (1885–1977) took on one of his father's stores and later traveled to the UK and US to learn about changing retail methods, particularly the concept of "five-and-dime" stores. In 1914, in partnership with his brothers, he opened the first Coles' "variety store" (a store selling a wide range of low-cost items). More stores followed. In 1927, the company went public, and by World War II there were 86 Coles stores across Australia; the brothers proceeded to buy other small family chains and the company now has more than 100,000 employees.

$78 million, and the company was listed on the New York Stock Exchange. Rapid expansion continued, with Walmart becoming a multinational.

Low prices were a part of the success story, but the customer service Walmart "associates" provided was also key to ensuring shoppers would return. Unusually for a leader at the time, "Mr Sam," as he was known, shared his vision with employees. He often dropped in to stores unannounced to chat to the team and, while doing so, would discover new ideas to take to other Walmart stores.

Small-town success
His wife's dislike of large towns heavily influenced Walton's small-town strategy, which also limited opportunities for incoming competitors. Walton ensured each store was only a day's drive from a Walmart regional distribution center, meaning that the store shelves were always well stocked. Selling American products, rather than cheap imports, was also crucial, and he sought US manufacturers who could supply the entire Walmart chain direct.

When *Forbes* magazine named him "the richest man in America" in 1985, Walton was still driving a red Ford pickup truck and proudly wearing Walmart clothes, including a store baseball cap. By the time Walton died in 1992, 1,000 Walmart shares bought in 1970 for $1,650 were worth $2.6 million, Walmart was employing 380,000 people, and yearly sales were around $50 billion.

Walton's first "five-and-dime" stores established his novel approach to retail. By selling a high volume of cheap products, he undercut competitors and generated a fast turnover to plow back into his business.

OFTEN BEGAN WORK AT 4:30 AM

LEFT AN ESTIMATED £100 BILLION FORTUNE

HAD HIS **FIRST $1-BILLION-** SALES WEEK IN **1993**

139

AWARD-WINNING LIGHT
Wins prize for excellence at the Paris Exhibition in 1933, for developing and patenting a neon light.

COFOUNDS BUSINESS
In 1946, sets up electronics company with Akio Morita, funded by around $500 from Morita's father.

GETS LICENSE
Pays $25,000 to the US company Western Electric in 1953 for the rights to make transistors in Japan.

SCIENCE ADVOCATE
Establishes the Sony Foundation for Education in 1972 to foster children's scientific knowledge.

The engineering genius behind such products as the tape recorder and the all-transistor television, Masaru Ibuka grew his small electronics business into the giant Sony Corporation with cofounder Akio Morita.

Masaru Ibuka was born in Nikko City, Japan, in 1908. He studied electronics at Waseda University, Tokyo, where he became known as a "student inventor of genius." After working for a series of scientific companies, he was employed by the Japanese Navy as a civilian radio engineer in its Wartime Research Committee, where he met Akio Morita. In 1945, Ibuka left the navy and started a radio repair shop in a bombed-out Tokyo department store. Morita joined him in 1946, and together they founded Tokyo Tsushin Kogyo (Tokyo Telecommunications Engineering Corporation), which they renamed Sony Corporation in 1958. Ibuka headed Sony's technological innovation and served as the company's president and then as its chairman until his retirement in 1976.

"To establish an **ideal factory** that **stresses a spirit of freedom** and **open-mindedness.**"

Masaru Ibuka, 1946, on establishing Tokyo Tsushin Kogyo (later Sony)

MASARU IBUKA

Japanese businessman Akio Morita established the Sony brand as a global leader in the electronics and entertainment industries, revolutionizing the way the world consumed music, television, radio, and film.

Born in 1921 in the village of Kosugaya, Japan, Akio Morita was expected to join his family's sake brewing business. Fascinated with technology as a child, he instead chose to study physics at Osaka Imperial University. When he entered the Japanese Navy as a student, Morita was assigned to avionic research as a technical officer. In this role, he worked with the civilian engineer Masaru Ibuka, testing and producing new equipment. Despite the 13-year age gap, Morita and Ibuka became good friends and later went into business together. Looking after the finance and marketing of Sony Corporation, Morita established Sony as a global brand, pushing for the development of new products to keep the company at the forefront of the electronics business. He retired in 1994 due to ill health.

MILESTONES

MEETS IBUKA
In 1945, while an officer in the Japanese Navy, meets Ibuka on a project to design heat-seeking missiles.

BIRTH OF A BRAND
Changes the name of Tokyo Tsushin Kogyo to Sony in 1958; lists the company on the Tokyo Stock Exchange.

AMERICAN MARKET
Moves to the US for a year in 1963 and gains valuable insight into the American consumer market.

MOVES INTO FILM
In 1989, sets up deal to buy Columbia Pictures for $3.4 billion, giving Sony a huge stake in the movie industry.

> "I have no use for **people that lack the desire** to go out and **earn success.**"
>
> **Akio Morita**, 1966

AKIO MORITA

"Creativity comes **from looking for the unexpected** and stepping **outside your** own **experience."**

Masaru Ibuka, 1992

Ibuka's founding prospectus for Tokyo Tsushin Kogyo, known today as Sony Corporation, stated that its aim was to establish a factory "where engineers with sincere motivation can exercise their technological skills to the highest level." Tokyo Tsushin Kogyo represented a perfect partnership: Ibuka was the

innovator behind the company's most iconic inventions, while business-savvy Morita made Ibuka's ideas commercially successful around the globe.

The pair's earliest notable innovation came in 1950 with Japan's first reel-to-reel tape recorder—the "G-Type." Initially used by the government, it later became an essential item in schools.

By 1952, the company had 120 employees, and Ibuka, in the hope of expanding their market, traveled to the US. There, he was introduced to the transistor,

Morita and Ibuka revolutionized the entertainment business. The Trinitron TV (1968) was lauded for its bright images, while the iconic Sony Walkman (1979) changed the way people listened to music.

which had been invented by American company Bell Laboratories. When Ibuka returned to Japan, he convinced Morita that working with transistors should be their new project.

Transistors take off

With the help of a friend in the US who spent months negotiating with the patent holder, Western Electric, Morita finally acquired a license to manufacture transistors in Japan in 1953. This was, however, subject to approval from the country's Ministry of International Trade and Industry (MITI), which had rejected Morita's original request. Luckily, a sudden change of personnel at MITI resulted in his gaining the permission he needed.

This development led to the company's first widely successful product: the transistor radio. At the time, radios were made using bulky vacuum tubes, and Ibuka wanted to replace these with transistors, which were much smaller and more durable. It was a gamble since this was both technically challenging and required a huge investment—in both funds and effort.

HAD 20 EMPLOYEES IN 1946

BOUGHT CBS RECORDS FOR $2 BILLION IN 1988

SOLD 200 MILLION SONY WALKMANS

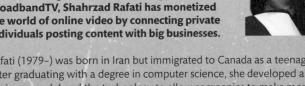

SHAHRZAD **RAFATI**

Founder of digital media technology company BroadbandTV, Shahrzad Rafati has monetized the world of online video by connecting private individuals posting content with big businesses.

Rafati (1979–) was born in Iran but immigrated to Canada as a teenager. After graduating with a degree in computer science, she developed a business model and the technology to allow companies to make money from fan-uploaded online content. Her first large client was the National Basketball Association (NBA), followed by businesses such as Sony Pictures. Passionate about gender equality, Rafati was appointed to represent Canada in the G20 Business Women Leader's task force.

"I only did the **things I enjoyed. Morita** took on **the difficult** side of **things.**"

Masaru Ibuka, 1989

Despite strong opposition from many of their staff members, Morita and Ibuka proceeded. Their efforts paid off in 1955 when Ibuka's engineers produced Japan's first transistor radio.

In advance of a planned sales trip to the US, Ibuka and Morita decided that their products should be branded with a name that could be remembered easily in the West. They came up with Sony, from the Latin word *sonus* meaning "sound," and the American expression "sonny boy."

Launching the brand

On his sales trip, Morita received an impressive offer for 100,000 units of the radio from a major American watch manufacturer, Bulova. However, Bulova told him that it wanted to rebrand the radios with its own name. Morita rejected Bulova's offer, saying that the Sony brand would one day be just as famous; he was right.

After producing the pocket-size TR-63 in 1957—at the time, the world's smallest transistor radio—in 1958, Tokyo Tsushin Kogyo released an even smaller model, the TR-610. It won global acclaim for its design and sold 500,000 units. The same year, Morita made the dramatic decision to change the company's name to Sony Corporation. It was another gamble, as the company was already well known in Japan under the Tokyo Tsushin Kogyo moniker. Morita was adamant that the name change was necessary in order to expand the business further overseas. In 1960, Sony Corporation of America was established in the US. The following year, it became the first Japanese company to be listed on the New York Stock Exchange.

In boosting Japan's postwar economic recovery, Ibuka and Morita transformed the world's view of products "made in Japan" from poor-quality goods to the epitome of cutting-edge technology. Morita became increasingly active in the international business community and was often involved in smoothing trade relations between Japan and the US. Meanwhile, Ibuka continued to oversee the design of more innovative products, including the world's smallest all-transistor TV, in 1962, and the first high-quality color TV—the Trinitron—in 1968.

Ibuka handed over his role as president to Morita in 1971 and remained chief advisor until his death in 1997. Morita died two years later. The pair's vision and entrepreneurialism had turned Sony into a global conglomerate and a market leader not only in the field of consumer electronics but also in the entertainment industry, where it is now one of the giants of music, movies, television, and gaming.

Ibuka and Morita's ability to focus on the future fueled Sony's groundbreaking designs, including their line of robotic pets (AIBO), first launched in 1999.

Sony brought out the world's first video tape recorder designed for home use in 1965. Recording picture and sound simultaneously, the tape could be played back immediately. ▶

1924–

Indian businessman and engineer F. C. Kohli pioneered the use of information technology in India from the 1960s and went on to advance adult literacy around the country.

Faqir Chand Kohli was born on February 24, 1924 in Peshawar, India (now Pakistan). After studying at Punjab University, Queen's University, Canada, and the Massachusetts Institute of Technology, Kohli began training in power system operation in the US. Returning to India in 1951, he joined Tata Electric Companies (now Tata Power) and oversaw the installation of a computer system to control the electricity network between Bombay (now Mumbai) and Pune in 1968. A year later, he was appointed general manager of Tata Consultancy Services (TCS), now India's largest software consultancy. Kohli transformed TCS into a multinational concern, pioneering its software systems. As part of this process, he was instrumental in introducing advanced technology and computerization to India. His contributions have led to him being referred to as the "Father of the Indian Software Industry." After retiring from TCS in 1999, he began focusing on using computer systems to promote adult education and literacy.

> "What matters is **the intelligence of the people** and how we help them to **take the country forward.**"

Faqir Chand Kohli, 2018

MILESTONES

COMPUTERIZES GRID	ADVANCES LITERACY	GAINS RECOGNITION
In 1968, masterminds the first computer system in Asia to manage an electricity network.	Creates software in 2000 that uses images to teach illiterate adults how to read common words.	Receives the title of Padma Bhushan—India's third highest civilian honor—in 2002.

US finance executive Charles Schwab established the largest brokerage company in the US, buying and selling shares. He pioneered the sale of equity securities to the wider public.

MILESTONES

STARTS OUT
Launches the *Investment Indicator* newsletter in 1963 to help people with their investments.

FOUNDS BUSINESS
Sets up a brokerage business in California in 1971; continues to publish his newsletter.

BUILDS BRAND
Buys out his business associates and changes the company's name to Charles Schwab Corporation, 1973.

GIVES BACK
With his wife, sets up a foundation concerned with education, health, and poverty in 1987.

Born in 1937 and educated at Stanford University, Charles "Chuck" R. Schwab founded an investment brokerage company in 1971. He became a trailblazer in the discount sector of the business after US policy changed in 1975 to allow variable commission rates to be charged. Schwab took an early lead in the industry by offering a combination of low prices and fast, efficient order executions—his company, Charles Schwab Corporation, soon became the US's largest discount broker.

Schwab made many innovations in the investment services industry, helping individuals make the most of saving and investing, such as 24/7 access to services, no-transaction-fee mutual funds (buying and selling shares without commission), and online trading. He also promoted cutting-edge technology. In 2008, Schwab retired as CEO of the company but as its chairman remained the largest shareholder and the driving force behind growth and diversification.

"**Do something**, because the **biggest risk** in investing is **doing nothing.**"

Charles R. Schwab, 1998

CHARLES SCHWAB

The founder of Swedish furniture business IKEA, Ingvar Kamprad had a talent for sales and marketing, and a mission to provide customers with well-designed, affordable products. Unassuming and frugal, his thrifty ethos inspired innovative, low-cost furniture with a minimalist aesthetic that transformed the world of homeware.

MILESTONES

FIRST CATALOG
Produces the first annual IKEA catalog in 1951, distributing it across Sweden.

SETS UP STORE
Opens a flagship store in Kungens Kurva, Stockholm, in 1965. After a fire in 1970, it reopens in 1971.

GOES GLOBAL
Launches IKEA stores in France, Belgium, the US, the UK, and Italy between 1981 and 1989.

TEACHES "IKEA"
Publishes *A Little IKEA Dictionary* in 1996. It contains words relating to the IKEA philosophy.

Ingvar Kamprad began his career as an entrepreneur when he was just five years old, selling matches and garden seeds to neighbors in the small Swedish village of Agunnaryd, Småland, where he lived. He bought a bicycle with the profits from his early endeavors, and by the age of 10, he had moved on to cycling door-to-door selling pencils and Christmas decorations that he had bought in bulk.

At 17, Kamprad was given a small sum of money for finishing school by his father, who was especially proud of his son because he was dyslexic. Kamprad used the money to found IKEA, a name he came up with using his initials and those of his home: Ingvar Kamprad from Elmtaryd, Agunnaryd. At first, IKEA was a mail-order business that sold products such as pencils and postcards. Kamprad soon added furniture made by local farmers to his catalog, and sales boomed.

Flat-pack furniture
In the 1950s, Sweden underwent a period of rapid modernization that resulted in people moving from rural to urban areas. Many new apartments were built to provide accommodations in towns and cities. People wanted furniture that was easy to transport and carry up flights of stairs, and Kamprad provided this with a timely innovation. He saw the potential of flat-pack furniture when an employee tried to take a table to a catalog photo shoot by car. Kamprad realized he could sell flat-pack items at more affordable prices because they would be cheaper to manufacture, store, and move; savings would also be made on assembly costs. This simple

> **"I see my task as serving the majority of people."**

Ingvar Kamprad, 2000

INGVAR KAMPRAD

1926–2018

"By **always asking why** we are **doing this** or that, we can find **new paths.**"

Ingvar Kamprad, 1976

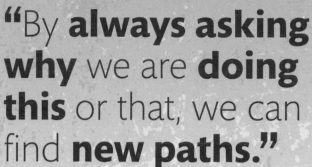

Kamprad had a light-bulb moment while watching an employee dismantle a table to fit it into a car. He realized that flat-pack furniture would be easier to transport and could be assembled at home.

concept of efficiency and economy became the driving philosophy behind IKEA and gave the company a significant competitive advantage over other furniture retailers.

At that time, IKEA was not the only mail-order business in Sweden. Among the many competitors were retailers that were squeezing prices and compromising on the quality of their products to gain a share of the market. To prove that IKEA was not just another poor-quality mail-order company, Kamprad offered potential buyers a chance to view his products in a showroom in the town of Almhult before they purchased them. As an added incentive to visit, browse, and buy, he also offered free coffee and buns. Opening in May 1953, the showroom was an instant hit with customers and also allowed Kamprad to collect valuable feedback on his furniture.

Cost and convenience

From the start, Kamprad's business ethos (later outlined in his 1976 manifesto "The Testament of a Furniture Dealer," written for IKEA employees) was to offer "well-designed, functional home-furnishing products at prices so low that as many people as possible will be able to afford them." Low cost and convenience were key to IKEA's success: customers could visit a showroom, choose a piece of furniture, transport it home, and assemble it themselves, all on the same day. Kamprad also held the belief that "no good business is done on an empty stomach." He moved on from serving coffee and

KARL ALBRECHT

Taking over his mother's grocery business in Essen, Germany, Karl Albrecht grew it into the global supermarket chain Aldi.

Albrecht (1920–2014) and his brother, Theo, started running the family store after serving in World War II (1939–1945) and soon opened more outlets. They kept their premises small, with warehouse-style fittings, and sold mainly nonperishable goods that were quickly replaced if they did not sell. This allowed them to cap prices. Today, Aldi (short for Albrecht Discount) has more than 11,000 stores.

buns to establishing restaurants in his showrooms that offered (among other things) Swedish meatballs, a ubiquitous and popular culinary feature of every future IKEA store.

Unfortunately, Kamprad's low prices provoked the ire of his larger competitors in the Swedish furniture market. By the mid-1950s, they had banned him from the country's furniture fairs, and the National Association of Furniture Dealers had put pressure on local manufacturers to stop supplying IKEA. To combat these issues, Kamprad moved production to Poland, where manufacturing costs were lower, and brought all furniture design in-house.

During the 1960s, Kamprad expanded IKEA, opening new outlets in Oslo and Copenhagen. His furniture quickly gained a reputation for its contemporary design and use of modern materials. In 1968, inexpensive particleboard became a common feature of IKEA products. The 1969 PRIVAT sofa, with its particleboard base, became especially popular. Like the sofa, other classic items, such as the POÄNG armchair, MASTHOLMEN coffee

CONDUCTED HIS FIRST BUSINESS DEAL AGED 5

FOUNDED IKEA AT THE AGE OF 17

DROVE THE SAME VOLVO CAR FOR 20 YEARS

WAS STILL ADVISING THE BUSINESS AGED 91

"I don't fly first class on the airplanes, and the stores' executives don't either."

Ingvar Kamprad, 1997

table, and EKTORP sofa used the names of Scandinavian places or words. This was a deliberate device initiated by Kamprad, who found them easier to remember than numbers because of his dyslexia.

The IKEA empire continued to grow, but in 1994, Kamprad was again dogged by controversy. Stories appeared in the press about his wartime affiliation with the Swedish fascist group Nysvenska Rörelsen and its leader Per Engdahl. Kamprad apologized for these links in a letter to IKEA employees but remained friends with Engdahl. He also developed an alcohol problem that lasted until 2004.

By 2000, IKEA had more than 50,000 employees and 155 stores in 30 countries. Kamprad reduced his responsibilities, giving each of his sons—Peter, Jonas, and Matthias—part of the IKEA empire to run. In 2013, aged 87, Kamprad finally stepped down as chairman of the board, and Matthias took over his role.

Thrifty billionaire

In 2004, Kamprad was reported to be one of the richest people in the world, although his personal fortune was the subject of conjecture. His full earnings were unknown because he ran IKEA through three holding entities: Inter IKEA Group, IKANO Group, and INGKA Group. *Forbes* magazine estimated that between 2005 and 2010, Kamprad had a net worth of around $28 billion (£22 billion).

Yet Kamprad was a billionaire who had little interest in the trappings of wealth. He chose to fly economy class, caught trains and subways instead of taking taxis, he trawled flea markets for clothes, and sought out cheap haircuts. He was famously refused entry to a gala dinner because the security guards had seen him arrive at the venue by bus.

Kamprad extended this democratic attitude to his company's staff, who were referred to as "coworkers," wore informal uniforms, and were regarded as extended family. Commenting on his frugality, Kamprad stated: "If I start to acquire luxurious things then this will only incite others to follow suit. It's important that leaders set an example. I look at the money I'm about to spend on myself and ask if IKEA's customers could afford it." Kamprad died in 2018, at the age of 91.

Kamprad issued his first IKEA catalog in 1951; it became the company's main marketing tool.

Self-reliant and determined, Italian businessman Leonardo Del Vecchio escaped his childhood poverty to found Luxottica, the largest producer and distributor of glasses and lenses in the world.

Dispatched to an orphanage by his widowed and impoverished mother at the age of seven, Leonardo Del Vecchio soon learned to rely on his own resources. At 14, he began work as an apprentice toolmaker in Milan, using his wages to attend design school at night. Discovering he had an aptitude for making parts for glasses, he moved to Agordo—the center of the Italian eyewear industry—and founded his own business, Luxottica, in 1961. Initially, the company made frames on contract for other firms, but in 1967, Del Vecchio began issuing his own brand designs. By the 1980s, he had global sales and licensing deals with fashion companies such as Armani. An inspired businessman, Del Vecchio's detailed knowledge of frame design, production methods, and the eyewear market allowed him to control every aspect of Luxottica's growth and to make canny acquisitions of other famous brands, including Ray-Ban and Oakley.

MILESTONES

ACQUIRES SKILLS
In 1949, as a 14-year-old apprentice, begins to learn the metalworking skills needed to make glasses.

FOUNDS LUXOTTICA
Establishes own glasses workshop in Agordo, north of Venice in 1961; it has 10 employees.

INITIATES TAKEOVERS
Begins acquiring famous brands after raising money by listing on the New York Stock Exchange in 1990.

LEADS THE WORLD
In 2017, brokers merger with French lens maker Essilor to create a giant multinational company.

1935–

"**When I started out** as a contractor, I **never thought** I would **come this far.**"

Leonardo Del Vecchio, 2011

LEONARDO DEL VECCHIO

Italian designer Giorgio Armani is the founder, CEO, and chief designer of the luxury fashion house that bears his name. For over four decades, he has grown it into a global fashion empire and made a significant impact on the evolution of modern clothing.

MILESTONES

MOVES INTO FASHION
In 1957, gains experience as a buyer at a Milan department store, before turning to fashion design.

ESTABLISHES BRAND
Founds the Giorgio Armani Corporation in 1979, aged 40; launches his trademark "deconstructed" look.

GLOBAL RECOGNITION
Attains worldwide fame by appearing on cover of *Time* magazine in 1982—only the second designer to feature.

FASHION ICON
Becomes the first living designer to have work exhibited at Guggenheim Museum, New York, in 2000.

Born in 1934, Giorgio Armani originally intended to become a doctor but gave up his medical degree at the University of Milan in 1953 to join the Italian army. He became a buyer for a Milan department store in 1957 and by 1964 had decided to pursue a career in fashion design. Armani gained experience in the fashion house of Nino Cerruti where, despite his lack of formal training, he designed a line of menswear. His work was soon in demand, and in 1970 he left Cerruti and set up as a freelance fashion designer and consultant. With friend and business partner Sergio Galeotti, Armani started his own company, Giorgio Armani S.p.A., in 1975, and launched his own label of ready-to-wear clothes for men and women.

Global reach
Armani founded the Giorgio Armani Corporation in the US in 1979, to produce clothes for the American market. With his innovative approach to styling, he transformed the fashion industry, softening the edge of men's clothing and modernizing clothes for women. In 1980, he designed the clothes worn by actor Richard Gere in *American Gigolo*. This made him popular in Hollywood and set the trend for celebrities to be dressed by fashion houses. Armani expanded his range, creating perfumes and launching Emporio Armani, a lower-cost line of clothes. With around 3,000 outlets worldwide, Armani retains total control of his privately owned company.

"[P]erfectionism, and the need to **always have new goals** and achieve them, is a state of mind that brings profound **meaning to life**."

Giorgio Armani, 2013

Armani's spring/summer men's collection in 2019
continued to highlight his talent for relaxed tailoring.

GIORGIO ARMANI

1934–

PHIL KNIGHT

A cofounder of the leading American sportswear brand Nike, Inc., Phil Knight channeled his love of running into first importing then manufacturing sneakers. He built Nike into one of the world's largest suppliers of sports shoes and clothing, serving as the company's CEO and chairman and amassing a huge fortune in the process.

Born in Oregon in 1938, Philip Hampson Knight enjoyed running from a young age. He was a key member of Cleveland High School's track team, and he also competed while studying at the University of Oregon. He trained as a middle-distance athlete with legendary track coach Bill Bowerman, who was already experimenting with improving the design of running shoes. When no footwear company would take up his ideas, Bowerman created his own design. Knight was the first to try the prototype.

While Bowerman continued to test his shoe ideas, Knight graduated with a degree in journalism. After serving in the army, he enlisted for an MBA at Stanford University, where one of his assignments was to devise a new business idea. Other students focused on electronics and technology, but Knight stuck to what he knew best. His business plan was based on sneakers—importing high-quality sports shoes from Japan and selling them in the US at a high profit margin. He got an A for his thesis—and the idea for his business.

First business steps

In 1962, Knight traveled to Japan and forged a relationship with Onitsuka, the manufacturer of Tiger running shoes. He and Bowerman invested $500 each in their company Blue Ribbon Sports, importing Tiger sneakers to the US. Early sales were made from the trunk of Knight's car—1,300 pairs in the first year, grossing $8,000. By 1969, with two stores, 20 employees, and sales of $300,000, Knight quit his accounting job to manage the company full time.

MILESTONES

PLANS FOR BUSINESS
Wins a contract in 1962 to distribute Onitsuka shoes in the US. The first samples take a year to arrive.

ESTABLISHES COMPANY
In 1964, sets up Blue Ribbon Sports with coach Bill Bowerman. Opens first store in California in 1967.

LAUNCHES NIKE BRAND
Changes company name to Nike in 1971; the first Nike-branded shoe is launched a year later.

"JUST DO IT"
In the 1980s, diversifies product lines and increases brand presence by using motivational slogans.

RETIRES FROM NIKE
Steps down as chairman in 2016, and continues with philanthropy; by now, Nike has revenues of $32 billion.

Jeff Johnson, Nike's first employee, suggested the company's new name, after the Greek winged goddess.

"Let everyone else **call your idea crazy ... just keep going.** Don't stop."

Phil Knight, 2016

157

The first Gap store opened by Donald and Doris Fisher in 1969 sold Levi's jeans and records. By 2018, the global brand had sales of $16.6 billion.

When he could not find a pair of jeans to fit him, Donald Fisher (1928–2009) set up The Gap in San Francisco with his wife Doris (1931–). Trading on the guarantee that they would always have every style and size of Levi's jeans in stock, the store had a ready market among teenagers. In 1972, The Gap started manufacturing its own brand basics, initiating a high-street branding revolution. Taking The Gap public in 1973, the Fishers continued to expand the business, acquiring Banana Republic and founding new divisions such as babyGap. Gap, Inc., is now a multibillion dollar business, with more than 3,700 stores worldwide.

In 1971, a dispute with Onitsuka ended links with the Japanese supplier. Knight then changed the company name to Nike and revised the business plan; instead of selling another brand, Nike was to start producing and selling its own shoes. Knight paid a graphic design student just $35 for the now famous swoosh logo, later giving her shares in the company.

Birth of a brand
The first Nike shoe—the Cortez—debuted at the Olympic trials in 1972 and went on to earn

1962
TIGER SHOES

1972
NIKE CORTEZ

1984
NIKE AIR JORDAN

the company more than $3 million. Product innovations such as the waffle sole and raised heel played a major role in Nike's early success.

Knight was not a fan of formal marketing. He wanted to shape Nike around the needs of athletes, such as long-distance runner Steve Prefontaine, who influenced other runners to wear the shoes. Further paid endorsements came from athletes such as basketball player Michael Jordan, tennis star John McEnroe, and golfer Tiger Woods. In the 1980s, the company began to use

Knight started selling Japanese sneakers from the trunk of his car at athletics events in 1964. He showed runners why he liked wearing them to initiate sales.

mainstream advertising, often with a motivational message, building the brand with the trademark slogan "Just Do It." Knight was determined to keep ahead of the competition at a time when fitness was gaining in popularity.

In the 1990s, Knight responded to anti-globalization protesters by initiating new supply chain reforms, such as assigning field managers to the various regions and making them responsible for monitoring compliance with labor laws. Nike has continued to steadily expand its business and diversify its product line through numerous acquisitions.

Knight stepped down as chairman of Nike in 2016. To date, he has donated billions of dollars to US educational institutions and also made significant contributions to charity.

ONCE RAN **1 MILE** IN **4 MINUTES 13 SECONDS**

STARTED COMPANY WITH JUST **$500**

HAS DONATED OVER **$2 BILLION** TO CHARITY

RETIRED AS COMPANY CHAIRMAN AFTER **52 YEARS**

1990 NIKE AIR MAX

DIRECTORY

In the aftermath of the Great Depression and World War II, the global economy was transformed and growth rocketed, leading to greater consumption of goods than ever before. Businesses used mass advertising and telecommunications to attract wider customer bases and make greater profits.

SILVIO SANTOS
(b. 1930)

A popular Brazilian media mogul and television personality, Silvio Santos was born Señor Abravanel in Rio de Janeiro, the son of Jewish immigrants. He took Silvio Santos as his name after moving into entertainment and becoming host of a television show. In 1981, he set up his own television network, Sistema Brasileiro de Televisão, while continuing to host his own variety program. Santos also set up the conglomerate Grupo Silvio Santos, which expanded into property, hotels, finance, and cosmetics. In 1989, he ran for president but was not successful.

ALVIN AILEY
(1931–1989)

African American Alvin Ailey was born in Texas and moved to Los Angeles in 1942. He began formal dance training in 1949, taught by Lester Horton, who became an important mentor. After Horton died in 1953, Ailey became director of his dance company and choreographed his own performances. In 1958, he founded the Alvin Ailey American Dance Theater in New York, where he developed some of the most influential works in modern dance. Ailey established his own dance school in 1969. An important civil rights activist, he was posthumously awarded the US's highest civilian honor, the Presidential Medal of Freedom, in 2014.

DHIRUBHAI AMBANI
(1932–2002)

Born in Gujarat, India, Dhirubhai Ambani emigrated to the Yemeni city of Aden aged 17. He worked as clerk for a trading firm then returned to India in 1958 to start a spice and yarn trading business. He later diversified into textile manufacture as well as other foods. In 1973, Ambani renamed his company Reliance Industries and took it public in 1977. Reliance expanded into a range of fields, including financial services, petrochemicals, plastics manufacture, and power generation. In the 1980s, Ambani officially stepped down but was involved in Reliance until his death.

AMANCIO ORTEGA
(b. 1936)

Briefly the wealthiest man in the world in 2015, the Spanish fashion executive Amancio Ortega started his retail career as a delivery boy and a tailor's assistant before becoming manager of a clothing store. Ortega set up his first business in 1963, selling bathrobes. In 1975, he launched Zara clothing and opened the first branch in A Coruña, Spain. Zara grew into a global chain with over 1,000 branches and was the most important part of Inditex, which Ortega founded in 1985 as a holding company for Zara and the other brands in his empire. Ortega served as Inditex's chairman until stepping down in 2011.

DIETMAR HOPP
(b. 1940)

Born in Heidelberg, Germany, Dietmar Hopp worked as an engineer for IBM but left in 1972 with four others to form a software company called SAP (Systems, Applications & Products). The firm offered customers accounting and payroll services and would eventually provide businesses worldwide with a full range of software products. After SAP went public in 1988, Hopp served as co-CEO until 1998; he became chairman of SAP's supervisory board from 1998 to 2003. Hopp has donated much of his wealth to his charitable foundation, involved in sporting, medical, and educational initiatives.

JUDI SHEPPARD MISSETT
(b. 1944)

A graduate of Northwestern University in Chicago, Judi Sheppard Missett, was a professional dancer and taught dance classes in the city. In 1969, she adapted her dance classes to target fitness and called them Jazzercise. She relocated to California in 1971, where her Jazzercise classes became so popular she had to hire additional instructors. By 1982, there were over 1,000 official Jazzercise instructors across the US, prompting Missett to franchise her business, which helped make it a global phenomenon. Missett remains the CEO of Jazzercise, which has more than 8,000 franchises.

HASSO PLATTNER
(b. 1944)

After gaining a degree in engineering, German Hasso Plattner worked for IBM. In 1972, he cofounded SAP (Systems, Applications & Products), providing software to businesses, and grew it into a worldwide company. In 1988, the business went public and Plattner became vice-chairman of the executive board before serving as chairman of the executive board and co-CEO from 1997 to 2003. He chaired SAP's supervisory board and started his own investment fund. In 1998, he also founded the Hasso Plattner Institute, focusing on IT education and research.

CAO DEWANG
(b. 1946)

Born in Shanghai, China, Cao Dewang left school aged 16. From 1976, he worked as a sales manager for a glass factory in Fuqing, southeastern China. He bought the factory in 1983 and three years later converted it to produce glass for cars, which China had previously had to import. In 1987, Cao established Yaohua Automotive Glass Co., later known as the Fuyao Group. Under Cao's leadership, Fuyao became a world leader in automotive glass production, as well as a manufacturer of other types of glass.

MOHAMMED IBRAHIM
(b. 1946)

Sudanese-born Mohammed Ibrahim moved to Egypt as a child, then to England, where he gained a PhD in mobile communications. He set up his own software company, MSI, in 1989. In 1998, he founded iMSI-Cellular Investments, later Celtel International, one of the first cell phone companies to focus on Africa. Ibrahim then sold Celtel for $3.4 billion to the Mobile Telecommunications Company of Kuwait. In 2006, he founded the Mo Ibrahim Foundation, targeting political change in Africa.

BOUDEWIJN POELMANN
(b. 1949)

After holding various roles with Oxfam in the Netherlands, Dutch-born Boudewijn Poelmann founded the media company Novamedia in 1983. In 1991, he cofounded Independent Media, which became Russia's second-largest publisher of newspapers and magazines until its sale in 2005. Poelmann helped devise and set up the Dutch National Postcode Lottery in 1989, which gives half of its proceeds to charity. Since then, Novomedia has started similar lotteries in Sweden, Britain, and Germany, raising more than $10 billion for charitable causes.

JAVIER MOLL
(b. 1950)

Spanish media proprietor Javier Moll was born in Zaragoza. In 1978, he and his wife acquired the company Prensa Canaria, which owned newspapers in the Canary Islands. From 1984, they began to purchase other newspapers in Spain, changing the name of the company to Editorial Prensa Ibérica. The group embraced the provision of digital news content and also owns two television channels and a radio station. Moll stepped down as CEO in 2015 and was succeeded by his son.

DEAN KAMEN
(b. 1951)

The US inventor Dean Kamen studied engineering at college but left early to concentrate on research in medical technology. He developed a pocket-sized device that delivered precise doses of drugs to the wearer. Kamen launched the company AutoSyringe to make and market the device in 1976 and sold it in 1981. He then started DEKA, a research and development corporation that created key medical devices, such as a portable kidney dialysis machine and the iBOT-powered wheelchair. Kamen's most famous invention is the Segway, an electronic personal transportation machine he unveiled in 2001. Kamen is also focused on water treatment, developing a purification device called Slingshot.

HOWARD SCHULTZ
(b. 1953)

US businessman Howard Schultz grew up in Brooklyn and, after working as a salesman for Xerox, became a manager for Hammarplast, which made plastic products, including coffee filters. In 1982, he joined Starbucks, a small Seattle-based coffee-roasting company, as marketing director but left in 1985 to start a chain of espresso bars. Schultz bought Starbucks in 1987 and expanded it across the US and Canada, going public in 1992. Starbucks opened its first outlet outside the US in 1996 and now has more than 30,000 outlets. Schultz remained CEO until 2017.

6

LEISURE AND ENTERTAINMENT

1960–2000

Self-made Mexican business tycoon, engineer, and philanthropist Carlos Slim Helú built a fortune from a wide portfolio of interests to become one of the wealthiest people in the world.

As a child, Carlos Slim Helú learned the value of sound accounting and management practice from his father; Slim made his first investment (in a government bond) at age 11 and his first stock purchase at age 12. In 1961, he graduated with a degree in engineering from the University of Mexico and became a stock trader. Amassing large profits from private investments, he used them to open his own brokerage firm in 1965.

Over the next two decades, Slim continued to reinvest in his expanding business empire. During the 1982 Mexican financial crisis, he bought many businesses at reduced prices, making huge gains when the economy recovered. Today his conglomerate, Grupo Carso, spans a variety of fields from education to manufacturing and financial services, and around 40 percent of Mexican Stock Exchange listings are those of companies over which Slim has some control. Renowned for his philanthropy, he has contributed to art and cultural preservation in Mexico City and set up the Carlos Slim Foundation to support health, sport, and education in Latin America.

"To take **poor people** out of poverty ... is very **good** for the **economy**, for the **country**, for **society** and for **business."**

Carlos Slim Helú, 2012

CARLOS SLIM HELÚ

Frederick W. Smith is the founder and CEO of FedEx, the world's first overnight express-delivery company. He revolutionized delivery services, introducing international transit and tracking.

MILESTONES

OVERNIGHT SUCCESS
Founds Federal Express in 1971, which by 1973 is serving 25 cities with a fleet of 14 aircraft.

BEATS THE ODDS
Survives falling profits during the recession of 2008, before posting record-high sales in 2013.

BUSINESS ACCOLADE
Forbes magazine names him one of the 100 Greatest Living Business Minds in 2017.

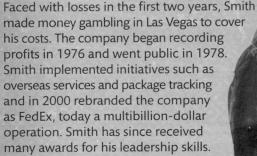

Born in Mississippi in 1944, Frederick Wallace Smith attended Yale University in the early 1960s, where he came up with a business model for an overnight delivery service—an idea that would later prove to be the key to his commercial success. From 1966, Smith served with the US Marine Corps in Vietnam, an experience he credited with teaching him how to build trust as a team leader. In 1971, having refined and developed his original idea, Smith founded Federal Express, an express-delivery service, after raising $91 million in venture capital. Faced with losses in the first two years, Smith made money gambling in Las Vegas to cover his costs. The company began recording profits in 1976 and went public in 1978. Smith implemented initiatives such as overseas services and package tracking and in 2000 rebranded the company as FedEx, today a multibillion-dollar operation. Smith has since received many awards for his leadership skills.

"Fear of failure must never be a reason **not to try something."**

Frederick W. Smith

FREDERICK W. SMITH

Economist and social entrepreneur Muhammad Yunus was moved to take action after seeing women struggling to escape poverty in his native Bangladesh. He established the concept of "microcredit"—small loans for people too poor to get traditional bank loans. The Grameen Bank he founded now has millions of beneficiaries around the world.

Born in Chittagong, Bangladesh, Muhammad Yunus studied for a PhD in economics in the US and taught there before returning to Bangladesh after it achieved independence. In 1974, he witnessed firsthand the horrors of a famine in which thousands of poor farming families perished, unable to buy food.

While heading the Economics department at Chittagong University, he set up a research project to look into rural poverty. He discovered that women making bamboo furniture were taking out high-interest loans to buy materials, which meant they could not save money. Yunus conducted an experiment: he lent $27 to 42 women in Jobra village; each one turned a small profit as well as paid him back. This convinced him that, given the opportunity, poor people would repay loans if the interest rate was very low—and their businesses could grow, in turn helping their families. He also believed that loans should be offered primarily to women because they were more likely to invest in the well-being of their families.

Groundbreaking bank

In 1976, Yunus secured a loan to set up his own bank for poor people around Chittagong. By 1982, 28,000 people were using his microcredit program. A year later, he established the Grameen Bank, which operated across Bangladesh.

Not everyone supported Yunus, and he had to defeat religious and political opponents. Some conservative clerics even told women that they would be denied a Muslim burial if they borrowed from Grameen. However, convinced

"Unless you have a financial system which includes the poorest person, sustainability doesn't exist."

Muhammad Yunus, 2018

MUHAMMAD YUNUS

1940–

LOANED $7.6 BILLION TO PEOPLE IN POVERTY BY 2008

FIRST BANGLADESHI TO BE AWARDED NOBEL PEACE PRIZE IN 2006

INSPIRED MICROLENDING PROJECTS IN OVER 100 COUNTRIES

that the program was morally right, he pressed ahead. Instead of asking for collateral, which he knew the women did not have, Yunus trusted in peer pressure. Typically, groups of five prospective borrowers met with Grameen field managers and two were granted loans. If, after a probation period, these two individuals met the repayment terms, then loans would be offered to the other three. Thereafter, these small "solidarity groups" were expected to support one another's efforts. By 2017, Grameen had 9 million borrowers, 97 percent of them women, and the repayment rate was more than 99 percent.

From the late 1980s, Yunus began to diversify Grameen's operations. Nonprofit companies such as Grameen Uddog (which has organized 10,000 Bangladeshi hand-loom weavers into a quality-controlled cooperative to export cotton fabric) and Grameen Motsho (which plays a similar role for poor fish and shrimp farmers) have been set up.

Global vision

In 2011, Yunus's vision went global when he launched Yunus Social Business (YSB) with fellow entrepreneurs Saskia Bruysten and Sophie Eisenmann. YSB supports and finances "social businesses"—which Yunus defines as those that are solely focused on solving problems rather than producing dividends for shareholders—in sub-Saharan Africa, South America, and South Asia. The social businesses YSB supports are committed to delivering health care, clean water and sanitation, and clean energy, but Yunus quickly points out that this is business, not charity. In India, for example, Waste Ventures has provided higher incomes and greater security for many waste pickers by broadening the range of items that they can collect for recycling, benefitting both the workers and the environment, while Women on Wings has created more than 260,000 sustainable jobs for Indian women working in agriculture, textiles, and forestry. Other projects have established affordable health care for poor people in Colombia and access to cleaning products at below market prices for half a million Haitians. In 2006, as a mark of his contribution to the fight against poverty, Yunus was awarded the Nobel Peace Prize.

JESSICA **JACKLEY**

A lecture by Muhammad Yunus in 2003 inspired Pennsylvanian Jessica Jackley to set up her own online microfinance operation. It has since loaned more than $1.3 billion to 2 million people.

Jackley (1977–) learned that the biggest problem facing would-be entrepreneurs in the developing world was a lack of start-up capital. In 2005, she and partner Matt Flannery set up Kiva—a microlending website—to act as a facilitator, enabling people with capital to loan to those without it. The personal stories of those needing a loan—more than 80 percent of the beneficiaries are women—are shared with those lending the money. There is no interest charged on the loans, and repayment rates exceed 96 percent.

"**For building** stable **peace** we must find ways to **provide opportunities** for **people to live decent lives.**"

Muhammad Yunus, 2006

Yunus's microlending projects have enabled poor entrepreneurs worldwide to invest in their own small businesses, creating profits that help raise them and their families out of poverty.

As an anti-establishment environmental crusader and champion of social issues, Anita Roddick made an unlikely cosmetics brand owner. However, the founder of The Body Shop successfully pioneered the concept of running a business ethically, while at the same time promoting the use of products made with only natural ingredients.

MILESTONES

BECOMES A DAME
Awarded the title of Dame in 2003 after being given an Order of the British Empire (OBE) in 1988.

CREATES FOUNDATION
Establishes The Body Shop Foundation in 1990 to fund animal and environmental protection groups.

GIVES GENEROUSLY
Announces that she plans to use her entire personal fortune for philanthropic purposes in 2005.

REMAINS CONSULTANT
Sells The Body Shop to L'Oréal in 2006 but still consults on ethical practices for the company.

Born in Littlehampton, England, to Italian café owners, Anita Roddick was a strong-willed youngster who took an interest in social and environmental issues. She worked in her parents' café until she finished her education then worked as a teacher before quitting to travel the world. On trips to Tahiti, Australia, and South Africa, Roddick learned about local customs that included washing hair with plant products and using cocoa bean fat as a body moisturizer. She was inspired by the practice of harnessing natural ingredients in this way and resolved to raise public awareness of it. Her first initiative was to open a cosmetics shop, called The Body Shop, in the seaside town of Brighton.

First store
When Roddick launched The Body Shop in 1976, she did not have large profits in mind. She hoped that the shop would merely survive by selling its line of cosmetics made from natural ingredients. Roddick planned to create a word-of-mouth buzz about her unperfumed, uncolored, and simply packaged products. Her first store was created on a shoestring, and she had no money for advertising

Roddick outside an early Body Shop store on Oxford Street, London. She wanted her business to attract customers who were eager to buy ethically sourced and environmentally friendly products.

ANITA

RODDICK

1942–2007

The Body Shop's ethos was to create ethically sourced products from fair-trade suppliers in underdeveloped countries. The company was opposed to animal testing and committed to recycling.

NO ANIMAL TESTING

FAIR-TRADE ETHICAL FARMING

RECYCLING

> **"If you think you're too small** to have an **impact**, try **going to bed** with a **mosquito."**

Anita Roddick, 1991

or marketing. She painted the store dark green to hide moldy patches on the walls, and the same color remains on The Body Shop's branding today.

The first Body Shop's customers were encouraged to bring in their own containers to the store for product refills. "Why waste a container when you can refill it? ... [In] the second World War, we reused everything, we refilled everything, and we recycled everything," Roddick later wrote.

She had pamphlets in-store giving information about the ingredients in her cosmetics and how they were ethically sourced, and within months, The Body Shop line became popular. There were 25 products initially, including cocoa body butter moisturizer, tea tree facial oil, and banana shampoo. The range later expanded to include such items as maca root shaving cream, vitamin E skin cream, and white musk shower gel.

Roddick opened another store in 1977, and by the end of the decade, there were stores across all of Europe. Roddick's husband, Gordon, came up with the concept of "self-financing" The Body Shop, which enabled the company to expand rapidly by franchising stores.

Roddick used her burgeoning fame to promote both her product line and her social policy. This included banning the use of ingredients tested on animals and promoting fair trade with suppliers

from developing countries. She also supported other social, political, and economic causes, including protecting the rain forest, giving voting rights to all people, and providing debt relief for impoverished nations. Roddick wanted to prove that a business could be run ethically, with "moral leadership," while still balancing the books.

Riches and rebukes

The Body Shop had 700 stores worldwide by 1991, and Roddick was one of the richest women in Britain. However, there was a backlash against some of her business decisions. In 1984, she had made the company public, which meant that investors could buy shares in it and the company's success was measured in terms of profit for its shareholders. For some of The Body Shop's customers, Roddick's passionate support for

GREW
THE BODY SHOP TO A VALUE OF
£652 MILLION,
WITH **2,000** BRANCHES **IN 55** COUNTRIES

GAVE AWAY HER **£51 MILLION FORTUNE** IN 2005 TO **GOOD CAUSES**

GORDON **RODDICK**

A supporter of social and community enterprise, Gordon Roddick was a trained agricultural scientist who traveled widely before focussing on The Body Shop operations.

In 1991, Gordon Roddick (1942–) cofounded The Big Issue, a charity that aims to combat homelessness through sales of its magazine. Six years later, he established The Roddick Foundation, which offers support for people involved in social change, environmental justice, and human rights. In 2009, he cofounded 38 Degrees, a campaigning group for human rights. He also helped create The Day Chocolate Company, which makes the fair-trade chocolate Divine.

"If you **do things well**, do them **better**. Be **daring**, be **first**, be **different**, be **just**."

Anita Roddick, 1999

ecological and human rights causes now seemed like a ruse for product placement. Roddick was also challenged about her fair-trade practices in 1994, which caused the share price of The Body Shop to fall. She successfully sued the makers of a TV documentary, who accused her of lying about animal testing on her products. In 1999, she was criticized for joining an anti-globalization march—an unusual stance for a company owner with 2,000 stores in 55 countries.

Roddick sold The Body Shop to French cosmetics company L'Oréal in 2006 for £652 million ($1.2 billion). She stated her intention to give most of her personal earnings from the sale to charity. Roddick also said that, despite L'Oréal's history of testing its products on animals, The Body Shop ingredients would still be ethically sourced. Roddick stayed on as consultant to ensure that this happened.

Charity campaigning

Roddick kept her word about giving her share of the profits from The Body Shop sale to worthy causes, donating sizable sums through her charitable Roddick Foundation. The foundation established Children on the Edge (COTE) to help disadvantaged children in Europe and Asia, led a campaign with Greenpeace against Exxon-Mobil for its denial that fossil fuels have an impact on climate change, and fought against the exploitation of workers in developing countries. Roddick herself became a campaigner for the Hepatitis C Trust after learning she had been infected with the disease through a blood transfusion in 1971, following the birth of her daughter.

On September 10, 2007, Roddick died from a brain hemorrhage. The capitalist campaigner who had refused to conform had given away her entire fortune—later disclosed to be approximately £51 million ($102 million)—to various charities.

L'Oréal sold The Body Shop in 2017 to the Brazilian cosmetics company Natura for £860 million ($1.11 billion). In 2019, The Body Shop received a B-Corp certification, awarded to for-profit companies considered to adhere to social, environmental, and sustainable standards.

Roddick (center) *marks the opening of a new branch of her chain in Huddersfield, UK, July 10, 1992.* ▶

Director, producer, and screenwriter George Lucas revolutionized 20th-century filmmaking with his iconic *Star Wars* movie franchise. By forming his own movie production company, Lucasfilm Ltd., he kept tight control over every aspect of his movies, ultimately making him one of the most financially successful filmmakers of all time.

The son of a stationery store owner, George Lucas had an early fascination with comic books, which provided the inspiration for his first feature-length movie, *American Graffiti*. Japanese director Akira Kurosawa also influenced his early filmmaking. Lucas avidly watched Kurosawa's movies along with other alumni of the University of Southern California film school—one of whom was Steven Spielberg.

Movie franchises

After Lucas graduated in 1966, he made *THX 1138*, a futuristic science-fiction robot movie. Even though it was not well received, Lucas persevered with his next project, *American Graffiti*. Released in 1973, it is one of the most successful low-budget features ever made about listless American youth. Lucas then repeated some of the themes from *THX 1138* in his 1977 film *Star Wars*. An exhausting labor of love for Lucas, *Star Wars* became an instant, surprising hit and remains today one of the top-grossing movies ever made and an intrinsic part of modern popular culture. Although it was produced by the movie studio 20th Century Fox, Lucas managed to retain many of the licensing rights for *Star Wars*. This was a shrewd business decision that has earned him millions through the sales of *Star Wars* toys and other merchandise.

After the success of *Star Wars*, Lucas wanted more executive control over future movies, so he created new movie projects under the auspices of his production company, Lucasfilm Ltd. These included the *Indiana Jones* movies, which Lucas created with his old friend Steven Spielberg. In 2012, Lucas sold Lucasfilm Ltd. and the rights to the *Star Wars* franchise to Disney for $4.5 billion (£3.5 billion).

MILESTONES

DREAMS BIG
Leaves home in 1962 to go to film school, declaring he will be a millionaire by the time he is 30.

FIRST STUDIO
Founds American Zoetrope, a studio for independent filmmakers, with Francis Ford Coppola in 1969.

LOSES FORTUNE
Divorces his first wife, Marcia Lou Griffin, in 1987, resulting in the loss of most of his money.

ESTABLISHES CHARITY
Founds the George Lucas Educational Foundation in 1991 to encourage innovation in schools.

Lucas directing C-3PO in Star Wars. *He is best known for creating six* Star Wars *movies, which are now owned by Disney.*

"**Dreams** are **extremely important.** You can't **do it** unless you **imagine it.**"

George Lucas

GEORGE

LUCAS

1944–

With a loan from a Chinese state-backed institute, Liu Chuanzhi founded the technology company Lenovo. Even though the loan came with many strings attached and Chuanzhi had little experience in business management, he successfully built the company into one of the world's largest personal computer manufacturers.

Born in 1944, Liu Chuanzhi studied at the People's Liberation Army Institute of Telecommunication Engineering in Xi'an, central China. In 1984, while a researcher at the Chinese Academy of Sciences in Beijing, he acquired a loan from the Academy to set up computer company Legend (now Lenovo) so that he could develop his work further. Chuanzhi boldly insisted that the Academy allow him to manage the business himself, but he still had to work under many government restrictions.

He found the early years of his enterprise a struggle. After a failed attempt to import televisions, he saw an opportunity to distribute foreign-made computers. Legend's first successful innovation improved the ability of these computers to process Chinese characters, which allowed many Chinese people to use a personal computer for the first time.

Chuanzhi's business success came largely as a result of studying and adapting the marketing and management strategies of successful international companies, particularly the US electronics and computer corporation Hewlett-Packard. He also took on young people who had earned their business qualifications at colleges overseas to lead parts of the company. In 1990, Legend began producing its own computers, becoming the market leader in China six years later. In 2005, Legend acquired IBM's Personal Computing Division, making it one of the world's largest computer manufacturers at the time. Now in his 70s, Chuanzhi stepped down as chairman of Lenovo's parent company, Legend Holdings, in December 2019.

"Without dedication, entrepreneurship is difficult to achieve."

Liu Chuanzhi

LIU

CHUANZHI

1944–

ROBERT L. JOHNSON

Businessman and investor Robert L. Johnson spotted a gap in the market for a television network that catered for an African American audience. His groundbreaking media company Black Entertainment Television (BET) quickly gained a dedicated following in the US.

Born in Hickory, Mississippi, Robert Louis Johnson attended the University of Illinois, graduating in 1968, before gaining a master's degree from Princeton University in 1972. After completing his studies, he became public affairs director at the Corporation for Public Broadcasting in Washington, DC, and later vice president of government relations at the National Cable and Television Association. These introductions to the world of television gave him crucial insights into the possibilities it could offer and the realization that it was not targeting the interests of a large African American audience.

Success and diversification

In 1980, with a $15,000 bank loan, Johnson launched Black Entertainment Television (BET)—the first cable TV network controlled by and aimed at African Americans. Initially, BET broadcast for only two hours a week on a Friday evening, showing music videos and sitcom reruns, but it soon grew into a successful network originating its own programming. By the 1990s, the company was reaching over 70 million households through its general and dedicated music and movie channels, website, and publishing streams. In 2001, Johnson was propelled into the billionaire league when he sold BET to communications and media giant Viacom for $3 billion. He remained CEO of BET until 2005.

Eager to diversify his interests, Johnson founded RLJ Companies in 2002, a holding company that owns a wide range of products, including hotels, financial services, sports, and entertainment. He also bought the Charlotte Bobcats basketball team in North Carolina, becoming the first African American owner of a major professional sports team.

"I was not afraid of **getting my hands dirty.**"

Robert L. Johnson, 2002

MILESTONES

BREAKS THE MOLD
Becomes the only person to attend college in his family, enrolling at the University of Illinois, 1964.

TAKES THE LEAD
Founds BET in 1980, the first and now leading TV network targeting African American viewers.

MAKES HISTORY
BET becomes the first African American company to be listed on the New York Stock Exchange, in 1991.

BUSINESS SALE
Sells BET to Viacom in 2001; earns over $1 billion, making him the richest African American in the US.

SUPPORTS AFRICA
Sets up the Liberia Enterprise Development Fund to help finance new Liberian businesses, 2007.

JAMES DYSON

British inventor James Dyson suffered a series of failures, which put him heavily into debt, before creating his first successful product: a bagless vacuum cleaner with "Cyclone Technology" that became an icon and revolutionized household cleaning. Despite controlling a global company, Dyson's interest remains focused on innovation.

When he was nine years old, James Dyson's childhood in Norfolk, England, was rocked by the sudden death of his father. Alec Dyson had been a teacher at a boarding school attended by his son, who stayed on as a pupil after his death. The loss of his father, coupled with living away from home, fostered Dyson's independence and his determination to prove himself. In his teens, he fell in love with long-distance running, which helped him build the grit and tenacity he later required to perfect his product designs.

After finishing school, Dyson applied to become a doctor, but a medic at the hospital where he was to train suggested he would be more suited to studying art. He transferred to the Byam Shaw School of Art in London, followed by the Royal College of Art, where he developed a passion for design and engineering.

It was here that Dyson met Jeremy Fry. Head of the engineering company Rotork, Fry began to give Dyson freelance design projects and became an inspirational mentor to him. One of these projects, submitted for Dyson's final-year assessment in 1970, was a prototype for a high-speed, flat-hulled craft that could land without a jetty or harbor. After graduation, Dyson was taken on by Fry to run the subsidiary that designed and sold the landing craft. Four years later, Dyson was ready to set up on his own.

Into business

Dyson's first attempt at entrepreneurship came in 1974. Frustrated with the wheelbarrow he was using to renovate his home, he devised the Ballbarrow, a wheelbarrow with a plastic ball instead of a wheel, making it easier to maneuver. Having spent all his money on developing the prototype, Dyson needed outside investment to fund production, but he made the mistake of

MILESTONES

DISCOVERS DESIGN
Enrolls in furniture design course at the Royal College of Art in 1966, moving into interiors and engineering.

STARTS INNOVATING
In 1974, uses a ball instead of a wheel to create the Ballbarrow, which wins a design innovation award.

DEVELOPS CYCLONE
After five years of refining his Dual Cyclone technology, launches the G-Force vacuum cleaner in 1983.

ESTABLISHES COMPANY
In 1991, founds Dyson Appliances Ltd; its first Dyson vacuum cleaner, the DC01, launches in 1993.

SUPPORTS ENGINEERS
Sets up The James Dyson Foundation in 2002, and in 2007, an annual award, to encourage new designers.

"**We** actually **get** quite **excited** when **something fails,** because that's **how we learn.**"

James Dyson, 2007

assigning his patent to his new company, Kirk-Dyson, instead of licensing it. He lost control of the company and his design in 1979 when his investors sold the business. Despite this setback, the Ballbarrow led Dyson to his most iconic invention and strengthened his resolve to maintain complete control of all future designs.

The vacuum revolution

Dyson had already built an industrial cyclone dust extractor, which used centrifugal force to separate dust from air, for his Ballbarrow factory. The extractor did not need a bag to collect the dust, and in 1978, Dyson realized that this technology could be used in a domestic vacuum cleaner. Exasperated by the dust-clogged bag in his inefficient cleaner at home, Dyson attached a basic cyclone device made out of cardboard and sticky tape onto the machine,

and it worked. Dyson spent five years creating more than 5,000 prototypes for a bagless vacuum cleaner; by the time his design was ready, he was almost bankrupt. Unable to find a manufacturer for the cleaner because it would reduce the market for vacuum bags, Dyson was forced to manufacture it himself.

Dyson eventually sold the cleaner—called the G-Force—in Japan, through a catalog company. It proved hugely successful, and in 1991, Dyson used his profits to set up a research center and factory in the Cotswolds, UK. There he developed the DC01 cleaner. It was engineered to maintain a suction so powerful that it could pull

Dyson utilized the Dual Cyclone technology of his bagless vacuum cleaner in his later, improved models as well as in his new products, including a fan that was developed with a cyclone accelerator.

"You are as **likely** to **solve a problem** by being **unconventional** and **determined** as by being **brilliant**."

James Dyson, 2004

CYCLONE TECHNOLOGY

cigarette smoke from the air. Dyson quickly patented this "Dual Cyclone" technology, but it was the lack of a vacuum bag that was revolutionary. The DC01 was cleaner, more efficient, and cheaper to run and soon became the most popular vacuum cleaner in the UK. It had been launched in the US by 2001.

Thirst for innovation

Dyson has continued to refine his vacuum cleaner, producing updated models, and to develop a range of new products, including the Airblade hand dryer, hair dryers, fans, and air purifiers.

As well as innovating himself, Dyson set up a charitable foundation in 2002 to support education and research in schools and universities. In 2014, he established the Dyson School of Design Engineering at Imperial College London.

NICK **GREY**

British inventor Nick Grey left his job with only a small amount of savings, but within a year he had founded Grey Technology (Gtech), producing innovative cordless appliances.

Grey (1968–) had no formal engineering education, but just a year after leaving his job as head of product design at vacuum cleaner manufacturer Vax in 2001, he had designed and sold a floor sweeper called the SW01 to US company Shark. It was an instant hit and, unlike the Dyson DC01, cordless. Grey developed other home and garden products, including his biggest seller, the cordless AirRam vacuum cleaner (2012), which uses little electricity compared to other leading machines.

Virgin Group founder Sir Richard Branson's flair for business, adventurous spirit, and willingness to flout corporate norms have made him one of the world's most successful entrepreneurs. Thriving on challenges, he has tackled diverse sectors from music to space tourism.

When Richard Charles Nicholas Branson left Stowe School, Buckinghamshire, at the age of 16, his headmaster predicted that he would either end up in prison or become a millionaire. Branson had dyslexia, which made school years a struggle, but he had already dabbled in two business ventures—growing Christmas trees and breeding budgerigars—both of which failed.

Two years later, in 1968, Branson had his first success with the launch of youth culture magazine *Student*. It featured interviews with famous musicians and opinion pieces, and Branson managed to sell enough advertising space to fund an initial print run of 50,000 copies.

Soon after, he started a mail-order record business from the magazine's offices, undercutting traditional high-street retailers. The company, named Virgin by Branson in an acknowledgment that he and his colleagues knew little about business, quickly expanded into a store on London's Oxford Street. A recording studio and record label followed in 1972. A year later, the label's first signed artist, Mike Oldfield, had a smash hit with the album *Tubular Bells*. Branson's willingness to take

RICHARD BRANSON

"You don't learn to walk by following rules. **You learn by doing** and **falling over.**"

Richard Branson, 2014

1950—

on innovative—and sometimes controversial—artists, such as the Sex Pistols, Peter Gabriel, and Culture Club, quickly made Virgin Records into the world's biggest independent label.

In 1984, Branson identified a new business opportunity—in the travel industry. While on vacation in Puerto Rico, his flight to the British Virgin Islands was canceled. Deciding to charter his own plane, he offered his fellow stranded passengers a

"Whatever your goal is, you will never succeed unless you let go of your fears and fly."

Richard Branson, 2006

Branson's success in the music business provided the capital for expansion into other areas, such as travel, banking, and telecoms. Yet he was forced to sell Virgin Records to Thorn EMI in 1992 to keep his other interests afloat.

ride for a small fee. This covered the flight costs, and he realized there was a gap in the airline market. Within a few months, he had set up Virgin Atlantic, flying between London Gatwick and Newark in the US. The airline took on established long-haul carriers by featuring innovative services, bright red branding, cheeky advertising, and strong PR.

Over the next three decades, Branson expanded his travel business into hotels, vacations, trains, a cruise line, and even spacecraft. In 2004, he set up Virgin Galactic, which aims to take paying passengers into space for what he has described as "the greatest adventure of all."

Willing to test any market, Branson also made Virgin a household name by setting up radio, telecoms, health care, fitness, energy, and financial services companies. Not all of his projects have been successful (Virgin Cola and Virgin Cosmetics failed, among others), but he gained a reputation for following his interests, recovering from mistakes, and continually challenging traditional business practices with his consumer-focused approach.

He was knighted for services to entrepreneurship in 2000.

Master of promotion

Branson's talent for publicity, and readiness to act as the "face" of his ventures, has sustained the profile of the Virgin brand. As enterprising in his personal life as he is in his business dealings, he has embarked on a series of record-breaking stunts, including crossing the Atlantic and Pacific oceans by hot-air balloon, making the fastest transatlantic journey by boat, and becoming the oldest person to kitesurf across the English Channel. In recent years, he has focused on tackling environmental and social issues and promoting the entrepreneurial efforts of others through his nonprofit foundation Virgin Unite. Aiming to support those wishing to start up grassroots companies, its centers offer mentoring and financial help. In addition to his commercial achievements, a series of books and a popular online blog have cemented Branson's role as an advisor on entrepreneurship.

LAUNCHED HIS **FIRST** VENTURE AGED **15**

BOUGHT NECKER ISLAND FOR **$320 K** IN **1978**

SET UP VIRGIN ATLANTIC IN **JUST 3 MONTHS**

HAD BROKEN **7 GUINNESS WORLD RECORDS** BY AGE **65**

"I BECAME AN ENTREPRENEUR BY MISTAKE. EVER SINCE THEN I'VE GONE INTO BUSINESS, NOT TO MAKE MONEY, BUT BECAUSE I THINK I CAN DO IT BETTER THAN IT'S BEEN DONE ELSEWHERE."

Richard Branson
Interviewed by journalist Martyn Lewis, 1997

Branson celebrates his record-breaking Atlantic crossing on Virgin Atlantic
Challenger II *with British Prime Minister Margaret Thatcher, July 1986.* ▶

ARIANNA HUFFINGTON

Greek-born Arianna Huffington is best known as the founder of leading news website the *Huffington Post* and CEO of Thrive Global. Her remarkable vision and business successes have earned her placings in *Time* magazine's list of the world's 100 most influential people and the *Forbes* list of the world's 100 most powerful women.

MILESTONES

STUDIES IN UK
Moves to England in 1966 to study economics at Cambridge University, aged just 16.

POLITICAL AMBITION
Runs for California governor in 2003 against Arnold Schwarzenegger; she withdraws but comes fifth.

SETS UP WEBSITE
Launches *The Huffington Post*, a free, liberal-leaning commentary and news website, in 2005.

PROMOTES WELLNESS
Sets up Thrive Global in 2016 with the goal of helping people avoid stress and burnout.

Arianna Huffington was born Ariadne-Anna Stasinopoulou in Athens, where she was raised in a one-bedroom apartment. She studied economics at Cambridge University, becoming the third female president of the Cambridge Union. In 1974, aged just 24, she wrote *The Female Woman*, criticizing some aspects of women's liberation, and has since published another 15 books.

In 1980, after working for BBC radio and television as a journalist and presenter, Arianna moved to New York and married merchant banker, later congressman, Michael Huffington in 1986. She made a career as a radio commentator in Los Angeles and in 2003 ran for governor of California. The campaign failed, but she learned about harnessing the power of the internet, having raised almost $1 million online.

Following the 2004 presidential election, Huffington and businessman Kenneth Lerer raised the capital needed to set up a 24/7 news platform and blog. The *Huffington Post* was launched in May 2005 with Huffington as editor in chief. It became one of the world's most recognizable media brands and effectively made Huffington a brand herself, securing her regular television appearances and a place at the annual World Economic Forum. Regional versions of the site were launched in 2007. In 2011, Huffington sold the site to AOL for more than $300 million, becoming president and editor in chief of the company's Huffington Post Media Group.

In August 2016, Huffington announced that she was leaving the *Huffington Post* to set up a digital platform dedicated to health and wellness. Having identified a need for strategies to tackle stress and burnout in order to improve performance, she launched Thrive Global in November 2016.

"You have to **do what you dream of** doing **even while you're afraid.**"

Arianna Huffington, May 2014

FOLORUNSO ALAKIJA

Multitalented businesswoman Folorunso Alakija has left her mark on industries as diverse as fashion, print, and oil. A committed Christian, she is known for her philanthropic work, particularly in her native Nigeria.

Folorunso Alakija was born in Ikorodu, Lagos State, in 1951, one of 52 children from her father's eight marriages. Educated in the UK and Nigeria, Alakija started out as an executive secretary in the banking industry. Twelve years later, she left to pursue her love of fashion and, after studying in London, set up her own company, Supreme Stitches. Renamed Rose of Sharon House of Fashion in 1996, it became hugely successful in promoting Nigerian culture. At this time, Alakija had also founded the Famfa Oil company and had won the rights to explore an offshore oil field. In partnership with a US oil company, full operations began in 1996 in what would prove to be one of the most productive oil fields in Nigeria. Wishing to expand her business portfolio even further, Alakija moved into printing, establishing Rose of Sharon Prints, followed by Digital Reality Prints in 2006. Alakija is one of Nigeria's richest women and a major philanthropist. Her Rose of Sharon Foundation funds scholarships and grants for widows and orphans.

"You create 'lucky' by working extremely hard. You create 'lucky' by going the extra mile. Especially women."

Folorunso Alakija, 2014

MILESTONES

STARTS IN BANKING	FASHION PIONEER	MOVES INTO OIL
Begins secretarial work at Sijuade Enterprises in 1974 in Lagos, then moves to FinBank.	In 1986, founds couture label Supreme Stitches, catering to wealthy Nigerian women.	Gets oil prospecting license in 1993; her family retains a 60 percent stake in oil field.

Founder of Biocon, the largest biopharmaceutical firm in India, Kiran Mazumdar-Shaw has developed cost-effective ways of providing people in poorer countries with affordable health care.

Born in Bangalore, India, Kiran Mazumdar-Shaw gained a degree in zoology and initially hoped to go to medical school. Encouraged by her father, who was head brewmaster at United Breweries, she instead attained a master's degree in brewing from the University of Ballarat in Australia. On returning to India, however, she found that, as a woman, it was difficult to secure a managerial position. In 1978, after meeting Leslie Auchincloss, founder of Irish-based Biocon Biochemicals, she began Biocon India in her garage. With just two employees, the company manufactured enzymes for use in alcoholic drinks and exported them to Europe and the US.

Mazumdar-Shaw has grown Biocon into a thriving multinational biopharmaceutical company. She has kept the business focused on affordable health care, reducing the costs of therapy for diseases such as cancer. In 2009, she established the Mazumdar-Shaw Medical Center, a research institute dedicated to developing more effective treatments for a wide range of diseases.

MILESTONES

SUCCESS IN BREWING
Graduates with a master's in brewing in 1975; she is top of her class and the only woman in the course.

MOVES INTO BIOTECH
In 1978, after working for Biocon Chemicals in Ireland, sets up Biocon India in her garage.

TAKES BIOCON PUBLIC
Lists Biocon on the stock market in 2004. On its first day of trading, it closes with a value of $1.1 billion.

FUNDS CANCER CENTER
Sets up a 1,400-bed cancer care center in 2009, in Bangalore, after a family illness and a friend's death.

"**Failure is temporary** but giving up is permanent."

Kiran Mazumdar-Shaw, 2014

KIRAN MAZUMDAR-SHAW

JOHN MACKEY

John Mackey's mission to get Americans eating a healthier diet eventually made organic food mainstream. In the process, the businessman created one of the biggest grocery store chains in the US, with hundreds of outlets.

After dropping out of college, John Mackey, a committed vegetarian, scraped together $45,000 from family and friends in 1978 to open the Safer Way natural foods store in Austin, Texas, with girlfriend Renee Lawson. The shop sold no meat, sugar, caffeine, alcohol, or white flour. Sales did not take off, and in its first year of operation, the store lost half of Mackey's investment. Mackey realized that it had been a mistake to limit his market by being too puritanical about what he sold. Two years later, Safer Way joined forces with Clarksville Natural Grocery, owned by Craig Weller and Mark Skiles. They moved to a larger building and changed the store's name to Whole Foods Market, with the motto "Whole foods, whole people, whole planet."

The food range was still organic—with no artificial flavorings, colorings, or preservatives—but it now included meat, sugar, and alcohol. Sales increased, but within a few months, a flash flood destroyed much of the premises and most of its stock. Undeterred, Mackey and his team enlisted the support of loyal customers, and the store was open again for business within a month.

Expansion amid tension

Whole Foods Market grew steadily in the 1980s, becoming a publicly traded company in 1992, but it still had only 10 outlets. Mackey began to acquire other organic retailers around the US, but the speed of growth created tensions with his father, Bill, who sat on the Whole Foods board. In 1994, believing his father's conservatism was holding the company back, Mackey asked him to resign.

The next two decades were a period of rapid expansion for Whole Foods Market. New products, such as the packaged "365 Everyday Value" range, which included everything from freeze-dried fruit to organic body lotion,

MILESTONES

OPENS FIRST STORE
In 1978, sets up Safer Way organic grocer's in Austin, Texas, after living in a vegetarian cooperative.

JOINS BUSINESSES
Whole Foods Market is formed when Safer Way merges with Clarksville Natural Grocery in 1980.

SURVIVES FLOOD
In 1981, rebuilds business after a flood destroys the uninsured Whole Foods Market store and its stock.

FUNDS EXPANSION
Takes Whole Foods Market public in 1992, raising $28 million; this funds expansion across the US.

SELLS UP
In the face of increasing competition, sells Whole Foods Market to Amazon for $13.7 billion in 2017.

"To learn and grow, one must take chances and be willing to make mistakes."

John Mackey, 2014

CUT HIS OWN PAY TO $1 IN 2006 | **DONATED 100% OF HIS STOCK PORTFOLIO TO CHARITY** | **OPENED THE 500TH WHOLE FOODS STORE IN 2019**

Whole Foods Market was built on Mackey's core values of improving the health of his customers, the community, and the environment. All products that are sold must meet the company's stringent quality standards for being as natural as possible.

NATURAL AND ORGANIC

SUSTAINABLE AGRICULTURE

FREE FROM ARTIFICIAL COLORS, FLAVORS, AND PRESERVATIVES

breakfast cereals, and shade-grown coffee, proved popular and helped build sales. Mackey also bought other regional natural foods chains to give the company a national profile. By 2004, new shops had even opened in Canada and the UK.

Food philosophy

Mackey argued that his mission in building Whole Foods Market was not simply about making money, because the chain's produce contributed to the well-being of society. In one interview, he said that most Americans' diet was so unhealthy that just a week of eating "real foods" would make a dramatic difference.

Mackey hired workers who bought into his philosophy of healthy eating and ethical capitalism, and their loyalty was secured with decent working conditions and an in-house health care program.

In 1998, *Fortune* magazine listed Whole Foods Market in its top 100 companies to work for. Executive salaries were capped at 19 times the average pay of a full-time employee, and from 2006 Mackey slashed his own pay and bonuses.

Although his stores sold meat products, Mackey insisted that all suppliers upheld stringent standards on animal welfare. This ethical policy did not prevent Mackey from

YVON CHOUINARD

An expert rock climber, American Yvon Chouinard grew his small outdoor equipment business into a billion-dollar company, Patagonia, while maintaining a strong environmental agenda.

In 1957, Chouinard (1938–) started making toughened steel pitons for his own use, going on to sell them to other climbers from the back of his car for $1.50 each. By 1965, he had set up Chouinard Equipment with fellow climber and engineer Tom Frost to redesign and manufacture stronger and lighter versions of a range of climbing equipment. When Chouinard discovered that pitons were damaging rock faces, he introduced reusable aluminum chocks, and the concept of "clean climbing" was born. In 1973, the company was renamed Patagonia, and it branched out into clothing as well as hardware. It pledges to give 1 percent of sales, or 10 percent of profits (whichever is greater), to environmental campaigns.

courting controversy, however, and his comments on trade unions, "Obamacare" health insurance, and climate change generated much negative press coverage.

Changing markets

The high point for Whole Foods Market came in 2013, when its shares were priced at $65. By this time, though, longer-established retailers had woken up to the importance of the organic food market and could offer goods more cheaply than Mackey. In 2016, annual sales of natural and organic products at Kroger, the largest mainstream US supermarket chain, surpassed those of Whole Foods Market, whose stock price plummeted to $30. Nevertheless, the following year, Mackey sold his company to Amazon for $13.7 billion while staying on as CEO.

"You gotta **catch the wave.** If there's **no wave, you can't surf.**"

John Mackey, 2014

OPRAH WINFREY

Offered the chance to rescue a failing TV program, Oprah Winfrey not only turned it into the world's most popular talk show but also went on to create a media empire worth billions of dollars. Her story is even more remarkable because she was born into poverty, the daughter of a teenage single mother in Mississippi.

Orpah (later Oprah) Gail Winfrey's childhood was divided between the homes of her grandmother, mother, and father. She suffered sexual abuse at the hands of various men from the age of nine and became pregnant when she was 14. Despite these adverse circumstances, she did well at school and had a particular talent for public speaking. This earned her a scholarship to Tennessee State University, where she studied speech communications and performing arts.

Winfrey's big break came when she was hired to host the faltering morning talk show *AM Chicago* in 1984. Her engaging, sharp, intelligent, and candid TV persona and probing yet empathetic interview technique dramatically turned around the show's ratings. She was persuaded to license the program for a national broadcast network in 1986, rebranded as *The Oprah Winfrey Show*, with a guarantee that she would receive 25 percent of its gross earnings. It quickly became the most watched daytime talk show in the US and earned her huge rewards; by 1987, she was a millionaire, the following year her income reached $30 million, and the show ran for 25 years.

Establishing the brand

In 1986, Winfrey was nominated for an Academy Award for playing the part of strong and assertive Sofia in a film adaptation of Alice Walker's novel *The Color Purple*. The Oprah "brand" became a burgeoning media empire. She invested her earnings wisely, establishing TV production company Harpo Productions in 1986 (Harpo is "Oprah"

MILESTONES

REVEALS TALENT
Wins a speaking competition in 1970 and is awarded a four-year college scholarship.

TRANSFORMS RATINGS
Takes over as the anchor of the *AM Chicago* talk show in 1984 and wins 1 million new viewers.

GOES NATIONAL
Launches the nationally syndicated *The Oprah Winfrey Show* in 1986. It is an overnight success.

BUILDS MEDIA EMPIRE
In 1986, forms Harpo Productions to make movies and TV dramas, as well as her own show.

"There is **no such thing** as **failure**. Failure is just **life trying to move us** in another direction."

Oprah Winfrey, 2013

Oprah Winfrey's weekly, live-audience TV program revolutionized talk shows with its mix of everyday and celebrity guests, discussions of current affairs, self-help features, and book club. By 2000, the show had won 47 Daytime Emmy Awards.

spelled backward). In doing so, she became the first African American to control her own major studio. Her show attracted more than 10 million viewers by the later 1990s, with annual revenues of $150 million and 200 staff in Chicago. A subsidiary, Harpo Films, began producing feature-length movies in 1993, including *Beloved* (1998) and *Selma* (2014). By 1995, with a net worth of $340 million, she was the richest woman in entertainment.

Global influence

A new venture in 1996 was the launch of Oprah's Book Club, in which Winfrey discussed a book on her TV show. Over 15 years, about 70 books were featured, and the exposure turned them all into bestsellers. It has been estimated that this publicity boosted sales in the publishing industry to the tune of about 55 million books. Further media initiatives followed. In 2000, she launched a magazine geared

"Real **integrity** is **doing the right thing**, knowing that **nobody's going to know** whether **you did it or not.**"

Oprah Winfrey

mainly for women, *O, The Oprah Magazine*. Winfrey has written books on diet and exercise, founded a cable TV network for women, and started Oprah Radio.

By the early years of the 21st century, Winfrey had become the first black female billionaire in history and was involved in various philanthropic projects. Between 1998 and 2010, she paid all the administrative costs of the Angel Network, which encouraged 150,000 people to donate $80 million to charitable causes. She also established the Oprah Winfrey Leadership Academy in South Africa, which offers education to disadvantaged girls and young women.

Throughout her life, Winfrey has battled with weight, and her involvement with Weight Watchers (WW), which offers products and services to assist weight loss, is another example of the "Oprah effect"—anything that she puts her name to increases in popularity. In 2015, she bought a 10 percent stake in WW for $43 million and agreed to be its global ambassador. Within three years, WW had gained 1 million new members, and

MARTHA **STEWART**

Lifestyle guru Martha Stewart was the first female self-made billionaire in the US.

Best known for her TV show and magazine *Martha Stewart Living*, New Jersey–born Stewart (1941–) rose to prominence in the 1980s as the author of books about cooking, entertaining, and decorating. Her media empire expanded to include other magazines, "how-to" and recipe books, and a radio show. Despite controversy regarding a stock sale in 2004, she bounced back with a series of successful TV and publishing projects.

her stake was worth $400 million. Winfrey's ability to turn adversity into success—and to encourage others to do the same—has underpinned the phenomenal growth of her global brand. With her media empire, business interests, and philanthropic projects, it has also made her one of the richest and most respected women in the world.

THE YOUNGEST
PERSON
TO ANCHOR
THE LOCAL NEWS
AGED 19

VOTED ONE OF
THE MOST
INFLUENTIAL
PEOPLE
IN THE WORLD
5 TIMES

"EVERYBODY HAS A CALLING. AND YOUR REAL JOB IN LIFE IS TO FIGURE OUT AS SOON AS POSSIBLE WHAT THAT IS, WHO YOU WERE MEANT TO BE, AND TO BEGIN TO HONOR THAT IN THE BEST WAY POSSIBLE FOR YOURSELF."

Oprah Winfrey
From Oprah's Lifeclass on the Oprah Winfrey Network, October 18, 2011

__Oprah Winfrey entertains__ an enthusiastic audience during the Canadian leg of her "Your Path Made Clear" tour, named after her bestselling book. ▶

Chinese businessman Wang Jianlin established himself as one of the wealthiest men in China by founding and chairing the Dalian Wanda Group. His vision was to expand his residential property development company into a global giant incorporating commercial property, the hotel trade, movie entertainment, retail, tourism, and sport.

MILESTONES

CREATES BUSINESS
In 1988, borrows $80,000 to take over an indebted property company, renaming it Dalian Wanda.

GROWS COMPANY
Expands into commercial developments all over China, opening the first Wanda Plaza in 2000.

INVESTS IN SOCCER
Spends $52 million on a 20 percent stake in Spanish soccer club Atletico Madrid in 2015.

REDUCES ASSETS
In 2017, sells his Chinese tourism portfolio for more than $9 billion. In 2018, sells part of AMC for $600 million.

Born in Sichuan Province, China, Wang Jianlin joined the People's Liberation Army in 1970, aged 15. Serving for 16 years, he reached the rank of regimental commander, managing to complete his education at the same time through correspondence courses. After leaving the army, he worked in the port city of Dalian, first as a government clerk and then as a residential property developer.

In 1988, Wang borrowed money and invested it in the property company where he was working, changing its name to Dalian Wanda. Described in *The Economist* magazine as "a man of Napoleonic ambition," Wang was eager to expand his interests beyond Dalian Wanda by taking on many commercial and residential building projects in cities all over China. These included large urban complexes known as Wanda Plazas, which combined housing, shopping centers, restaurants, and hotels. He built more than 260 such developments, transforming Dalian Wanda into the largest property development company in China.

Determined to diversify further, Wang turned his attention to investing in the entertainment industry. Already the owner of around 6,000 cinema screens in China, he acquired the AMC Entertainment group in 2012 for $2.6 billion, making Dalian Wanda the world's biggest cinema operator. Then he made a big move into the global movie industry by purchasing Legendary Entertainment, the movie and production studio behind the *Batman* trilogy. In 2016, he opened his $3 billion Wanda City, a cultural theme park in Nanchang, as a rival to Disney's Shanghai theme park. An advocate of philanthropy, Wang donated more than $197 million to charitable causes in 2011 and has contributed toward earthquake relief efforts and public building programs in China on behalf of Dalian Wanda.

"It's never about the wealth but the process of pursuing wealth."

Wang Jianlin, 2015

A rendering of the 400-acre movie studio complex in Qingdao, backed by Wang's company. It opened in 2018 aiming to boost the Chinese movie industry.

WANG

JANLIN

DIRECTORY

Between 1960 and 1995, advances in telecommunications and computing gathered pace, creating new modes of entertainment and consumption and new opportunities for entrepreneurs. By the 1990s, mobile telephone technology and the internet had become vital parts of the economy.

ERIC SCHMIDT
(b. 1955)

US software engineer Eric Schmidt was born in Virginia and gained a PhD in computer science from the University of California in 1982. He joined the IT company Sun Microsystems, becoming chief technology officer. In 1997, he was named CEO of the computer software company Novell. Schmidt was recruited by Google in 2001 as CEO and oversaw its fast development into one of the dominant tech companies in the world. In 2011, Schmidt became executive chairman and remained in the role until 2018. He left the board of directors of Alphabet (Google's parent company) in 2019 but remains a technical advisor.

VINOD KHOSLA
(b. 1955)

Born in New Delhi, Vinod Khosla moved to the US, where he completed a master's degree and an MBA. In 1982, he cofounded the IT company Sun Microsystems, then in 1986 he joined the venture capital firm KPCB as a partner, working in computing and telecommunications investments. In 2004, he started his own firm in Silicon Valley, Khosla Ventures, specializing in experimental and innovative high-tech investments, particularly start-ups. Khosla strongly promotes more environmentally friendly technologies and is a prominent supporter of microfinance in Africa and India.

VIJAY MALLYA
(b. 1955)

The son of Indian entrepreneur Vittal Mallya, Vijay Mallya succeeded his father in 1983 as chairman of the United Breweries Group, a conglomerate that manufactured alcoholic drinks before diversifying into other sectors. Mallya further expanded the group's holdings into air travel, chemicals, and film. Twice elected to India's Parliament, he owns Royal Challengers Bangalore cricket team and was co-owner of a Formula One racing team. In 2016, he moved to London but is wanted for extradition by the Indian government on charges of financial crime.

MEG WHITMAN
(b. 1956)

After gaining an MBA from Harvard in 1979, New Yorker Meg Whitman worked for many companies, including Procter & Gamble, Walt Disney, and Hasbro. In 1998, she became CEO and president of online auction company eBay, overhauling its website and helping it successfully go public that year. Under Whitman's leadership, eBay became a major corporation. She left eBay in 2008 and, after an unsuccessful bid to be governor of California, was made president and CEO of Hewlett-Packard, overseeing its 2015 split into two firms. In 2018, she moved to be CEO of Quibi, a mobile video platform.

EIKE BATISTA
(b. 1956)

Brazilian-born Eike Batista attended college in Germany. By 1980, he had returned to Brazil to trade gold and diamonds and was later involved in gold mining in the Amazon. In 1985, Batista became CEO of the Canadian mining company TVX Gold. He also founded EBX Group, a conglomerate with interests in mining, oil and natural gas extraction, power generation, property, shipbuilding, and logistics. By 2012, he was the richest man in South America, but the following year EBX's profits collapsed. Later found guilty of bribery, he was jailed in 2018.

MASAYOSHI SON
(b. 1957)

Born in Japan and of Korean descent, Masayoshi Son was educated in the US. In 1981, he founded SoftBank in Japan, which first sold computer parts then branched out into telecommunications and magazine publishing. The firm went public in 1994. Two years later, Son became involved in internet services, entering into a joint venture to create Yahoo! Japan, of which he was CEO and president. In 1999, SoftBank was made a holding company, investing billions in many other firms globally, notably Alibaba, the Chinese internet and technology company. Son remains SoftBank's chairman and CEO.

SUNIL MITTAL
(b. 1957)

Born in the Punjab region of India, Sunil Mittal started Bharti Enterprises with his two brothers in 1976. It initially made bicycle parts then diversified into other sectors and in 1984 began making telephones and fax machines. In 1992, Mittal successfully pitched Bharti as a mobile telephone services provider and three years later formed Bharti Airtel, which expanded out of India and now operates in 18 countries in Asia and Africa. Under Mittal's chairmanship Bharti has expanded into a range of industries, including food, financial services, and property.

STRIVE MASIYIWA
(b. 1961)

Zimbabwean-born Strive Masiyiwa attended college in Wales, gaining a degree in electrical engineering in 1983. He returned to Zimbabwe and in 1993 set up Econet as a cell phone network, but the government refused him a license to operate. After a five-year legal battle, Econet won the right to begin business and became highly successful. To avoid state persecution, Masiyiwa left Zimbabwe in 2000. The Econet group expanded across Africa, Europe, and Asia, diversifying into internet provision, banking, and power.

YURI MILNER
(b. 1961)

After abandoning his PhD in physics, Yuri Milner left Moscow to do an MBA in the US. He never finished the MBA but worked at the World Bank before returning to Russia in 1995. He started his own venture capital firm, NetBridge, which specialized in the internet. It merged with the internet company Port.ru in 2001, taking the name Mail.ru. With Milner as CEO, Mail.ru became the dominant force in Russian-language internet, until 2003. He set up a holding company, Digital Sky Technologies, that purchased Mail.ru in 2006 and owns the tech investment firm DST Global.

ARKADY VOLOZH
(b. 1964)

Born in Guryev (Atyrau) in the USSR (now part of Kazakhstan), Arkady Volozh founded several computing, telecommunications, and IT businesses, including CompTek International. In 1993, he codeveloped a search engine and four years later founded Yandex, a technology company, becoming CEO in 2000. It became Russia's largest technology company and search engine, expanding into other online services, including advertising, data storage, and retail. Volozh oversaw its successful bid to go public in 2011 and, as CEO, has also helped it develop free online courses in data science.

ILYA SEGALOVICH
(1964–2013)

A Russian computing pioneer, Ilya Segalovich cofounded the software company Arkadia in 1990 with school friend Arkady Volozh. In 1993, they developed a product, Yandex, which could search the entire internet. Yandex's website went online in 1997, with Segalovich as chief technological officer. One of the key Russian-language search engines, it uses advertisements to generate profit. Segalovich was involved in many charitable endeavors, including his own organization for orphans.

DAMIEN HIRST
(b. 1965)

British artist Damien Hirst graduated from Goldsmiths College, London, in 1989. During the 1990s, he was part of the "Young British Artists" movement, gaining fame for his provocative works, some displaying animals preserved in formaldehyde (most famously, an entire tiger shark). A key early patron and promoter of Hirst was the advertising executive and collector Charles Saatchi. In 1995, Hirst won the Turner Prize, the most prestigious award in British contemporary art. With a flair for publicity, Hirst made his work highly profitable and in 2008 sold a collection for around $200 million. He is now the UK's wealthiest living artist.

MICHAEL DELL
(b. 1965)

American Michael Dell started his first computer business in 1984 while at college. He changed its name to the Dell Computer Corporation (later Dell, Inc.), and took it public in 1988. During the 1990s, Dell, Inc., became the leading manufacturer of PCs in the world. Dell stepped down as CEO in 2004, keeping his role as chairman of the board but returned as CEO in 2007. He oversaw, in 2016, its $67 billion acquisition of computer storage company EMC. Dell became CEO of the parent company that was established, Dell Technologies.

GLOBALIZATION AND E-COMMERCE

1980—PRESENT

American business magnate, computer software developer, investor, and philanthropist Bill Gates is best known for cofounding Microsoft. The global computer business ushered in the personal computer era, transforming almost every aspect of modern life, from work to personal communication.

An inquisitive student, William Henry Gates discovered his interest in computers while attending the private Lakeside School in Seattle. He began writing software programs at the age of 13 with his friend Paul Allen. Two years later, Gates and Allen developed a computer program to monitor traffic patterns in Seattle. They wanted to set up a company, but Gates's parents, hoping that he would become a lawyer, encouraged him to finish school and go to college.

In 1973, Gates went to Harvard University. After reading a magazine article on the new Altair 8800 microcomputer made by Micro Instrumentation and Telemetry Systems (MITS), he and Paul Allen contacted the company, claiming they could create a version of the BASIC programming language that would work on the Altair 8800. MITS expressed interest, and the pair embarked on developing the software, which they then licensed to MITS.

Software revolution
In 1975, Gates dropped out of Harvard to work with Allen, who had joined MITS. The pair took an office in Albuquerque and called their partnership "Micro-Soft." Gates realized that their software could be used on any microcomputer, and within a year, they had become independent of MITS and amended their name to Microsoft. By 1979, Gates was heading a business that had 16 employees and was grossing around $2.5 million.

Personal computers (PCs) were in their infancy, and Gates bought an existing operating system that he developed into MS-DOS (Microsoft Disk Operating System) and licensed to IBM. Other companies began to develop PCs, and as

"Power comes not from knowledge kept but from knowledge shared."

Bill Gates, 1999

1955–

BILL

GATES

WROTE HIS FIRST **SOFTWARE** **PROGRAM** AGED **13**

SET UP MICROSOFT AGED **23**

HAS **DONATED** OVER **$36** BILLION TO **CHARITY**

EARNS **$114.16** EACH SECOND

MS-DOS was ready and available, it became the industry standard. Microsoft's revenue from the program jumped from $7 million in 1980 to $16 million in 1981.

Gates believed that the PC would become an invaluable business tool, and the growing Microsoft team focused on developing new software for it. While Gates was Microsoft's spokesperson, other people were involved in the company's phenomenal growth, including Allen and Steve Ballmer. By 1983, an estimated 30 percent of the world's computers ran on Microsoft software.

The growth of Microsoft appeared unstoppable until the advent of Apple's Macintosh computer in 1984, which had a simpler interface that used graphics. In response, Gates developed the Windows operating system and took Microsoft public in 1986. By 1993, Windows was

"THE INTERNET

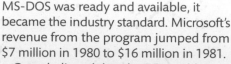

estimated to be on nearly 85 percent of the world's computers. The company strengthened its industry dominance in the mid-1990s by combining Windows with its other applications to create Microsoft Office and persuading manufacturers to preload their software on every new computer. The strategy worked—by 1999, Microsoft was posting sales of $19.7 billion.

Move to philanthropy

After 25 years at the helm, Gates stepped down as CEO of Microsoft in 2000 and set up a charitable foundation with his wife, Melinda. Focusing on improving health and well-being in developing countries, the foundation has given more than $50 billion in grants to date. Gates also founded the Giving Pledge in 2010, with Melinda and businessman Warren Buffett, which aims to encourage other extremely rich individuals to commit half of their wealth to philanthropic causes.

NAGAVARA RAMARAO NARAYANA **MURTHY**

Indian IT industrialist N. R. Narayana Murthy cofounded the multinational corporation Infosys Ltd., a global leader in IT outsourcing services, software technology, and consulting.

After working in the IT industry in India and overseas, Murthy (1946–) set up Infosys with six colleagues and just $250 in 1981. Their first client was in New York, and within six years, Infosys opened a US office. Murthy's concept of the Global Delivery Model (GDM)—a system of outsourcing IT solutions around the world—has become the backbone of the Indian software industry. He also introduced the notion of the 24-hour working day. Today, Infosys is a global software services company with annual revenue of more than $12 billion, and Murthy has been the recipient of numerous international business awards.

Gates realized the great potential of the web from the start. In 1995, a memo sent to Microsoft staff titled "The Internet tidal wave" outlined his company vision for dominating the new online arena.

"Patience is a key element of success."

Bill Gates, 2004

TIDAL WAVE"

STEVE JOBS

US inventor, designer, and investor Steve Jobs was the cofounder of Apple, Inc., and a pioneer of the personal computer age. His many groundbreaking products, which include the iPod, iPhone, and iPad, revolutionized music, mobile communication, and media and are considered the blueprint for modern computer technology.

Steven Paul Jobs was adopted as an infant and raised in the area of California that later became known as Silicon Valley. At 13, a mutual friend introduced him to 18-year-old Stephen Wozniak, and the pair bonded over a shared love of electronics. Jobs dropped out of college and worked as a video game designer before teaming up with Wozniak, who had built his own computer; together they would set in motion a personal computer revolution.

The birth of Apple

In April 1976, Jobs and Wozniak set up the Apple Computer Company and began assembling Apple I computer boards in Jobs's parents' garage, selling them to independent dealers in the area. Wozniak developed the Apple II, an expandable, more powerful system that supported color graphics, while Jobs sourced venture capital. The immediate success of Apple II enabled the company to go public in 1980. Aged just 25, Jobs was worth over $200 million.

Competition in the industry was fierce, and computer giant IBM was a key rival. In 1984, Jobs launched the Macintosh (Mac) computer to huge acclaim. Aimed at the ordinary user rather than experts, its graphic interface and mouse were revolutionary advances; however, its slow speed and limited software meant that it failed to match sales of IBM's personal computer.

After falling out with Apple's management board over control of the company, Jobs was ousted from Apple in 1985 and sold all but one of his shares. Taking with him a team from Apple, Jobs set up software company

MILESTONES

EARLY SUCCESS
Cofounds Apple Computer Company in 1976; its first Apple I computer goes on sale for $666.66.

MAJOR INNOVATION
Launches the Macintosh computer in 1984; it is the first user-friendly PC with a built-in screen.

NEW PURSUITS
Sets up NeXT in 1985; buys Pixar in 1986, and helps develop it into a major digital animation studio.

RETURNS TO APPLE
Takes over as Apple CEO in 1997; reinvigorates the company, saving it from bankruptcy.

LAUNCHES PRODUCTS
Oversees innovations from 1998 at Apple, including iMac, iTunes, Apple Store, iPod, iPhone, and iPad.

"Don't be **trapped** by **dogma**, which is **living** with the **results** of other people's thinking."

Steve Jobs, 2005

to Disney in 2006. Jobs joined the board and, with 7 percent of Disney shares, was the largest single shareholder.

In 1997, Apple bought NeXT in an attempt to revive its now failing business. Competitors were releasing cheaper, more innovative products, and Apple had failed to match Microsoft's Windows 95. Apple needed NeXT's novel operating system, and Jobs agreed to return as CEO.

Revival of Apple

Jobs reorganized the business, simplified the range of products, and launched a successful "Think Different" marketing campaign that enticed new customers. In 1998, he unveiled the iMac—the first in a series of innovations. His insistence on the high quality of hardware and software were key to Apple's new success: products had to be technically brilliant as well as aesthetically desirable. The company's stylish computers became covetable fashion items and offered high-speed processing for relatively low prices.

When Jobs launched the iPod in 2001, followed by iTunes, he transformed the music industry and also the way that

NeXT. He developed a new operating system and targeted the education market. While NeXT computers had limited sales, the operating system proved innovative.

Digital animation was another of Jobs's interests. He had bought animation studio Pixar in 1986 and invested heavily in the company. In 1991, Pixar began work on *Toy Story*, the world's first fully computer-animated movie, which was released by Disney in 1995. Pixar floated on the New York Stock Exchange in 1995 and was sold

"Saying **we've done something wonderful ...** that's what **matters to me.**"

Steve Jobs, 1993

Jobs allegedly suggested the name "Apple" to future business partner Steve Wozniak when he returned from a stint picking apples at a commune in Oregon after dropping out of college.

people accessed and stored music. Jobs soon realized that the new touch-screen technology could also be used in phones. The iPhone, released in 2007, allowed users to make calls, listen to music, surf the internet, and purchase a growing range of apps from a dedicated app store. The first touch-screen tablet—the iPad—

followed in 2010. By the time of his death, a year later, Jobs was lauded as an innovator and one of the pioneers of the digital revolution. His unique, user-friendly products had launched a new era of personal technology and had established Apple as one of the world's leading and most iconic brands.

WORKED AS AN **INTERN** AT HEWLETT **PACKARD** AGED **12**

STARTED APPLE IN **HIS PARENTS' GARAGE** AGED 21

AWARDED OVER **450** PATENTS

BECAME A **BILLIONAIRE** IN 1995 WHEN **PIXAR** WENT PUBLIC

"YOUR WORK IS GOING TO FILL A LARGE PART OF YOUR LIFE, AND THE ONLY WAY TO BE TRULY SATISFIED IS TO DO WHAT YOU BELIEVE IS GREAT WORK. AND THE ONLY WAY TO DO GREAT WORK IS TO LOVE WHAT YOU DO. IF YOU HAVEN'T FOUND IT YET, KEEP LOOKING."

Steve Jobs

From his commencement address to graduates at the University of Stanford, June 12, 2005

Jobs's obsession with detail and form fed into the minimalist aesthetic of Apple products, making them desirable as well as functional. ▶

Debbi Fields went from handing out her home-baked cookies during baseball games to becoming the founder of Mrs. Fields Cookies, one of the largest international retailers of freshly baked cookies in the US. The author of a number of books, Fields is known for her philanthropy and as a motivational speaker who believes that "good enough never is."

Born Debra Jane Sivyer in Oakland, California, in September 1956, Debbi Fields became one of the first ball girls for the Oakland Athletics baseball team as a young teenager. She had a passion for baking, and the "cookie kid," as she was known, would hand out her home-baked cookies at the game. She used the $5 an hour she earned to buy more baking ingredients.

In 1976, Debbi married financial consultant Randall Fields. The following year, dissatisfied with being a "tagalong" housewife and wanting to make money from doing something she loved, Fields set up her first store. Armed with a business loan from the Bank of America, she opened Mrs. Fields' Chocolate Chippery in Palo Alto, California, selling cookies straight from the oven. A second store, named Mrs. Fields' Cookies, followed in 1979 and was a huge success, with long lines of customers stretching out the door. By 1983, her company had expanded to 70 stores across the US and was recording sales of $30 million.

In 1989, Fields introduced a computer system to keep track of production schedules and operations—the first company in the food retailing industry to do so. Eventually, the business grew to several hundred outlets in the US and worldwide. Fields sold Mrs. Fields' Cookies for $100 million in the early 1990s but retained her position as spokesperson for a number of years afterward.

> "I knew **I loved making cookies** and every time I did, **I made people happy.** That was **my business plan.**"
>
> **Debbi Fields**

DEBBI FIELDS

1956–

Even as a schoolboy, Nigerian Aliko Dangote exhibited an entrepreneurial spirit when he sold sweets to his classmates. He began his career trading in agricultural commodities before moving into manufacturing and establishing the Dangote Group, with business interests in cement, sugar, flour, and oil production.

Born in Kano State, Nigeria, Aliko Dangote's ambitious nature was first sparked by his maternal grandfather, a wealthy man who had made his fortune selling commodities such as oats and rice. Dangote's grandfather then became his guardian in 1965 following his father's death. Aged 21, Dangote borrowed $3,000 from his uncle to become an agricultural commodities trader himself, importing goods such as sugar, rice, millet, and cocoa. He was so successful that he paid off the loan within three months.

It was while visiting factories in Brazil in 1995 that Dangote became convinced he should move from trading into manufacturing; if he could produce goods in his own country, he would not need to import them. In 1999, he set up Dangote Flour, followed in 2000 by Dangote Sugar, and was soon meeting 90 percent of Nigeria's demand for sugar. In 2005, with a $479 million loan from the World Bank and $319 million of his own money, Dangote built a cement factory. Within 13 years, his company was Africa's leading cement producer, manufacturing 50.3 million tons of cement each year, and with subsidiaries in 14 African countries. Determined to diversify further, Dangote announced plans in 2013 to build one of the world's largest oil refineries and move into the telecommunications industry.

Since establishing his own charitable foundation in 1994, Dangote has donated more than $100 million to education and humanitarian relief efforts. In 2011, his contribution was recognized with the award of Grand Commander of the Order of the Niger, Nigeria's second highest national honor. *Forbes* magazine also named him African of the Year in 2014.

MILESTONES

STARTS TRADING
In 1977, uses a loan to set up a small firm trading mainly in sugar from Brazil and rice from Thailand.

SHIFTS FOCUS
Moves into manufacturing in 1999, building sugar refineries and a flour mill to replace imports.

MOVES INTO CEMENT
Sets up Dangote Cement in 2005; becomes Africa's wealthiest man with an 85 percent company stake.

BUILDS REFINERY
In 2016, begins work on an oil refinery; aims to produce 650,000 barrels of oil per day.

"When you are raised by an entrepreneurial parent or grandparent **you pick that aspiration. It makes you ... think anything is possible.**"

Aliko Dangote, 2015

225

From small beginnings designing and selling activewear for the snowboarding, surfing, and skating communities in Calgary, Canadian Chip Wilson entered the growing market of yoga clothing. Credited with starting the "athleisure" retail category, he transformed his yoga clothing range into a global business now worth more than $30 billion.

MILESTONES

EARLY SUCCESS
Opens Westbeach Snowboard Ltd. in 1979, selling technical clothing to snowboarders, skaters, and surfers.

DISCOVERS YOGA
Sells Westbeach in 1997 and founds Lululemon in 1998, capitalizing on the growing popularity of yoga.

INNOVATES FABRIC
Trademarks an original four-way stretch fabric, Luon, for use in Lululemon products in 2005.

GROWTH SPURT
Between 2011 and 2013, Lululemon becomes one of North America's fastest-growing companies.

TAKES IT PUBLIC
Floats Lululemon on stock market in July 2007, selling 18.2 million shares and raising over $320 million.

Born in southern California, Dennis "Chip" Wilson's interest in both sport and clothing manufacture began in childhood. Wilson's parents were college athletes, his father later becoming a physical education teacher and his mother a seamstress. An excellent swimmer, Wilson spent his early years immersed in sport but also learned how to sew, helping his mother cut patterns at the kitchen table.

While studying economics at Calgary University in Canada, Wilson took a job on the trans-Alaska oil pipeline. Making $175,000 in just under two years, he funded his college studies and also had enough to start a clothing business. Still working for an oil company, he began stitching together squares of Hawaiian-style fabric to make baggy, brightly colored cotton shorts, selling them from a stall in the local shopping center. Radically different to the tight, dull-colored shorts available at the time, his designs were an instant hit with the growing skateboarding community. Wilson soon left his oil company job to concentrate on clothing full time, setting up Westbeach Snowboard Ltd. in 1979 to design, manufacture, and sell activewear for surfers, skateboarders, and snowboarders.

Enters yoga market
By the 1990s, Wilson was ready for another challenge. He sold Westbeach in 1997 and, while considering his next move, became hooked on yoga. Noticing that attendance at his yoga class was increasing rapidly, Wilson realized there was a growing market of young, professional, sporty women who might buy yoga clothes that could transition from a class to the street. Drawing on his

"[A] big part of success is sometimes just getting out of the way once the base has been set."

Chip Wilson, 2012

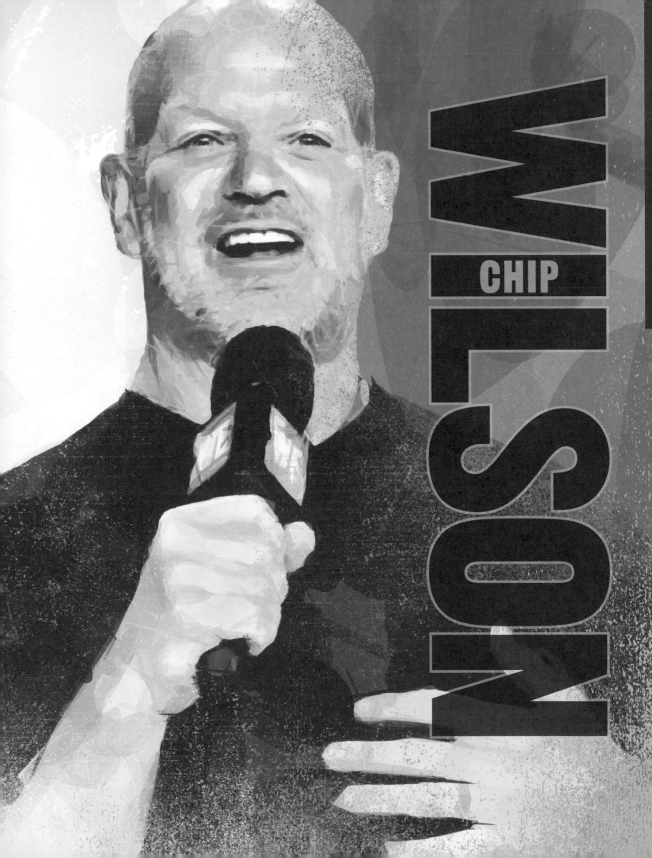

1956–

CHIP

WILSON

huge online sales. Wilson remained chief executive until 2005, when he stepped aside and brought in investors, including former Reebok executive Robert Meers, to oversee Lululemon's 2007 launch as a public company. Wilson resigned from the board of directors in 2015 to concentrate on philanthropic interests and other business ventures.

Function and fashion

Wilson's talent for spotting emerging trends and his fascination with technical clothing created a new type of garment for a new market. His introduction of flat seams, high-quality fabrics, and bright colors created functional, comfortable clothes that minimized sweat and odors and were also stylish. For the first time, it became acceptable to wear workout clothes before or after exercise—or even if no exercise was involved.

These clothes also prefigured a new era of brand loyalty. Wilson used word-of-mouth recommendations in place of conventional marketing and linked his clothing range to a community and a philosophy, fostered by free meditation and yoga classes at his stores. Rather than purely promoting exercise, wearing Lululemon signaled a lifestyle choice and a level of aspiration that was soon copied in the wider world of "athleisure" wear.

experience of producing and selling skate and snowboard clothes, Wilson set up Lululemon Athletica in 1998.

Initially, Wilson sold the company's clothing range from a yoga studio in Kitsilano, Vancouver, with class-goers providing a ready market and his yoga teacher acting as an ambassador for the brand. Two years later, he was ready to set up his first stand-alone store.

Using the same protocol, Wilson expanded his business by selling clothes in yoga studios and enlisting the support of teachers and clients before establishing a store. In fewer than 20 years, Lululemon had more than 400 retail outlets and

ASKED **100** PEOPLE TO PICK BETWEEN **20 OPTIONS TO CHOOSE THE COMPANY NAME**

OPENED THE **FIRST** STORE **OUTSIDE CANADA IN 2004**

IN 2014, SOLD **13.85%** OF HIS **STAKE** IN LULULEMON FOR **$845 MILLION**

"IF YOU START MAKING SOMETHING FOR EVERYBODY, THEN YOU MAKE SOMETHING FOR NOBODY IN BRANDING. WE FOCUSED IN ON JUST THAT 32-YEAR-OLD PROFESSIONAL WOMAN WHO OWNED A CONDO, AND TRAVELED, AND WAS FASHIONABLE, AND ATHLETIC."

Chip Wilson
Interview on KIMT3 News website, 2018

Known in China as the Queen of Trash, Zhang Yin—who also goes by her Cantonese name, Cheung Yan—made her fortune by buying up wastepaper and recycling it into paperboard to create packaging for exported goods. She owns the largest paper mill in the world.

MILESTONES

TRADING IN PAPER
Gains experience in paper trading before moving to Hong Kong to set up her own company in 1985.

AMERICAN DEALINGS
Drives around California trash dumps in 1990, setting up deals to acquire wastepaper.

BUSINESS IN BOXES
Returns to Hong Kong in 1995 to expand the business into packaging for exporting goods.

BUILDS PAPER GIANT
Cofounds Nine Dragons Paper Holdings with her husband and her younger brother in 1995.

TOPS THE LIST
Becomes the first woman to head China's rich list in 2006 after Nine Dragons floats in Hong Kong.

Born Zhang Xiuhua (she later changed her name to Yin) in 1957, the eldest of eight children, Zhang had to begin working at an early age when her father was imprisoned during China's Cultural Revolution. She worked as a bookkeeper in a textile factory and studied accounting at a trade school, before taking a managerial position at a paper-trading company in the city of Shenzhen, Guangdong province. During her time there, she heard about the opportunities in the wastepaper trade between China and Hong Kong.

In 1985, aged 28, Zhang used her savings of $3,800 to open her own paper-trading company, Ying Gang Shen, in Hong Kong. China's export industry was booming, and paperboard (a thick cardboard) for packaging was in high demand. Since there was a lack of wood, the industry was turning to wastepaper that could be recycled into paperboard. Realizing that she needed better resources of wastepaper, Zhang looked to the US for supplies. In 1990, she traveled to Los Angeles, where she set up deals to obtain the necessary supplies for shipping back to China, taking full advantage of the spaces left in the container ships that had brought Chinese-made goods to California. In partnership with her husband, Zhang cofounded America Chung Nam, which grew to become the largest exporter of paper in the US.

Returning to Hong Kong, Zhang set up Nine Dragons Paper Holdings in 1995. Today, Nine Dragons has the world's biggest production capacity for the manufacture of paperboard products from recovered paper supplies, making some 14.3 million tons of packaging materials each year.

"Without leveling a single Chinese tree, **I turned American trash into Chinese gold.**"

Zhang Yin

ZHANG

YAN

1957–

CHER WANG

Often described as one of the most powerful women in technology, entrepreneur and philanthropist Cher Wang cofounded the Taiwanese consumer electronics company HTC. Always keen to anticipate market trends, she grew HTC into a global tech giant.

Cher Wang was born in Taipei, Taiwan, in 1958, one of the nine children of the plastics and petrochemicals billionaire Wang Yung-Ching. Her father taught her about business practices and philanthropy from a young age and encouraged her to further her education overseas. She first studied music but then switched her degree to economics.

In 1982, Wang joined First International Computer, which had been cofounded by her sister, Charlene. Here, Wang sold motherboards and ran the personal computer division. Her work took her to Europe, where she would have to carry big, bulky computers through train stations en route to her clients. This gave her the idea to create a more portable, handheld device. In 1987, she founded VIA Technologies, Inc., developing silicon chip technology in California and later moving the company to Taiwan to take advantage of opportunities in its burgeoning IT industries.

Together with her friend H. T. Cho and an electrical engineer, Peter Chou, Wang set up HTC in 1997. They started out manufacturing notebook computers but found the business volatile and competitive. For Wang, the market for handheld devices offered more opportunity, and very soon HTC was producing smartphones and working in partnership with Microsoft, Google, and T-Mobile, among others. Keeping abreast of consumer, market, and technological trends has been key to her company's success. Going forward, Wang has said that she intends to explore new technologies, such as XR (extended reality), with a view to making HTC what she describes as "a complete ecosystem company."

MILESTONES

STUDIES ABROAD
Graduates in economics from the University of California, Berkeley, in 1981.

THINKS SMALL
Joins First International Computer in 1982. Dreams of developing a light, portable computer.

MOVES TO CHIP TECH
Founds VIA Technologies, Inc., in 1987, which designs, develops, makes, and distributes computer chips.

MOBILE EXPANSION
Cofounds HTC in 1997; it becomes, for a time, the world's third-largest cell phone manufacturer.

SUPPORTS SCHOOLS
Donates more than 5,500 HTC Flyer tablet PCs to 60 secondary schools in Taipei in 2012.

"It takes humility to realize that we don't know everything ... we must keep learning and observing."

Cher Wang, 2012

After struggling to get into college, then finding it impossible to sustain his first small business, Jack Ma had an epiphany when he visited the US and discovered the potential of the internet. Although his first two online commercial ventures proved unsuccessful, his persistence paid off—he went on to establish Alibaba, one of the giants of world e-commerce.

MILESTONES

TOUGH TIMES
Establishes a translation company in Hangzhou in 1994 but struggles to make an income.

DIGITAL COMPANY
Sets up China Pages to build websites for Chinese businesses after visiting the US in 1995.

E-COMMERCE SUCCESS
In 1999, starts Alibaba in Hangzhou with a group of friends; it quickly wins international investment.

MULTIBILLIONAIRE
Alibaba goes public on the New York Stock Market in 2014. The share issue raises a record $21.8 billion.

Jack Ma (born Ma Yun) grew up in Hangzhou, in eastern China, a city he has remained loyal to. His family had little money, and he struggled academically. He did realize the importance of communication, however, and set about learning English. He improved his skills by acting as a tour guide for English-speaking visitors—practicing the language and earning money at the same time.

Success did not come easily for Ma; he failed his college entrance exam twice and was rejected by many potential employers, including Kentucky Fried Chicken. After eventually qualifying as an English teacher, he taught at the Hangzhou Institute of Electronic Engineering for six years, then set up the Hangzhou Hope Translation Agency in 1994, although he still had to supplement his income by selling gifts and flowers.

His big break came on a visit to Seattle in 1995, where he discovered the internet. A friend told him about search engines, and Ma recalls that his first online search was for Chinese beer—which brought up no results. It seemed obvious to him that Chinese companies could benefit from accessing the internet, and on his return to China, he established China Pages to create websites for businesses. He was involved with the company for three years, but it lost its place in the market to rival Hangzhou Telecom, and he sold it. From 1998 to 1999, Ma headed an internet company in Beijing backed by the Chinese

Ma established his philanthropic foundation in 2014. One of its aims was to help improve education in China's rural and impoverished areas.

JACK MA

Ministry of Foreign Trade and Economic Cooperation. Feeling he might be limited by the constraints of government, he left after two years. With several false starts and now in his mid-30s, Ma might have been tempted to give up on the idea of starting a successful business, but, thanks to his characteristic determination, he did not.

Internet innovation

Ma returned to Hangzhou and, with 17 friends and former coworkers, launched the Alibaba Group, an e-commerce site that would go on to transform business in China and beyond. It was an online marketplace that made it easy for businesses to buy from and sell to each other. Ma believed this small-business-to-small-business model had more potential than business-to-consumer websites. Businesses paid one fee to be certified as trustworthy sellers, and a greater sum if they wished to sell to customers outside of China.

Ma's vision paid off. Growth was rapid enough for American internet giant Yahoo! to take a 40 percent stake in 2005, and two years later, Alibaba launched as a publicly traded company in Hong Kong. The initial

public offering (IPO) raised $1.7 billion. The company grew at a phenomenal pace, its IPO on the New York Stock Exchange in 2014 raising $21.8 billion. Alibaba was valued at $168 billion.

A few years earlier, in 2003, Ma had also launched an online marketplace for consumer-to-consumer transactions. Named Taobao ("searching for treasure"), it differed from competitors in that it did not charge a transaction fee but instead made money from online advertising. At the

Jack Ma created a global e-commerce giant. From its origins as a trading platform for businesses, Alibaba has grown to include a consumer e-commerce site and a digital payment platform. It also has interests in a multitude of other sectors, from Hollywood movies and sports to cloud computing.

time, American rival eBay had an 80 percent share of the Chinese market, but within four years, Ma's strategy had won Taobao a 67 percent share. It seemed everything he touched in the world of e-commerce turned to gold—quite an achievement for someone with no technical knowledge or training. Ma stepped down as Alibaba chairman in 2019, by which time the company was valued at more than $400 billion.

KATHRYN **PARSONS**

When British digital technology entrepreneur Kathryn Parsons founded the education company Decoded, her stated aim for it was to demystify the digital world. She promised that it would teach anyone to code in a day.

Parsons's (1982—) vision has paid off. In August 2011, there were just 10 trainees in the first Decoded workshop in London. The numbers attending increased exponentially in the following years. By 2019, 250,000 had received training, there were 500 teachers, and permanent or pop-up offices had been established in more than 80 cities globally. Parsons's advice is now sought by the UK government, and she sits on the board of the Department for Business, Energy, and Industrial Strategy.

"INSTEAD OF LEARNING FROM OTHER PEOPLE'S SUCCESS, LEARN FROM THEIR MISTAKES. MOST OF THE PEOPLE WHO FAIL SHARE COMMON REASONS, WHEREAS SUCCESS CAN BE ATTRIBUTED TO VARIOUS KINDS OF REASONS."

Jack Ma
Interview at the World Economic Forum, September 2018

◄ *A natural entertainer, Jack Ma* performed on stage during Alibaba's 20th anniversary gala at Hangzhou Olympic Center Stadium on September 10, 2019, in Hangzhou, China.

JEFF **BEZOS**

American businessman and e-commerce pioneer Jeff Bezos is best known for founding the online retail giant Amazon, in 1995, a company that dominates the sector today. Bezos's foresight and exceptional commercial skills have made him one of the most successful entrepreneurs in modern history.

Jeffrey Preston Jorgensen was born in 1964 in New Mexico. His mother remarried when he was four, and when his stepfather later adopted him, he changed his surname to Bezos. At Princeton University, Bezos studied computer science and electrical engineering, receiving multiple job offers on graduating. Becoming the youngest senior vice president at a Wall Street investment bank, 30-year-old Bezos was already successful before he had the idea for Amazon.

Bezos had been at his banking job for four years when, in 1994, he came across an article about the rapid growth in usage of the newly created internet. The enormous potential for online retail was obvious to him. Devising a business plan, he took a huge risk and quit his six-figure New York job. Bezos moved to Seattle, where he rented a house and set up business in the garage.

Twenty potential products were on his first list, but he saw an opportunity in books—recognizing that while a physical bookstore was limited by space, an online store could offer a much greater range of titles. Bezos raised the initial investment capital from family and friends. With five employees, he began sourcing books, developing the technology, and creating a user-friendly website

"You **earn reputation** by doing hard things well."

Jeff Bezos, 2004

MILESTONES

SPOTS POTENTIAL
Capitalizing on the nascent internet, quits his high-flying bank job in 1984 to set up an online business.

FOUNDS AMAZON
With five employees, builds the technology to create Amazon. Launches the site in July 1995.

GOES STRATOSPHERIC
In 1997, floats Amazon on the stock market; the company has a market value of over $400 million.

KEEPS INNOVATING
Ventures into music and videos in 1998, clothes in 2002, then electronics, toys, and groceries.

ESTABLISHES FUND
Launches the Earth Bezos Fund in 2020 to fight climate change. Commits an initial $10 billion.

BLUE MOON

Bezos's Blue Moon lander was unveiled in 2019. Part of his mission to create a human colony in space, the robotic carrier is designed to deliver equipment to the surface of the moon.

Bezos's original vision for Amazon was to stock every book ever published, including out-of-print titles, in order to create a comprehensive catalog.

"I knew the one thing **I might regret** is **not trying.**"

Jeff Bezos, 2001

with innovative resources such as purchase recommendations and customer reviews. Originally called Cadabra, Bezos changed the company's name to Amazon, after the river, because of its scale.

Instant online success

Amazon.com launched in July 1995 as the "Earth's Biggest Book Store," with more than one million titles. Within 30 days, the site was selling books across the US and around the world, and, in just over 12 months, Amazon had more than $15 million sales and 100 employees.

Bezos floated the company in 1997, in the face of market skepticism because many traditional retailers were rushing to compete with their own websites. Bezos outflanked them by expanding his product range to include CDs and videos. Amazon became an e-commerce leader as it ventured into electronics, games, and toys, and became a portal for third-party retailers, selling goods on commission.

During the dot-com crash, Bezos borrowed from banks to keep Amazon afloat. At one stage, he was forced to lay off staff and to close warehouses, but the company turned a corner and made its first profit in 2004.

Continual innovation has been key to Amazon's success and has included video on demand, the Kindle e-reader, Amazon's virtual assistant Alexa, grocery deliveries, the convenience stores Amazon Go, and experimenting with drone delivery. The

NIKLAS **ZENNSTROM**

A cofounder of Skype, Swedish technology entrepreneur Niklas Zennström has become one of the leading investors in the technology sector, helping fund others setting up tech businesses.

Zennström (1966–) cofounded Skype with Janus Friis in 2003, the first successful global online company outside the US. In 2005, eBay bought Skype for $2.6 billion. He has also cofounded other globally successful technology businesses, such as Kazaa and Joltid. His venture capital firm Atomico, founded in 2006, helps entrepreneurs expand their businesses. Zennström Philanthropies, which he set up in 2007 with his wife, Catherine, focuses on human rights and environmental issues.

launch of the loyalty program Amazon Prime in 2005 allowed Bezos to steal even more customers from rival retailers.

Personal vision

As president, chief executive officer, and chairman of Amazon, Bezos has never been far from media headlines—for his "Get Big Fast" mantra, the taxes Amazon pays, or his phenomenal personal wealth.

In 2000, Bezos began to invest heavily in the aerospace industry, publicly declaring his vision for the human colonization of space in 2016. His spaceflight company Blue Origin has since launched several suborbital rocket missions.

In 2013, Bezos bought *The Washington Post* for $250 million, aiming to give it an online platform. He made the newspaper profitable by 2016, attracting more readers in both the US and globally.

WORKED AT **MCDONALD'S** AGED **16** | **WARNED** INVESTORS IN 1994 THAT **AMAZON** HAD A **70%** CHANCE OF **FAILING** | MAKES ALMOST **$9 MILLION** PER HOUR

"IF YOUR CUSTOMER BASE IS AGING WITH YOU, THEN EVENTUALLY YOU'RE GOING TO BECOME OBSOLETE ... SO YOU NEED TO BE CONSTANTLY FIGURING OUT WHO ARE YOUR NEW CUSTOMERS AND WHAT ARE YOU DOING TO STAY FOREVER YOUNG."

Jeff Bezos
ABC News interview, September 25, 2013

Amazon has more than 175 fulfillment centers worldwide, *covering more than 150 million sq ft (139 million sq km).* ▶

WU YAJUN

Wu Yajun is the cofounder and chairperson of Longfor Properties, which she transformed from a small residential property company into a hugely successful commercial concern.

Born in Chongqing, China, in 1964, Wu Yajun graduated with a degree in engineering in 1984 before working for four years in a state-owned factory earning around $16 a month. Between 1988 and 1993, she was employed as a journalist for a publication affiliated with the Ministry of Construction, covering property.

After experiencing a number of problems while trying to buy herself an apartment—including delays in completion, poor lighting and gas supplies, and a sporadic elevator service—Wu set up the company that would become Longfor Properties. Longfor sold its first residential project in Wu's home city in 1997 and grew rapidly from there, constructing large shopping centers, high-rise apartment buildings, and business complexes in cities across China. The "China property queen," as Wu came to be known, set up Wu Capital in 2013; it invests in companies involved in technology, education, and health care, and has offices in Beijing, Hong Kong, and California's Silicon Valley.

> "I am **just** a person **focusing on my own business.**"
>
> **Wu Yajun**

MILESTONES

TECHNICAL TRAINING	FOUNDS LONGFOR	BUSINESS GROWTH
Studies engineering at Northwestern Polytechnical University, graduating in 1984.	Sets up own property company in 1993. Four years later, sells first residential project.	By 2018, the company's revenue reaches $17.5 billion with operations in more than 48 cities.

Harvard graduate Seth Goldman left a promising career in politics to undertake a management course at Yale, where he became interested in the beverage industry. A few years later, he teamed up with a former Yale professor to create the company Honest Tea.

MILESTONES

POLITICAL INTEREST
Works on Michael Dukakis's presidential campaign in 1988. Leaves politics to study management at Yale.

FIRST THOUGHTS
Shares his idea for a low-calorie drink with Nalebuff, who had attended a tea auction in India, in 1997.

LAUNCHES BUSINESS
Cofounds company with Nalebuff—who gives it the name Honest Tea—in 1998. Distributes the tea himself.

MAKES MILLIONS
Sells 40 percent of Honest Tea to Coca-Cola in 2011. Invests in meat substitute company Beyond Meat.

Seth Goldman was born in 1965 and grew up in Massachusetts. He studied government affairs at Harvard University, and, after being involved in politics for a few years, he attended the Yale School of Management in 1995. Goldman's idea for a low-calorie beverage first came about while he was working on a case study of the beverage industry at Yale; he saw there were many types of sugary drinks and bottled water on the market, but nothing in between. After a run in New York's Central Park, Goldman could not find a suitable drink to buy. As a consequence, in 1998, he cofounded the beverage company Honest Tea with Barry Nalebuff, one of his professors at Yale, initially producing organic, not-too-sweet, bottled teas. In 2011, Coca-Cola bought 40 percent of the company for $43 million.

In 2015, Goldman became executive chair of Beyond Meat, a producer of plant-based meat substitutes. He stepped down as "TeaEO" of Honest Tea at the end of 2019 to pursue his interest in environmental activism and climate change.

SETH GOLDMAN

PETER THIEL

One of software entrepreneur Peter Thiel's early investments was an expensive failure, but he learned from the experience and went on to establish PayPal as the first and most successful digital money transfer service. He famously invested in social networking start-up Facebook, making millions when he sold his shares.

Although he was born in Germany, most of Peter Andreas Thiel's early years were divided between the US and southern Africa. He was a bright student, graduating in philosophy from Stanford University, California, in 1989, and then gaining a law degree at Stanford Law School three years later. In his 20s, he worked as a judicial clerk, a securities lawyer, and a speechwriter for politicians but found none of these jobs fulfilling. In the mid-1990s, he moved to the Bay area of California, determined to go it alone.

With financial support from his family and friends, Thiel raised $1 million and in 1996 founded Thiel Capital Management (TCM) as a vehicle to invest in start-up businesses. TCM was a venture capital project, designed to take on the risk of financing tech-based start-up businesses with the potential for high growth but also with an above-average risk of failure. It was no overnight success; the company lost $100,000 after investing in a web-based calendar project put forward by one of Thiel's friend's, which failed.

Confinity and PayPal
Thiel was not easily deterred. In September 1998, he cofounded Confinity (a wordplay on "confidence" and "infinity") with graduates Max Levchin, Ken Howery, and Luke Nosek, whose average age was 21. Aged 30, Thiel was the veteran of the quartet and helped fund the start-up. The aim of Confinity was to develop software that allowed the digital transfer of money, and it proved to be phenomenally successful. In mid-1999, Confinity launched PayPal—a product that enabled users to send money to each other via pagers and cell phones. Confinity had convinced other companies that it was a good investment. At the launch party, Nokia Ventures used the PayPal software to

"Today's 'best practices' lead to dead ends; the best paths are new and untried."

Peter Thiel, 2014

249

"[PayPal] will become one day just like your wallet."

Peter Thiel, 1999

send $3 million of venture funding to Confinity through Thiel's PalmPilot (a handheld device that was at the cutting edge of technology at the time). In 2000, Confinity merged with online bank X.com and investment continued.

Within five months of its launch, PayPal had one million customers, and a year later, the service was available in 26 countries. During 2001, an average of 20,000 new customers signed up daily. PayPal was launched as a public company in

PAYPAL

FACEBOOK

PALANTIR TECHNOLOGIES

CLARIUM CAPITAL

FOUNDERS FUND

February 2002. Its shares sold initially for $13 each, but by the close of trading, they were changing hands for $20 and the business was valued at $800 million. Just five months later, Thiel sold the ever-expanding PayPal to eBay for $1.5 billion, and by 2015, PayPal was valued at a staggering $50.8 billion.

New ventures

After his direct involvement with PayPal ended, Thiel helped finance the new Facebook social networking service in 2004. His $500,000 investment bought him a 10.2 percent share in the business. Eight years later, he sold most of his shares, making a handsome profit.

Thiel has also invested in other companies, including Clarium Capital—a global hedge fund that made millions speculating on the rise and fall of the dollar—and Palantir Technologies—a private software company that specializes in big data analysis, including counterterrorism and anti-fraud analytics. Several of Thiel's former PayPal colleagues have also gone on to successfully invest in other start-up companies, leading some to refer to Thiel as the "don of the PayPal mafia." In 2005, Thiel joined forces with ex-PayPal coworkers Ken Howery and Luke Nosek to establish the venture capital firm Founders Fund. Thiel's investment business has continued to thrive, and he is considered to be one of the world's top technology investors.

Funding the future

Thiel set up The Thiel Foundation in 2006, a philanthropic organization that has allocated grants to a range of cutting-edge projects, including artificial intelligence and antiaging research. Through its Thiel Fellowship, established in 2011, it also funds young entrepreneurs who want to start their own businesses rather than go to college. In 2014, Thiel coauthored the book *Zero to One*, based on a lecture he gave at Stanford University about computer history, start-ups, and the future of technology.

WAS **RANKED A**
TOP-10
UNDER-13
CHESS
PLAYER
IN THE US

NAMED **6**
OF HIS COMPANIES
AFTER **PEOPLE**
OR **PLACES**
IN *THE LORD OF THE RINGS*

PATRICK AND JOHN **COLLISON**

In building their software company Stripe, Irish brothers Patrick and John Collison facilitated businesses to talk directly with banking systems.

Patrick (1988–) enrolled at the Massachusetts Institute of Technology in 2006 to study math. He did not finish his course but instead teamed up with John (1990–) to create software company Auctomatic that same year. Two years later, after selling this for $5 million, they created software that enabled businesses to plug in to websites and apps to instantly connect with credit card and banking systems. Marketed through their company Stripe, this made online financial transactions quicker and easier and particularly helped start-up companies. By 2018, more than 100,000 businesses were using the product.

PIERRE OMIDYAR

US entrepreneur Pierre Omidyar changed e-commerce forever when his experimental online auction service quickly grew into the world's largest digital marketplace: eBay. Creating a platform and a community for people to buy and sell products directly, his company fueled the success of individual businesses as well as his own.

When Pierre Morad Omidyar was six, his Iranian parents moved from Paris, France, to Baltimore, Maryland. He developed an interest in computer coding while at school and wrote his first program at the age of 14. After graduating with a degree in computer science, in 1991, he set up a software company called Ink Development Corporation with three friends. Omidyar added an e-commerce shop to the company's website, which proved so successful that Microsoft bought the business, renamed eShop, in 1996.

Intrigued by the possibilities offered by e-commerce, Omidyar began to develop code to build an online marketplace where people could buy and sell their own items. Over the Labor Day public holiday in 1995, he added a page to his personal website offering an online service called AuctionWeb. The site quickly took off, with customers selling a range of collectibles and household items. By charging sellers between 25 cents and $2 for posting their items online, and taking a small percentage of each sale, Omidyar soon began accruing more money than his salary at internet phone company General Magic.

The digital marketplace he had set up aided both sellers and buyers—who could give feedback by assigning positive or negative ratings to one another—and also provided him with income every time a transaction took place. Within nine months, AuctionWeb was so successful that Omidyar gave up his day job to focus on the business, acquiring an office in San Jose, California, in 1996. In 1997, Omidyar moved the auction site to a new platform called eBay.

"Everyone is **born equally capable** but **lacks equal opportunity.**"

Pierre Omidyar, 2011

MILESTONES

STARTS PROGRAMMING
In ninth grade in 1981, writes his first computer program to catalog books in his school library.

FINISHES STUDIES
Graduates from Tufts University, Massachusetts, in 1988 with a computer science degree.

STARTS AUCTION SITE
Develops the code for AuctionWeb in 1995—an online marketplace that will become eBay.

PUBLIC OFFERING
Floats eBay on the New York Stock Exchange in 1998; share prices almost triple within 24 hours.

INNOVATES IN GIVING
With his wife, Pam, establishes philanthropic investment firm Omidyar Network in 2004.

253

He had wanted to name the site after Echo Bay in Nevada, but that domain name was already taken.

By mid-1997, eBay was hosting up to 800,000 auctions a day; a year later, it had 2.1 million registered customers and annual revenues of $750 million. Realizing his strengths lay more in innovation than in management, Omidyar appointed skilled businesswoman Meg Whitman as chief executive in 1998; during

Omidyar recruited business expert Meg Whitman in 1998 to help him grow the business. She increased eBay's revenue from $4 million to $8 billion over 10 years.

her 10-year tenure, the company grew exponentially. On September 24, 1998, eBay went public. The initial public offering was a phenomenal success—shares were expected to trade for $18 but reached $53.50 within 24 hours.

Despite the scale of the company's growth, it maintained a strong ethos of customer care. In 1999, a 22-hour

eBaY
Your Personal Trading Community

...tions every day,

24 ho...

Se...

eBay is the *biggest* trading place anywhere in the world

Collect

service interruption threatened to destroy eBay's reputation, but this was avoided by individually calling the site's top 10,000 sellers to apologize for the problem.

Over the next decade, eBay diversified and expanded its business, adding a car marketplace, a website advertising rental housing, the Gumtree classified listing site, and companies PayPal, Skype, and StubHub to its portfolio. While Omidyar remained eBay's majority shareholder, he began to focus on philanthropy and a range of new online media interests.

Market philanthropy
Seeing that eBay had enabled millions of people to set up their own thriving businesses, Omidyar considered this model might be transferrable to the philanthropic sector. In 2004, he and his wife, Pam, launched the Omidyar Network, pioneering what have become known as "impact investments." Funding for-profit businesses, as well as nonprofit organizations, the foundation has given millions of dollars to help small-scale entrepreneurs and community projects.

What had started as an experiment in online shopping ended up transforming the digital commerce industry. Omidyar's personalized marketplace democratized the process of buying and selling—anyone could profit from auctioning their items. It also took full advantage of the boom in internet usage to create new business opportunities, and trading communities, around the world.

MIKE **LAZARIDIS**

Dropping out of college to set up a computer software company, Mihal "Mike" Lazaridis transformed the personal communications industry when he developed the BlackBerry.

In 1984, Lazaridis (1961–) left his electrical engineering course at the University of Waterloo, Canada, to set up Research in Motion (RIM), a wireless technology company, with his friend Douglas Fregin. By 1999, he had developed the BlackBerry. A two-way pager, it was the first wireless device that could link with company mail systems, giving users access to their emails on the move. By 2003, it had an integrated phone—the first modern smartphone—and millions of users worldwide.

> "I want people to be entrepreneurs ... **because they think they can change the world** ... Not because they think they can make a lot of money."

Pierre Omidyar, 2000

ROBIN LI

Chinese computer scientist and digital entrepreneur Robin Li cofounded Baidu, China's first search engine. Developing pioneering search engine technology, as well as innovative web advertising, he transformed internet usage and access to information, creating one of the most widely used search portals in the world.

MILESTONES

ACADEMIC PROWESS
Improves his life chances by securing a place at China's renowned Peking University in 1988.

EARLY ALGORITHMS
Develops the RankDex algorithm while working at Dow Jones in 1996; this forms the basis of Baidu.

FOUNDS BUSINESS
In 2000, cofounds Baidu, China's first search engine company; by 2004, it has become profitable.

LOOKS TO THE FUTURE
Opens a research facility in Silicon Valley in 2013 to develop artificial intelligence products.

Robin Li Yanhong was the fourth of five children born to factory workers in the city of Yangquan, Shanxi Province. Despite his family's modest circumstances, Li excelled at school, and, with his mother's encouragement, he enrolled at Peking University, graduating in 1991 with a bachelor's degree in information management. He then traveled to the US, where he gained a master's degree in computer science at the State University of New York, Buffalo, in 1994. From this initial platform, Li would rise to become one of the most skilled and innovative internet search engineers in the world.

Early endeavors
Li joined Dow Jones's IDD Information Services Division in 1994, working on search engine algorithms and helping develop a software program for the online edition of *The Wall Street Journal*. During his time there, Li invented RankDex, an algorithm that ranked internet search listings according to how many other websites they linked to. Li's patent for RankDex, filed in 1997, predated the very similar algorithm PageRank, the patent for which was filed in 1998 by the founders of Google, Larry Page and Sergey Brin (see pp.284–289). Li offered his search engine to Dow Jones, but it turned it down; it was this technology that Li would later use to create his own Chinese search engine.

In 1997, Li joined the search engine company Infoseek as a software engineer. He was introduced to John Wu, head of Yahoo!'s search engine team, by Eric Xu, his friend and later business partner. However, Yahoo! at the time did not recognize the commercial potential of search engines and nothing came of

"Entrepreneurship only bears fruit when you plant the seeds at the intersection of passion and ability."

Robin Li, 2017

JACK **DORSEY**

US internet entrepreneur and computer programmer Jack Dorsey cofounded social networking phenomenon Twitter, which revolutionized the way people communicate.

Born and raised in St. Louis, Missouri, Dorsey (1976–) wrote software in his teens that is still used by taxi companies today to organize dispatches. By 2000, he realized that there might be a use for a service that could combine the reach of his dispatch software with instant messaging so that friends could share what they were doing. He cofounded Twitter in 2006; at its peak, it handled over 600 million tweets a day. In 2010, he started a new technology venture, the mobile payment platform Square.

site, which they named Baidu (meaning "countless times"). Their first office was a hotel room near Peking University.

From 2001, they charged advertisers to appear at the top of Baidu search results and also whenever a customer clicked on an advertisement. This increased web traffic and therefore business for advertisers as well as revenue for Baidu. By 2003, Li had also added news and picture search engines to the company.

Meteoric success
Xu left the company in 2004 to start up his own venture capital business, and Li became CEO of Baidu. After receiving billion-dollar takeover offers from Yahoo!,

the meeting. After Disney acquired control of Infoseek in 1998, it began to steer the business away from searches and toward content. Determined to follow his instincts and pursue search technology, Li decided to leave Infoseek and set up his own company with Eric Xu in 1999.

Birth of Baidu
Li set about building a Chinese search engine using the software he had developed while at Dow Jones. With $1.2 million in venture capital seed money from contacts in Silicon Valley, and later funding of $10 million from two tech media companies, Li and Xu returned to Beijing. They licensed their search indexing software to Chinese web companies Sina and Sohu.com. Each time a user ran a query, it generated revenue for the business partners.

Then in January 2000, following a dispute over licensing payments, Li and Xu set up their own search

Microsoft, and Google, on August 5, 2005, Baidu made its initial public share offer on the US stock exchange NASDAQ. When trading closed that day, the company's stock had risen by 354 percent; Li's shares were worth more than $900 million.

Under Li's leadership, Baidu became one of the world's most used websites. Globally recognized as a pioneer in modern search technology, his ability to see the early potential of internet search engines, and then to commercialize the technology as China's digital usage exploded, was key to his success.

Li has continued to tap into this vast new market by adding products for Baidu users, such as access to music files, mapping, discussion forums, and mobile web browsing. Today, he is diversifying into internet TV and artificial intelligence technologies, including self-drive vehicles and voice assistants.

CHOSE THE NAME **BAIDU** FROM AN **800**-YEAR-OLD POEM

BAIDU HAS FILED 2,368 **AI** PATENT APPLICATIONS

NAMED IN *FORBES'* LIST OF MOST **POWERFUL** PEOPLE **3** YEARS IN A ROW

Li has widened Baidu's interests to include artificial intelligence. With plans to eventually build "smart" cities, products already include robotic helpers, self-driving vehicles, the Little Fish voice-controlled home assistant, and the Raven R smart speaker.

259

When electrical engineering graduate Jerry Yang met fellow student David Filo, their mutual interest in cataloging websites led them to found internet portal Yahoo! The entrepreneur then went on to set up AME Cloud Ventures, investing in data-based start-up companies.

JERRY YANG

Born Yang Chi-Yuan in Taipei, Taiwan, in 1968, Jerry Yang moved with his family to the city of San Jose, California, aged 10. He earned a Master's degree in electrical engineering from Stanford University, where he met fellow graduate David Filo. In 1994, while studying for their PhDs, the pair set up a website directory arranged in categories and subcategories and according to specific criteria, in order to record what interested them on the internet. They called it Jerry and David's Guide to the World Wide Web—a name they later changed to Yahoo! They introduced a search engine function in 1995, and it grew rapidly from there. By April 1996, Yahoo! had become a public company and was the internet's most popular gateway. Yang was named one of the world's top 100 innovators under the age of 35. In 2005, Yang oversaw an investment in Chinese conglomerate Alibaba, described by hedge fund founder Eric Jackson as "the best investment an American company ever made in China," and he became Yahoo!'s CEO in 2007. During that same year, he set up the Yahoo! Human Rights Fund.

> "Success doesn't come from a high IQ or innate talent. It takes a **willingness to work hard.**"
>
> **Jerry Yang**, 2009

MILESTONES

LAUNCHES YAHOO!	INVESTS IN ALIBABA	FUNDS START-UPS
Yang and Filo agree on the name Yahoo! and receive nearly $2 million in capital investment in 1995.	Arranges for Yahoo! to buy 40 percent of Chinese e-commerce giant Alibaba in 2005.	Leaves Yahoo! in 2012 to create AME Cloud Ventures. Funds more than 50 tech start-ups.

When the tech company she was working for went bankrupt, Ana Maiques bought it, convinced that the research part of the business had a future. She created the cutting-edge neuroscience technology spin-off Neuroelectrics and became its CEO.

Ana Maiques was born in Valencia, Spain, in 1972. After gaining an MBA in European Economy at London Metropolitan University, Maiques joined the Barcelona-based research division of tech company Starlab. In 2001, Starlab was declared bankrupt. Maiques, her husband—physicist Giulio Ruffini, who was also working there—and another colleague bought the research side of the company, believing that neuroscience technologies offered business potential. In 2011, Maiques set up spin-off company Neuroelectrics to market the research conducted by Starlab into brain health and to provide technology to help treat various neurological problems through affordable brain stimulation devices. One of these devices, which patients can take home and use under supervision, resembles a wired swimming cap. It sends small electrical currents into the brain and is said to help with conditions such as depression, chronic pain, stroke rehabilitation, and sleep disorders. Maiques continues to demonstrate the device at international conferences and science events, and the company has sold it in more than 40 countries.

"**[The] most important thing to learn** is to **never lose sight of why you started** a company."

Ana Maiques, 2019

ANA MAIQUES

Jay-Z's childhood and adolescence were marred by poverty, drugs, and exposure to gang violence. However, he succeeded in escaping the ghetto through his talent for rap, becoming a global hip-hop star. Investing profitably in a number of entertainment and clothing ventures, he later became the world's first billionaire rap artist.

Shawn Corey Carter, or Jay-Z—as he would later be known—grew up in the notoriously violent Marcy Houses housing project in Brooklyn, New York. His father abandoned the family when Jay-Z was 11, leaving his mother, Gloria, to bring up four children. Jay-Z's adolescence was tough, and he became involved with drug gangs, claiming in interviews that he sold crack cocaine, dabbled in gun violence, and was shot at three times. Gloria encouraged her son's love of music by buying him a boom box, after which he began writing lyrics and freestyle rap.

In 1989, he joined local rapper Jaz-O, hoping to escape his impoverished background, and soon adopted the nickname Jay-Z. Unable to get a recording contract, however, Jay-Z had to sell CDs from the back of his car. Determined to succeed, he set up an independent record label, Roc-A-Fella Records, with friends Damon "Dame" Dash and Kareem "Biggs" Burke in 1995. The following year, he released his debut album, *Reasonable Doubt*; although it did not achieve immediate commercial success, it is now considered a hip-hop classic and was named by *Rolling Stone* magazine in its list of 500 Greatest Albums of All Time.

In 1998, *Hard Knock Life (Ghetto Anthem)*, one of the songs on his third album, reached number 15 on the US Billboard chart and was an international hit. The album from which it was taken, *Vol. 2... Hard Knock Life*, was a phenomenal success, selling more than 5 million units in the US alone. It made Jay-Z the

MILESTONES

RECORD LABEL
Cofounds Roc-A-Fella records in 1995. Releases the critically acclaimed *Reasonable Doubt* in 1996.

CHART-TOPPER
Achieves multimillion global sales with his third album, *Vol. 2... Hard Knock Life*, in 1998.

BROADENS INVESTMENTS
Cofounds Rocawear in 1999. Invests in other industries, including beauty, sports, beverages, and property.

WEDS BEYONCÉ
Marries recording artist Beyoncé in 2008. They form one of the most successful partnerships in music.

MAJOR SUCCESS
Inducted into the Songwriters Hall of Fame in 2017. Becomes the first billionaire rapper in 2019.

"**Rosa Parks sat** so that Martin Luther King could walk. **Martin Luther King walked** so that Obama could run. **Obama's running so we all can fly.**"

Jay-Z, 2008

BANG **SI-HYUK**

South Korean Bang Si-hyuk was discouraged by his parents from making a career in music because it was too risky. Ignoring their advice, he spectacularly proven them wrong.

"Hitman" Bang (1972–), as he is known professionally, worked as a composer, arranger, and music producer for JYP Entertainment before founding his own company, Big Hit Entertainment, in 2005. Si-hyuk's stable of artists includes globally successful Korean boy bands BTS and TXT. Not content with being just a record executive, "Hitman" continues to write and arrange songs, including six on BTS's critically acclaimed 2016 album *Wings*. By 2019, he had 16 industry awards to his name.

SET UP THE SHAWN CARTER FOUNDATION IN 2003 TO PROMOTE FURTHER EDUCATION

A 22-TIME GRAMMY AWARD WINNER

---

biggest name in hip-hop and very wealthy, and kick-started a succession of hit singles and albums.

In 2003, Jay-Z took a three-year break from recording and used his business acumen and knowledge of the music world to focus on other projects. He sold Roc-A-Fella Records to American record label Def Jam and then, in 2008, signed a contract with gig and festival promoter Live Nation worth $150 million; nine years later, this relationship was renewed, with the deal now worth $200 million for Jay-Z over 10 years.

Branching out

Jay-Z invested his wealth in a variety of music, clothing, and sports projects that were of personal interest to him, most of which also became moneymakers. Crucially, he chose to build his own brands rather than to promote someone else's. The first was the Rocawear urban clothing brand, which he established with fellow rapper Dame in 1999; he sold it to the Iconix Brand Group for $204 million eight years later, by which time it had annual sales of $700 million.

In 2003, Jay-Z opened the first of a chain of 40/40 Clubs in New York City; these featured live music and sports-themed memorabilia. A big fan of baseball and basketball, he invested in the New Jersey Nets basketball club in 2004 and was part of the investment group that moved them back to his native borough in 2012, renaming them the Brooklyn Nets. He later sold his stake to found Roc Nation Sports, an agency that represents the interests of sportsmen and -women. Then in 2014, his company acquired the top-selling champagne brand Armand de Brignac.

As part of his philanthropic ventures, he has helped send supplies to Hurricane Maria survivors in Puerto Rico, allegedly paid bail for many jailed Black Lives Matter activists in Baltimore, and helped finance a project to reunite incarcerated men with their children on Father's Day.

Jay-Z turned to rap music as a way to get out of the ghetto. His business acumen has helped him invest successfully in other areas, such as nightclubs, fashion, and sports.

ROC NATION

ROCAWEAR

40/40 CLUB

ROC-A-FELLA
RECORDS

Technology pioneer, engineer, and philanthropist Elon Musk is best known for heading the electric car manufacturer Tesla. His diverse entrepreneurial successes also include cofounding web maps company Zip2, the internet payment system PayPal, and aerospace company SpaceX, which launched a landmark commercial spacecraft in 2012.

MILESTONES

SEIZES ON INTERNET
In 1995 quits Stanford PhD course to grasp an internet opportunity; founds Zip2 with his brother.

INVESTS IN SPACE
Founds SpaceX in 2002 and wins a NASA contract to supply the International Space Station with cargo.

GIVES TO CHARITY
Sets up the Musk Foundation with his brother in 2002 to fund renewable energy research.

CONTROLS TESLA
In 2014 becomes CEO of Tesla, aiming to accelerate the world's transition to sustainable energy.

Born in South Africa in 1971, Elon Reeve Musk showed a keen interest in computers from childhood. He lived with his father from the age of nine, and had developed and sold his first video game by age 12. In 1989, Musk left Pretoria to attend college in Canada. He went on to study at Stanford University but left when he spotted a great opportunity to set up in business.

It was 1995 and California was abuzz with news about the burgeoning internet. With his brother, Kimbal, Musk started Zip2, one of the first internet map and web direction services, which helped print media such as *The New York Times* get online. Four years later, the brothers sold Zip2 to Compaq, making them multimillionaires.

Investing in ideas
Musk's next business venture with his brother was in online financial services. Using the money made from Zip2, they set up internet payment company X.com. This went on to become PayPal, which was acquired by eBay in 2002. Musk, who had owned 11 percent of the company, was now a billionaire.

Space discovery was Musk's next idea. In 2002, he cofounded aerospace company Space Exploration Technologies (SpaceX), which attracted world attention because of its significant breakthroughs. These included developing

Musk has overseen the development of all products at Tesla, including a network of fast-charging stations introduced from 2012.

ELON

MUSK

1971–

Commercial spacecraft are seen orbiting Earth in these 3-D illustrations. Musk is pioneering the development of fully and rapidly reusable rockets and spacecraft to reduce the cost of space travel.

innovative rocket engines and, in 2012, operating the first commercial spacecraft to deliver cargo to and from the International Space Station. Interested in the prospect of creating a self-sustaining community on Mars, and the launch of space tourism, Musk has continued to oversee the development of new spacecraft in his roles as lead designer and CEO.

Initially as an offshoot of SpaceX, Musk founded The Boring Company in 2016. Combining fast, affordable tunneling technology with an all-electric public transportation system, Musk aims to improve travel between and within cities.

Taking over Tesla

A true polymath, Musk has also become involved in companies associated with sustainable energy. Tesla Motors was

MARC **BENIOFF**

American technology pioneer and leading philanthropist Marc Benioff changed the way we access and use software when he founded Salesforce, his cloud computing company.

Benioff (1964–) wrote and sold his first software application at the age of 14. He went on to study business administration and then spent 13 years at Oracle, becoming their youngest vice president. In 1999, he founded Salesforce, pioneering cloud computing and software as a service. He has received numerous innovation awards and become a leader in corporate philanthropy, creating the 1-1-1 model—where companies commit 1 percent of product, time, and resources to help communities.

founded in 2003 by Martin Eberhard and Marc Tarpenning with the aim of building and commercializing an all-electric car. In 2004, Musk joined as chairman and major investor. The first Tesla product, the Roadster sports car, was released in 2008. Following collaborations with major car manufacturers, including Daimler and Toyota, Tesla went public in 2010, raising $226 million for the company. In 2016, Tesla acquired SolarCity, the leading provider of solar power systems in the US. This reflected Musk's vision of giving people the means of producing, storing, and using their own energy.

Musk is the CEO and public face of Tesla, overseeing product design and the engineering and manufacture of electric vehicles, battery products, and solar roofs. However, he was forced to step down as chairman for three years in 2018 and pay a $20 million fine, after sending misleading tweets about Tesla funding.

Neural technology

In 2015, Musk established the artificial intelligence (AI) company OpenAI to promote positive developments in the field. His interest in the relationship between the human brain and technology has also been reflected in his involvement

> ## "Failure is an option here. If things are **not failing, you're not innovating** enough."

Elon Musk, 2005

with Neuralink; he cofounded the company in 2017 to develop ultra-high bandwidth brain-machine interfaces that can be implanted in the brain and linked to a computer.

Musk's pioneering work in multiple fields has won him many awards and accolades. In 2019, he was ranked co-first with Jeff Bezos in *Forbes's* list of the world's most innovative leaders. His diverse interests have also been echoed in his charitable giving, which includes funding research into renewable energy, AI, space exploration, and education through the Musk Foundation.

STARTED COMPUTER PROGRAMMING AGED 9 | DONATED 1 MILLION TREES TO CHARITY #TEAMTREES | HAS OVER 6,000 EMPLOYEES AT SPACEX

US businesswoman Sara Blakely created Spanx, innovative body-slimming underwear and shapewear for women. Her brand sells in 65 countries, and she owns her company outright, with no partners, shareholders, or board of directors. The world's youngest female self-made billionaire, she is also known for her philanthropy.

Born in Florida in 1971, Sara Blakely attended Clearwater High School. At the end of each week, her father, a trial lawyer, would ask Sara where she had failed, rather than about her achievements, to help her understand how to learn from failure. Blakely completed a communications degree at Florida State University and, after an unsuccessful application to law school, worked at Walt Disney World for three months in various roles. Her next job was selling fax machines for office supply company Danka. A natural salesperson, Blakely was so successful that she was appointed national sales trainer at the age of 25.

It was while Blakely was getting ready for a party that the idea for Spanx was born. She lacked the right underwear to provide a smooth look underneath her white trousers, and so, after finding a pair of scissors, she cut the feet off her control top tights. She immediately realized that she had created a garment that, when worn beneath clothes, could help women achieve a slimmer appearance. Not only that, her invention allowed her to wear sandals without showing a seamed foot. Blakely knew she was on to something. By day, she continued selling fax machines, and by night, she began researching designs, patents, and trademarks. She started with her first idea of footless hosiery.

Spanx superheroes carry out good deeds on London's Oxford Street in 2010 to promote the launch of Spanx for Men at Selfridges department store.

"Don't be **intimidated** by **what you don't know.**"

Sara Blakely

SARA

BLAKELY

1971–

> **"**Having a mental snapshot of **where you are, where you are going, and what you are moving toward is** incredibly powerful.**"**

Sara Blakely

in 2000. Using $5,000 of her own savings, Blakely eventually found a North Carolina factory willing to manufacture her design.

The Oprah effect

Blakely applied for the patent, designed the logo, and also put forward the name Spanx for her hosiery. The first major order came from the prestigious American department store Neiman Marcus. A consummate salesperson, Blakely gave up her day job and went out selling Spanx to retailers, modeling the hosiery herself. The breakthrough moment came when talk show host Oprah Winfrey listed Spanx as one of her favorite things in 2000, its first year of production. Sales rocketed, and other US department stores,

including Bloomingdales and Saks, were soon stocking Spanx. Later, First Lady Michelle Obama would also endorse the brand.

The Spanx range grew from footless hosiery to bras, underwear, leggings, and a wide range of women's clothing. Blakely famously shunned advertising, not placing any advertisements until 2016. Instead, she worked relentlessly as the face of the brand she had created and has been continually active in making public appearances. In 2004, Blakely took part in the reality television program *Rebel Billionaire*, traveling the world with Virgin Group founder Sir Richard Branson. Branson was so impressed with her entrepreneurialism that he gave her $750,000. Blakely used the money to set up the Sara Blakely Foundation, a philanthropic organization providing scholarships and grants to aspiring female entrepreneurs.

By 2012, just 12 years after Spanx was founded, the company was valued at $1 billion. That same year, Blakely opened her first stand-alone Spanx store in Virginia and graced the cover of *Forbes* magazine as the youngest self-made female billionaire.

Blakely signed the Giving Pledge, started by Bill and Melinda Gates, in 2013 to donate half of her personal wealth to charitable causes.

CATH **KIDSTON**

Catherine Isabel Audrey Kidston is a British designer who founded the eponymous home furnishings retail business Cath Kidston.

Initially working as an interior designer's assistant, Kidston (1958–) opened her first store in London's Holland Park in 1993. She filled it with vintage items, decorative fabrics, and renovated finds from car trunk sales, creating her distinctive concept of "modern vintage." Kidston soon began to design and produce her own prints and household products, the first being a floral-patterned ironing board cover. A mail-order business followed, the number of UK stores grew, and, by 2015, there were more than 200 Cath Kidston stores worldwide. Kidston received an MBE for services to business in 2010.

Sara Blakely attends the launch of Spanx's Haute Contour Collection at Saks Fifth Avenue in New York City in 2009.

FAILED 2
ATTEMPTS AT ENTRANCE
EXAM TO
STUDY **LAW**

CAME **2ND** ON
RICHARD BRANSON'S
REBEL BILLIONAIRE
TV SHOW IN 2004

INVESTED
$5,000
OF HER OWN MONEY TO
KICK-START SPANX

Ma Huateng—often known as "Pony Ma"—cofounded the successful software company Tencent in 1998. With his passion for computer software and talent for spotting opportunities in the growing Chinese online market, Ma helped turn Tencent into one of the biggest internet conglomerates in the world.

MILESTONES

FOUNDING FRIENDS
Cofounds with friends the software company Tencent in 1998; becomes CEO, despite natural shyness.

INSTANT MESSAGING
Unveils messaging service OICQ (later QQ) in China in 1999. It gains immediate popularity.

ONLINE GAMING BOOM
Launches Tencent Games in 2003. By 2019, it is the largest online gaming company in the world.

STARTS APP
Presides over the launch of WeChat messaging service in 2011, which has over 1 billion users by 2018.

Born in Chaoyang, in the southern Chinese province of Guangdong, Ma Huateng moved to Shenzhen, near Hong Kong, when his father found work there as a port manager. As a child, he had a keen interest in science, which he channeled into computing, graduating with a degree in computer science from Shenzhen University in 1993.

After graduation, Ma took a job at telecoms company China Motion Telecom Development, creating software for pagers. Although he was working in the field he loved, he was earning less than $200 a month, so he moved to a competitor and began to harbor hopes of establishing his own company. At the time, only around one in 100 people in China had a computer, but Ma recognized the potential of the imminent digital revolution. Seeing that there were great opportunities for those who had ideas and were prepared to finance them, Ma, along with four former university classmates, founded software company Tencent in 1998.

Tencent takes off
A couple of years earlier, Ma had attended an event to publicize ICQ—the world's first personal computer-based instant messaging service. Determined to recreate this in China, he launched Tencent's version, the instant messaging service OICQ, in February 1999. A lawsuit brought by American giant AOL, which owned ICQ, quickly followed, but Ma renamed his product QQ, and it proved an instant hit with the Chinese public. By the end of 1999, the service had more than 1 million registered users. Realizing that cell phone use was

"Try bravely, without hesitation."

Ma Huateng

274

MA
HUATENG

1971–

their interest. Online and mobile gaming, social networking, e-commerce, and entertainment services were added over the next 10 years, with the aim of making the Tencent portal an integral part of everyday life. In 2011, this approach culminated in the launch of the app WeChat. Swiftly becoming one of the most popular instant messaging services in the world, it offered chat and mobile payment facilities, as well as social media functions, allowing users to fulfill all their daily digital needs through a single application.

Ma's success has been based on his expert understanding of these user needs and his ability to respond quickly to a changing digital landscape with relevant services. Focusing on product quality and design, he has used internal competition and a young, technology-savvy workforce to fuel innovation, and is renowned for his "10/100/1,000" rule—whereby product managers

increasing exponentially, Ma expanded QQ's service to provide a mobile messaging platform in 2001. Three years later, with profits soaring, he floated Tencent on the Hong Kong stock exchange, raising $200 million.

As internet use exploded worldwide, Ma began to supply Tencent's QQ users with a growing range of products to keep

Ma Huateng's launch of a range of successful mobile apps capitalized on Chinese consumers' preference for using their smartphones rather than computers as a means of accessing internet services.

"A service starts with the **satisfaction and needs of its users** in mind and is defined by those two things."

Ma Huateng

must run 10 end-user surveys, read 100 users' blogs, and collect feedback from 1,000 people on their user experience each month.

Knowing what people want, and then being able to deliver these services via cell phone, has allowed Ma to dominate the digital market and become one of China's most influential tech developers and industry leaders. With ambitions to move into artificial intelligence, robotics, and space technology, he is looking to continually expand Tencent's products and reach globally and beyond.

AllPay

QQ Music

Tencent Games

WeChat

EARNED JUST
$176
PER MONTH
IN HIS
FIRST JOB

SET UP
TENCENT AGED
27

DONATED
SHARES
WORTH
$2
BILLION
TO CHARITY
IN 2016

"WEALTH WON'T GIVE YOU SATISFACTION; CREATING A GOOD PRODUCT THAT'S WELL RECEIVED BY USERS IS WHAT MATTERS MOST."

Ma Huateng
Facebook post, October 2019

Ma Huateng has expanded Tencent's influence and product lines by acquiring stakes in companies with related interests. These include artificial intelligence (AI) specialists BTech Robotics, which produces humanoid robots. Tencent provided funding of $120 million for the company in 2018. ▶

Australian businesswoman Abigail Forsyth is the cofounder and managing director of KeepCup—the world's first barista-standard reusable cup. Her tireless campaign to eliminate single-use cups has helped transform consumer habits across the globe.

Born in Scotland in 1971, Abigail Forsyth has spent most of her life in Melbourne, Australia. Her entrepreneurial instincts were first sparked when, aged 11, she raised the money for a pair of roller skates by selling homemade sandwiches in the office park where her father worked. Forsyth later studied a combined law and arts degree at the University of Melbourne. While practicing as a solicitor, she volunteered at a pro bono legal center, giving legal advice to refugees and immigrants. However, her natural flair for business and creativity propelled her to take a bold leap and leave law to pursue her own interests.

Starting afresh

In 1998, Forsyth and her brother Jamie launched Bluebag, a health-concept café, based in Melbourne, specializing in fresh, seasonal food along with high-quality coffees. The Forsyths turned Bluebag into a thriving business, opening six shops across Melbourne as well as a linked catering company. Yet as the operation grew, so did the waste it generated—the single-use, polyethylene-lined cups in which Bluebag's coffee was dispensed were not recyclable, resulting in thousands of cups being sent to landfill each week.

Forsyth sought reusable alternatives, but the range available was designed for US-style filter coffee, would not fit under espresso machines easily, and had unappealing designs. Forsyth knew that she had only one option—to design and manufacture her own reusable cups.

Groundbreaking product

In partnership with her brother Jamie, Forsyth went on a mission to reduce the landfill impact of their business. Getting support was not easy—one designer even told her it was the "stupidest idea ever"—yet she persisted with her goal. In 2007, she and Jamie set up KeepCup and spent two years developing a cup

"Many small acts make a phenomenal difference."

Abigail Forsyth, 2019

FORSYTH

design that would work for baristas and coffee drinkers alike—one that was environmentally sustainable, practical, and attractive.

In June 2009, with its stylish, tactile, and brightly colored designs, KeepCup was launched at the Melbourne Design Market. In just six hours, 1,000 KeepCups had been sold. It was the combination of a great product design and a clear business purpose that set KeepCup apart. The product is part of a campaign to reduce single-use plastics and the

"We are all about **local manufacture,** putting ourselves in the community and **reducing the environmental footprint** of the business."

Abigail Forsyth, 2018

IN 2017, **LLOYDS BANK GROUP** REPORTED SAVING

43,489 CUPS

FROM LANDFILL DUE TO **KEEPCUP INITIATIVE**

USING A **KEEPCUP**
24 TIMES

OFFSETS THE EMISSIONS AND ENERGY
NEEDED TO **MANUFACTURE THE CUP**

Forsyth has estimated that, since its launch in 2009, KeepCup has saved 3.5 billion disposable cups from going to waste.

environmental damage of convenience behavior. Forsyth also ran a successful campaign to persuade coffee outlets to sell the product themselves, greatly increasing the cups' distribution network and also the brand's presence.

Changing the world

In 2010, the Forsyths sold Bluebag to focus on KeepCup. The sole owner of the company since 2014, Abigail Forsyth keeps its carbon footprint as low as possible, opting to manufacture products locally where volumes allow and where the manufacturing capacity exists. KeepCups are hand-assembled in Australia, the UK, and the US for local markets. More than 10 million KeepCups had been sold in 65 countries by 2019, saving the production and waste of billions of disposable cups. While maintaining sustainability as a core business principle, rather than cutting corners to increase profit margins, in less than 10 years, Forsyth had succeeded in securing an annual turnover of more than $15 million.

In 2015, she launched KeepCup Reuse HQ, an online platform to help users measure their environmental impact. Forsyth has received global acclaim for her work, recognizing both her financial and environmental successes.

The son of two computer programming experts, American internet entrepreneur Larry Page cofounded the world-leading search engine Google with Sergey Brin while they were both students. The site immediately transformed access to information on the web.

MILESTONES

MEETS SERGEY BRIN
Enrolls in PhD in computer science in 1995; meets Sergey Brin on his first visit to Stanford campus.

DEVELOPS PAGERANK
Creates website ranking algorithm in 1996, which becomes the basis of the Google search engine.

ESTABLISHES GOOGLE
Incorporates Google.com in 1998, moving into its first office—a garage in Menlo Park, California.

GLOBAL ENTERPRISE
Announces the creation of the holding company Alphabet in 2015 to control Google's diverse portfolio.

Lawrence Edward Page spent his childhood surrounded by computers. Born in Michigan in 1973, his father was a computer science professor and his mother was a computer programming instructor. Technology magazines and science books were strewn around his home, and, with the encouragement of his older brother, the young Page often took household goods apart to see how they worked. He was also keen on music, studying the flute, saxophone, and composition, later claiming that music inspired his obsession with timing and speed in computing. In 1995, Page enrolled in a PhD program in computer science at Stanford University, where he met fellow student Sergey Brin. The two went on to develop the search engine Google as part of Page's PhD research project.

Page's fascination with technological advances has continued through his involvement with "flying car" start-ups Kitty Hawk and Opener, and a space exploration venture that aims to mine valuable resources from asteroids.

LARRY PAGE

American computer scientist and mathematician Sergey Brin cocreated Google while studying for a PhD at Stanford University. The search engine's ability to rank pages according to popularity revolutionized internet usage and made Brin a billionaire.

Born in Moscow in 1973, Sergey Mikhaylovich Brin left Russia with his family to escape Jewish persecution when he was six years old. His parents, both well educated at Moscow State University, found work in the US—his mother as a researcher at NASA's Goddard Space Flight Center and his father as a professor of mathematics at the University of Maryland. Brin's father encouraged his numerical ability, and Brin graduated with a degree in computer science and mathematics at the young age of 19. In 1993, Brin enrolled for a PhD in computer science at Stanford University and, while participating in an orientation event for new students, met Larry Page. Despite the mutual antipathy between the pair, Brin soon joined Page's project to investigate how websites linked to each other. His mathematical skills helped create a system for ranking the links by importance. By 1996, the pair had created the search engine algorithm to power Google.

Since establishing Google.com in 1998, Brin has concentrated on developing new technologies as part of the company's "moonshot" innovation program, including self-driving cars, smart glasses, sustainable energy sources, and the use of drones for deliveries.

MILESTONES

MOVES TO THE US
In 1979, emigrates with his parents and brother to the US; his father encourages his interest in math.

STUDIES AT STANFORD
Wins National Science Foundation scholarship in 1993 to study at Stanford, where he meets Larry Page.

CRAWLS THE WEB
Helps Page develop system for counting web page links, resulting in the Google search engine in 1998.

LOOKS TO THE FUTURE
Debuts innovative face computer Google Glass in 2012, as part of his ongoing product research.

SERGEY BRIN

"We want **Google** to be the **third half of your brain.**"

Sergey Brin, 2010

Page and Brin added mapping to their Google products in 2004 when they acquired satellite imaging company Keyhole and relaunched it as Google Earth. Their Street View and Google Map functions were introduced in 2005 to aid route planning.

PAGE BUILT AN INKJET PRINTER FROM LEGO WHILE AT COLLEGE

PAGE'S **IDEA** FOR A **SEARCH ENGINE** CAME TO HIM IN A **DREAM**

BRIN AND PAGE PLANNED TO **SELL** GOOGLE FOR **$1 MILLION**

FORBES NAMED BRIN AND PAGE THE JOINT **5TH MOST POWERFUL** PEOPLE IN THE WORLD IN 2009

Brin was already in his second year at Stanford University when he met Page and had been working on a variety of projects, including a movie-rating platform and a tool for converting academic papers into HTML files. Allegedly, they disagreed about everything at first, but within a year, they had formed a firm friendship and research partnership.

Together with another student, Scott Hassan, who left the group before Google was established, they built a search engine named BackRub. This used an algorithm to count and rank the "backlinks" of individual web pages, allowing pages to be listed in order of importance. Other less efficient search engines at the time used keywords to rank sites. Initially, BackRub operated on Stanford's servers, but it quickly took up too much bandwidth.

Soon after, they changed the name to Google and registered it in September 1997. The name originated from the mathematical term for Googol—a number 1 followed by 100 zeros—which referenced their search engine's ability

to access and organize vast amounts of information. Google soon caught the attention of the academic community at Stanford and investors in Silicon Valley.

The cofounder of Sun Microsystems, Andy Bechtolsheim, provided $100,000 of investment in August 1998, and the company Google, Inc., was formed. Page and Brin moved out of Stanford and into their first office—a garage in suburban Menlo Park, California, owned by Susan Wojcicki (one of Google's first employees and later CEO of YouTube).

Nonconformist business

Page and Brin attempted to sell Google to rival search engines in 1999, but, failing to find a buyer, they decided to build the business themselves. With its first server encased in Lego bricks, diverse "doodle" logos, and a "serious without a suit" culture, Google was unconventional from the start.

The company expanded rapidly, moving from its garage in 1999 to an office in Palo Alto and finally to a complex known as Googleplex in Mountain View, California. Around 2000, Page and Brin adopted the slogan "Don't be evil" to

the business—Page as president of products and Brin acting as president of technology.

Over the next decade, the acquisition of companies such as YouTube, Motorola Mobility, Waze, and DeepMind greatly expanded Google's reach. In 2015, Page and Brin announced a new conglomerate, Alphabet, as an umbrella organization for Google's different businesses. Separate ventures such as research lab Google X, biological research company Calico, and home products company Nest became distinct firms under Alphabet. Page was appointed CEO with Brin as president. However, they both stepped down from these roles in 2019, while retaining a large shareholding in the organization.

sum up the company's anti-corporate spirit, but as Google's popularity grew, its investors demanded a stronger management culture, and Google began selling advertisements associated with search keywords. Eric Schmidt was hired as chairman and CEO of Google, and under his leadership, the company began a period of major expansion.

An initial public offering (IPO) of Google shares in August 2004 made Page and Brin billionaires at the age of 31, but they continued to remain closely involved with

Beyond the internet

In addition to their core Google business, developing new technologies to improve daily life has remained a focus for Page and Brin. In 2004, they formed the philanthropic organization Google.org with a start-up fund of $1 billion to focus on the issues of climate change and global poverty. They have also continued to invest in diverse research and development projects, including digitizing books, exploring renewable energy sources, artificial intelligence, and driverless cars.

With Google, Page and Brin created one of the most influential and powerful companies of the digital era, and established the verb "to google" as an everyday term. The initial aim of improving access to information has now expanded into global businesses that touch on every aspect of modern living, from how we communicate and navigate to the way that we manage the heating and lighting of our homes.

Google's Home Mini smart speaker was released in 2017 under its Nest brand.

"OBVIOUSLY EVERYONE WANTS TO BE SUCCESSFUL, BUT I WANT TO BE LOOKED BACK ON AS BEING VERY INNOVATIVE, VERY TRUSTED AND ETHICAL, AND ULTIMATELY MAKING A BIG DIFFERENCE IN THE WORLD."

Sergey Brin
ABC News "Person of the Week" interview, 2004

1973–

MARTHA

LANE FOX

British businesswoman Martha Lane Fox cofounded Europe's largest travel and leisure website, Lastminute.com. She now devotes her time to developing digital projects for the greater good of society and is the founder of Doteveryone, a charity that advocates responsible technology and helps people navigate the digital world.

Daughter of well-known historian and gardening writer Robin Lane Fox, Martha Lane Fox was born in London in 1973. Despite teenage ambitions to join the prison service, her first job after college was with media and telecoms consultants Spectrum Strategy. A work assignment to write a paper on the emerging internet gave her insight into the rapidly changing technology and the new opportunities it offered. While employed at Spectrum, Lane Fox met fellow Oxford graduate Brent Hoberman. After they had both left the company, and Lane Fox was working for a television channel, Hoberman invited her to join his new internet business venture. His concept for Lastminute.com was a simple one—to offer late online deals on anything from flights to concert tickets. It was 1998, the internet was in its infancy, and initially Lane Fox rejected the idea; but Hoberman was persuasive, and Lane Fox resigned from her job.

Rise of Lastminute.com
The pair's first challenge was to raise £600,000 ($994,000) from venture capital and investors. Their next was to encourage travel industry suppliers to work with them. Both young and with no experience in the travel sector, they had to be tenacious, personally calling airlines hundreds of times. To give the company credibility, they assembled a board of travel experts and invited the ex-chairman and CEO of Dutch airline KLM to act as chairman. Despite fears that no one would buy items over the internet, the website took off immediately. In just two years, Lastminute.com had more than 650,000 regular users.

"I have never seen a tool that is as phenomenally empowering as the Internet."

Martha Lane Fox, 2015

By 2000, the company had offices in London, Paris, Munich, and Stockholm, and Lane Fox and Hoberman decided to float it on the stock market. They raised $152 million from across the UK, US, and Europe, just weeks before the dot-com bubble burst. Despite the ensuing stock market crash, the business thrived, with a growing customer base and the shrewd and timely acquisitions of several smaller travel businesses and websites. In 2004, Lane Fox stepped down as the company's managing director, and the following year, the business was sold to Sabre Holdings for $1.06 billion. Aged just 32, and a highly regarded multimillionaire, Lane Fox had everything to look forward to. She was due to join retailer Selfridges but was involved in a serious car accident in Morocco, which left her in the hospital for more than a year. Her determination helped her through the ordeal, but it was a life-changing experience.

She cofounded karaoke company Little Voice in 2005 but became increasingly focused on the social rather than the commercial aspects of technology and the internet.

Inclusive technology

In 2009, Lane Fox moved into a public service role and accepted the post of Digital Champion for the UK. Tasked with increasing internet usage among the general population and taking government services online, she also advised on technological reform and policy. As part of this initiative, she set up the charity Go ON UK in 2012 to help people acquire digital skills. Lane Fox

BELINDA **PARMAR**

British entrepreneur Belinda Parmar is CEO of The Empathy Business and pioneer of the world's first Empathy Index, which rates corporations according to empathy and performance.

Parmar (1974–) set up Lady Geek in 2010 with the aim of getting more women into technology but soon found that it was empathy, not gender, that affected corporate performance. The business changed its name, and Parmar began advising companies on how to increase empathy across all aspects of their operation. She was appointed a Young Global Leader in 2014 by the World Economic Forum and has also founded the Little Miss Geek campaign, which inspires girls to become technology pioneers.

> **"Be ambitious in** terms of **the problems you** are trying to **solve;** make it count.**"**

Martha Lane Fox, 2019

*With **lastminute.com, Lane Fox** cleverly harnessed the immediacy of the internet to bring customers continuously updated last-minute entertainment, travel, and accommodation offers that were not available all in one place elsewhere.*

resigned from her government role in 2013 and became the youngest female member of the House of Lords as the crossbench peer Baroness Lane-Fox of Soho.

In 2015, Lane Fox had the idea for Doteveryone, an organization to campaign for a fairer internet and for responsible technology that benefits everyone. She is a patron of a number of charities and sits on the boards of companies, including Twitter and Chanel.

Lane Fox is unusual among her peers in that over the course of her career, she has changed her focus from being a tech entrepreneur to a social one.

Canadian tech pioneer Garrett Camp founded the on-demand car service Uber to solve the cost and timing issues of using taxis. A serial innovator, he also developed the web-exploring tool StumbleUpon and Expa, a platform to help entrepreneurs start up new companies.

Born to entrepreneurial parents who had established a successful home-building business, Garrett Camp launched his first company while still a student. In 2002, while studying for a master's degree in software engineering at Calgary University, he set up the "discovery engine" StumbleUpon. Designed to help people find websites that were more targeted to their interests, the company attracted investment from Silicon Valley. Relocating to San Francisco in 2006, Camp sold the business to eBay the following year.

In 2008, he came up with an idea for an app that would save his friends' time when traveling across town. This developed into Uber. Launched by Camp and fellow businessman Travis Kalanick (see p.309) in 2009 with just a few cars, Uber quickly expanded across the US and then globally. By 2019, more than 100 million people were using the Uber app to book on-demand taxi services from drivers using their own cars. With experience of his own start-ups to share, and continually looking for new ideas, Camp founded Expa in 2013, an enterprise to assist entrepreneurs in launching new businesses.

> ## "Every time I make a mistake with a company, I write it out and try and figure out why it happened."

Garrett Camp, 2013

MILESTONES

STUDIES TECHNOLOGY
Gains a degree in electrical engineering in 2001, followed by an MSc in software engineering.

SETS UP STUMBLEUPON
Develops the web-discovery tool StumbleUpon in 2002, selling it to eBay in 2007 for $75 million.

FOUNDS UBER
Launches transportation service UberCab in 2009, shortening it to Uber in 2011 to placate taxi operators.

PROMOTES NEW IDEAS
Establishes "start-up studio" Expa in 2013 to help develop, launch, and finance new companies.

Camp acquired JUMP bikes in 2018 to provide bicycles and scooters for rent via the Uber app.

Leader of one of the world's most successful girl groups in the 1990s, Beyoncé Knowles-Carter used her exceptional talent and charisma as an R&B singer, songwriter, and dancer to build a global profile and attract millions of fans. She then established herself as a successful businesswoman and role model for black women around the world.

Growing up in Houston, Texas, in the 1980s, Beyoncé Giselle Knowles-Carter was encouraged by her parents to perform from an early age. At nine, she teamed up with cousin Kelly Rowland and two classmates to form girl group Girls Tyme. Although the girls made it to the TV talent show *Star Search*, they did not win the competition. Beyoncé's father, Matthew, convinced of their genius, gave up his day job to manage them, which proved to be a turning point.

The years of voice and dance practice that followed finally paid off when the group—renamed Destiny's Child and fronted by Beyoncé—won a recording contract with Columbia Records in 1997. Their first, eponymous album was a success, but nothing compared to their second, *The Writing's on the Wall*, which sold six million copies in the US alone and won two Grammy Awards. The track "Bills, Bills, Bills," written by Beyoncé, became the girls' first Billboard number 1. A string of hits and international acclaim followed.

Pursuing success

Beyoncé launched her solo career in 2003 with the album *Dangerously in Love*, on which she is credited as cowriter and coproducer, cementing her reputation as more than just a performer. The album received five Grammy Awards and sold more than 11 million copies globally. Beyoncé had already launched her acting career with a lead role in the 2001 TV film *Carmen: A Hip*

"We all have our purpose; we all have our strengths."

Beyoncé, 2012

MILESTONES

SHOWS EARLY TALENT
In 1990, forms Girls Tyme (later Destiny's Child); the group appear on talent show *Star Search* in 1992.

GETS RECORD DEAL
Destiny's Child signs to Columbia Records in 1997; their first single reaches number 3 in the US charts.

STARTS SOLO CAREER
Releases her first solo album in 2003, which sells more than 300,000 copies in its first week.

MARRIES JAY-Z
In April 2008, gets married to megastar rapper Jay-Z; they are dubbed pop's first billionaire couple.

FEMINIST

Beyoncé's On the Run Tour II in 2018—the second that she co-headlined with husband, Jay-Z—grossed more than $250 million.

Hopera, and the following year she costarred with Mike Myers in the film *Goldmember*. In 2019, she lent her voice to the role of Nala in Disney's *The Lion King* animation.

Other ventures

Music and acting are not the only sources of Beyoncé's wealth. Her association with global brands such as Pepsi, L'Oréal, Samsung, Tommy Hilfiger, and Giorgio Armani has guaranteed her millions. In 2006, wanting to launch her own fashion brand, Beyoncé established the House of Deréon with her mother, Tina. Diversifying further, in 2010, Beyoncé released the first of a line of fragrances.

Heat broke department store Macy's sales record with $75,000 worth of the scent sold in one day when it launched.

Taking control

Determined to be in control of all aspects of her career, Beyoncé set up Parkwood Entertainment in 2010 to produce music, videos, and movies and oversee other projects. Parkwood went on to release three of her albums.

Eager to extend her presence in the fashion industry, Beyoncé worked on a collaboration between Parkwood and Topshop, resulting in athletic streetwear line Ivy Park in 2014. However, following controversy surrounding Topshop boss Philip Green, Parkwood took full control of the business, later launching a line with sportswear company Adidas. In addition to fashion, Beyoncé has business interests in the food industry, investing in a beverage start-up company and a vegan-based meal delivery service.

Beyoncé has been involved in many philanthropic projects. She cofounded the Survivor Foundation in 2005, which provided housing for the victims of Hurricane Katrina and gave financial aid to survivors of the 2010 Haiti earthquake. In 2013, Beyoncé founded BeyGOOD, a fundraising initiative that works with charities to raise awareness of local causes.

THE HIGHEST-PAID BLACK MUSICIAN IN HISTORY

HER PERFUME **HEAT** SOLD 72,000 BOTTLES WITHIN THE **FIRST HOUR** OF LAUNCH

"I CAN NEVER BE SAFE;
I ALWAYS TRY AND GO AGAINST
THE GRAIN. AS SOON AS I
ACCOMPLISH ONE THING,
I JUST SET A HIGHER GOAL.
THAT'S HOW I'VE GOTTEN
TO WHERE I AM."

Beyoncé
From an interview with *Billboard* magazine, 2011

Computer programming prodigy Mark Zuckerberg progressed from coding games for his friends to founding Facebook, now the biggest social media company in the world, at the age of 19. One of the world's youngest self-made billionaires, he has committed a large proportion of his profits to philanthropic causes.

Born in New York in 1984, Mark Elliot Zuckerberg was first taught how to code by his father at age 11. A great student, he excelled at school, while spending his free time creating computer games. Around 12 years old, he developed his first networking software, ZuckNet, which connected his family's computers with those in his father's dental surgery. This was followed during high school by a music system that used artificial intelligence to understand people's listening habits and recommend music. Microsoft and AOL both offered to buy the system and hire Zuckerberg, but he enrolled at Harvard to study psychology and computer science.

The Facebook
At Harvard, Zuckerberg soon earned a reputation for his programming wizardry and began launching sites from his student room. In his second year, he set up Course Match to help students form study groups and select classes based on other students' choices. FaceMash followed—a site that allowed users to rate the attractiveness of students by asking "Who's hotter?" It landed Zuckerberg in trouble, crashing the campus network and eliciting criticism for being offensive. Harvard shut down the site and Zuckerberg apologized, claiming it had been an experiment.

One semester later, in 2004, Zuckerberg set up "The Facebook." Inspired by the student directories often created by private schools, the idea was developed with the help of roommates and fellow students Eduardo Saverin, Andrew McCollum, Dustin Moskovitz, and Chris Hughes. On the night the site went

> "Move fast and break things. **Unless you are breaking stuff,** you are **not moving fast enough.**"

Mark Zuckerberg, 2009

Zuckerberg and Facebook cofounder Chris Hughes set up the site on laptops in their Harvard dorm room in February 2004.

MILESTONES

BEGINS CODING
In 1996 builds first chat service, ZuckNet, for his father's dental practice using Atari BASIC.

STARTS THE FACEBOOK
In February 2004 launches The Facebook; by December it has one million users over four college campuses.

TAKES IT PUBLIC
A public offering (IPO) in 2012 raises $16 billion for Facebook—the largest technology IPO to date.

DIVERSIFIES BUSINESS
Buys Instagram in 2012, followed by WhatsApp and Oculus in 2014, to expand influence into new areas.

MARK ZUCKERBERG

1984–

> "**Helping a billion people connect** is amazing, humbling, and by far the thing **I am most proud of in my life.**"

Mark Zuckerberg

Zuckerberg purchased virtual reality (VR) headset maker Oculus in 2014, with the aim of making VR the next major computing and communications platform.

live, hundreds signed up and within the first month, more than half of the Harvard undergraduate population had registered.

That summer, Zuckerberg rented a house in Silicon Valley, California, to focus on The Facebook (soon changed to just "Facebook") and dropped out of Harvard to build the business. By the end of the year, membership was open to nearly every university in the US and Canada, with students eager to join.

The strength of the idea was clear, and venture capital investment followed. Facebook began to grant access to schools and to employees of Microsoft and Apple, moving the network from its original student base. Zuckerberg turned down numerous offers to buy the company and continued to expand membership.

Global influence

In September 2006, Facebook was opened up to everyone over the age of 13 with a valid email address. It became a global phenomenon, helped by constant new features such as Timeline, the "Like" button, and Facebook Messenger.

In May 2012, Zuckerberg took the company public, launching it on NASDAQ. It was one of the most anticipated initial public offerings in history, and, as the largest shareholder, Zuckerberg became a multibillionaire. His success has not been without controversy, however, in particular

JAN KOUM

Ukranian American computer programmer Jan Koum cofounded WhatsApp, the world's biggest mobile messaging service in 2009. By 2014, he had sold it to Facebook for $19 billion.

Emigrating to California aged 16 from a poor village near Kiev, Koum (1976–) taught himself to program computers using manuals from second-hand bookstores. While at college, he began working for Yahoo!, dropping out to work there full time with Brian Acton, his WhatsApp cofounder. In 2009, Koum bought an iPhone and realized the potential for creating new apps. His idea for a messaging service that synced phone numbers and showed status updates quickly became a global success.

because of the scale of Facebook and its massive influence. Zuckerberg has settled with three Harvard students who claimed he had stolen their idea and has faced accusations of promoting fake news and misusing personal Facebook data in the Cambridge Analytica scandal.

Despite this, his stated aim of fostering world communication has continued to find expression in business terms through company acquisitions such as Instagram and WhatsApp and through philanthropy. Pledging most of his wealth to charity, he cofounded an initiative with his wife, Priscilla Chan, in 2015 to use technology to solve some of the world's most pressing challenges—from eradicating disease to improving education for children.

CREATED **HIS FIRST** COMPUTER PROGRAM AGED **12**

FOUNDED FACEBOOK AGED **19**

PAYS HIMSELF AN **ANNUAL** SALARY OF **$1**

"BUILDING A MISSION AND BUILDING A BUSINESS GO HAND IN HAND. THE PRIMARY THING THAT EXCITES ME IS THE MISSION. BUT WE HAVE ALWAYS HAD A HEALTHY UNDERSTANDING THAT WE NEED TO DO BOTH."

Mark Zuckerberg
Interview at TechCrunch Disrupt conference, 2012

Facebook's long-awaited launch on the NASDAQ stock exchange on May 18, 2012, was broadcast live in Times Square, New York. ▶

1990–

ANNE-MARIE

MAFEIDON

While attending a conference celebrating women in computing, Anne-Marie Imafidon was concerned to learn that the numbers of women entering industries related to science, technology, engineering, and mathematics (STEM) were falling. So the former child mathematics and computer prodigy set up a program to try to reverse the trend.

Anne-Marie Imafidon was born in Britain in 1990 to Nigerian parents and grew up in Walthamstow, London. By the age of 10, she could speak six languages. A year later, she had earned an AS-level in mathematics and become the youngest girl ever to pass an A-level in computer science. At 13, she had won a scholarship to study mathematics at John Hopkins University in Baltimore, Maryland. When she was 20, Imafidon became the youngest person to be awarded a master's degree in mathematics and computer science from the University of Oxford in the UK.

After graduation, Imafidon worked in financial services for global banks such as Goldman Sachs and Deutsche Bank. It was while attending a conference in Baltimore that she first became aware that the number of women involved in STEM was dwindling. Despite girls regularly outperforming boys in STEM subjects at school, less than a quarter of the UK workforce in these fields was female. Determined to do something about it, Imafidon founded social enterprise STEMettes in 2013, funded through corporate partnerships.

STEMettes organizes workshops in the UK and Europe for girls, upward of five years old, and young women, encouraging them in the pursuit of careers in science and technology. Within its first six years of existence, STEMettes had given support to 40,000 young females with free events, exhibitions, and mentoring programs. In 2014, Imafidon set up the Outbox Incubator program, a residential program aimed at teaching people about product development and introducing them to investors. Three years later, she was awarded an MBE for services to young women in the STEM sectors.

"Technology is at the forefront of the economy and women have a vital role to play."

Anne-Marie Imafidon, 2013

DIRECTORY

The rapid growth of the internet over the last three decades has created challenges and opportunities that transcend national borders for entrepreneurs, as well as for social and business networks. The ubiquity of smartphones has made for a global platform that links consumers with products.

LAURA TENISON
(b. 1967)

Welsh-born Laura Tenison founded British retail chain JoJo Maman Bébé in 1993, selling maternity wear and products for children. She initially sold via mail order, then launched a website four years later. By 1999, the company had grown so much that Tenison moved her head office to a warehouse in Wales. The first store opened in London in 2002; the company now has 90 outlets in the UK and Ireland and has recently expanded into the US. Tenison was awarded an MBE in 2003.

SERGEY GALITSKY
(b. 1967)

Born Sergey Arutyunyan in southern Russia, Galitsky adopted his wife's surname after they married. In 1998, during a severe recession in Russia, he opened his first Magnit shop in the city of Krasnodar. Galitsky attracted customers with low prices and grew Magnit into a nationwide chain of supermarkets, convenience stores, and cosmetics retailers. He took the company public in 2006 and two years later founded his own soccer club, FC Krasnodar, building the club a stadium

and state-of-the-art facilities. In 2018, he sold 29.1 percent of his Magnit shares to the state bank VTB for $2.4 billion and stepped down as CEO.

PHIL HUNT
(b. 1967)

After working in advertising and as a music photographer, British-born Phil Hunt began his career as a film producer in the 1990s, focusing on small independent films. In 2002, he cofounded Head Gear, which provides production services and investment funding for a range of media, including film, television, and video games. Hunt cofounded Bankside Films in 2007, a media company that sells, finances, and internationally distributes independent films for production companies. With Hunt as comanaging director, it has invested in over 50 films since 2010.

SAHAR HASHEMI
(b. 1968)

In 1995, Londoner Sahar Hashemi left her career as a corporate solicitor to cofound the coffee bar chain Coffee Republic with her brother. After the first branch opened in London, Hashemi

expanded the business to over 100 outlets across the UK. In 2001, she stepped down from Coffee Republic and in 2005 started a second major business, Skinny Candy, which makes low-fat confectionery. Hashemi was awarded an OBE in 2012 for services to the economy and charity work. She has advised the British government and written two business books.

SEAN COMBS
(b. 1969)

Born in New York, media mogul Sean "Puffy" Combs left college after two years to pursue an internship at Uptown Records, which specialized in hip-hop and R&B. He became vice president, then founded his own label, Bad Boy Entertainment, in 1993. Combs discovered, signed, and produced major artists, including the Notorious B.I.G. In 1997, under the name "Puff Daddy," Combs released the first of six studio albums and the next year launched his own clothing and lifestyle company, Sean John. In 2001, Combs assumed the stage name "P. Diddy" (then dropped the "P" in 2005). He is one of the most influential figures in US entertainment.

MARTIN LORENTZON
(b. 1969)

Swedish-born Martin Lorentzon studied economics and engineering while at college. He moved to California in 1995 to work for the search engine website AltaVista. He met fellow Swede Felix

Hagnö, and in 1999 they founded online advertising company Netstrategy (later TradeDoubler). In 2006, Lorentzon met Daniel Ek, founder of an advertising website, and they cofounded the music streaming service Spotify, launching in 2008. Lorentzon served as chairman of its board of directors until 2016.

SHONDA RHIMES
(b. 1970)

US writer and producer Shonda Rhimes grew up in suburban Chicago. Her first major writing project was a television movie that aired on HBO in 1998. Rhimes then wrote two feature films before returning to television, creating the highly popular medical drama *Grey's Anatomy*, which debuted in 2005. It was produced by Rhimes's own production company, Shondaland, which has since brought numerous successful series to air, including *Scandal* in 2012 and *How to Get Away with Murder* in 2014. In 2017, Rhimes signed a production deal to develop projects for online streaming.

TAMARA HILL-NORTON
(b. 1972)

British self-made businesswoman Tamara Hill-Norton worked as a buyer for retailer Knickerbox but was made redundant in 1997. She cofounded Sweaty Betty with her husband, making and selling women's exercise clothing. The first Sweaty Betty store opened in London in 1998, launching a range of attractive activewear for women. It gained a huge following and, with Hill-Norton as creative director, has expanded its range of products, all of which are designed and made under its own label. There are now more than 60 Sweaty Betty outlets across the UK and, more recently, within the US.

STEWART BUTTERFIELD
(b. 1973)

Brought up on a commune in Canada, Dharma Jeremy Butterfield changed his name aged 12. Initially a website developer, he founded the photo-sharing website Flickr in 2004. It was bought by Yahoo! the following year, with Butterfield as general manager until 2008. He cofounded Tiny Speck in 2009, which focused on gaming but was renamed Slack in 2014, after the workplace messaging app it launched that year. Slack has been used by over 600,000 organizations to communicate.

KELSEY RAMSDEN
(b. 1976)

After completing an MBA, Canadian Kelsey Ramsden became president of the contracting firm Belvedere Place Development. Under her leadership, it expanded into large civil construction and infrastructure projects across Canada and the Caribbean. She later started a property development and residential management company. After recovering from cervical cancer, Ramsden founded SparkPlay in 2012, a monthly subscription service that provides boxes of toys and educational items to encourage learning and interaction between children and parents. She mentors for the Branson School of Entrepreneurship, started a management consulting agency, and has written a book about her life and experiences in the business world.

TRAVIS KALANICK
(b. 1976)

American Travis Kalanick left college in 1998 to work on Scour, a searching and file-exchanging service he cofounded with classmates. Scour was sold in 2000, and the next year Kalanick cofounded another file-sharing company, RedSwoosh, which sold for $19 million in 2007. With this capital, in 2009 Kalanick co-launched the ride-hailing service Uber, with computer programmer Garrett Camp (see p.294–295). It grew into a global operation, and Kalanick became CEO in 2010 but stepped down in 2017 amidst controversy. In 2019, he sold his remaining Uber shares for $2.5 billion and left the company board.

PIERRE ANDURAND
(b. 1977)

French businessman Pierre Andurand was an oil trader for Goldman Sachs in 2000 before working for the Bank of America from 2002. Andurand later cofounded BlueGold, a hedge fund that launched in 2008. At its peak, BlueGold managed $2.4 billion but closed in 2012 due to declining returns. Andurand then launched Andurand Capital, a hedge fund that specialized in oil and energy investments. He is cofounder of Glory World Series, a martial arts promotion company.

JULIANA ROTICH
(b. 1977)

Born in Kenya, Juliana Rotich studied computer science in the US. She cofounded nonprofit company *Ushahidi* in 2008 in response to Kenya's election crisis. Using web, mobile, and geolocation data, it crowdsourced data about violence and mapped it. Rotich founded BRCK in 2013 to help provide internet connections in areas where power was unreliable, and it is now the largest Wi-Fi provider in sub-Saharan Africa. Rotich continues to develop free open-source software.

OSCAR SALAZAR
(b. 1977)

Born in Mexico, Oscar Salazar earned a PhD in telecommunications at Canada's University of Calgary, where he met computer programmer Garrett Camp (see p.294–295). In 2008, Camp pitched Salazar an idea for a ride-sharing start-up, then called UberCab, that he was setting up with Travis Kalanick. Salazar helped develop the app's prototype and was paid in equity. This proved very profitable when Uber, as it was renamed, launched in 2011 to become a successful global business. After leaving Uber, Salazar invested in and founded several tech companies.

MATT FLANNERY
(b. 1977)

In 2005, US computer programmer Matt Flannery cofounded Kiva, a nonprofit organization, with Jessica Jackley (see p.166). Kiva crowdfunds small loans to people with low incomes, particularly women, business owners, and students. The first loans were repaid in 2005, and Flannery became Kiva's CEO. Kiva is active in more than 80 countries, funding over 1.6 million loans to a value of over $1.3 billion. In 2015, Flannery stepped down at Kiva, and is now CEO of Branch, a bank using smartphone technology to lend money.

BHARGAV SRI PRAKASH
(b. 1977)

As a student in the US, Indian engineer Bhargav Sri Prakash set up his company CADcorporation, which researched automotive engine design. He sold it to General Motors in 2005, then founded Vmerse, which was a gaming platform for universities to recruit students and encourage donations. Sri Prakash sold Vmerse in 2009, and in 2011 set up FriendsLearn, using mobile devices to promote public health. It launched the app Fooya! in 2012, which uses gaming to encourage children to eat healthily and learn about nutrition.

QAIS AL KHONJI
(b. 1978)

Born and raised in Muscat, Oman, Qais Al Khonji was educated in the UK, then worked in banking. In 2010, he started his own business in Oman, Qais United Enterprises Trading, which imported goods from China. He is the founder of Genesis International, an IT company, and also founded Genesis Projects and Investments, which analyzes oil and works with many of Oman's biggest petrochemical corporations. Al Khonji is highly active in the education sector, promoting local projects for young people and helping Omani students to study at colleges abroad.

SHAWN FANNING
(b. 1980)

While still at high school, American computer programmer Shawn Fanning began working on a file-sharing service to download music from the internet. He later dropped out of college to complete the software. Fanning and his friend Sean Parker co-launched the software, called Napster, in June 1999. It gained millions of users but was shut down in 2001 due to legal challenges from the music industry. In 2002, Fanning cofounded Snocap, an online music company, which he left in 2006. He has also cofounded two social networking services, Rupture and Path.com, both of which he sold. In 2012, he reunited with Parker to launch the video chat platform Airtime.com.

HERNÁN BOTBOL
(b. 1981)

Argentinian Hernán Botbol founded his first company, Wiroos Internet Hosting, with his brother and an associate in 2005. The next year, they acquired Taringa!, a social networking website aimed at Latin American users. With Botbol as CEO, Taringa! grew across the Spanish-speaking world to around 30 million registered users. In 2015, Botbol and Taringa! partnered with bitcoin wallet producer Xapo, enabling Taringa! users to earn bitcoin for posting popular content. Known as Taringa! Creators, this system drove advertisement revenue and almost doubled the volume of content being uploaded to the website.

BRIAN CHESKY
(b. 1981)

While studying at the Rhode Island School of Design, American Brian Chesky met fellow student Joe Gebbia. They later shared an apartment in San Francisco and in 2007 rented it out to conference delegates. Their enterprise, named "Airbed and Breakfast," was the foundation of Airbnb, which the pair formally founded in 2008 with another friend, Nathan Blecharczyk. Chesky became CEO of Airbnb, which gained start-up capital from investors and has grown into a global business offering a rental platform to property owners.

JOE GEBBIA
(b. 1981)

Born in Atlanta, American Joe Gebbia is one of the three cofounders of peer-to-peer lodging company Airbnb. After working in publishing, he started the business in San Francisco in 2008 with two friends Brian Chesky and Nathan Blecharczyk. Airbnb expanded globally and now lists properties in nearly 200 countries. Gebbia, still a key part of the company, is head of Samara, Airbnb's in-house product design team, which develops innovative projects. Gebbia has also designed a range of modular furniture that launched in 2017.

NATHAN BLECHARCZYK
(b. 1983)

A computer engineer from Boston, Nathan Blecharczyk created his first IT business while still at high school. He studied at Harvard University while continuing to code and develop websites then, after graduating, worked as a computer engineer. In 2008, Blecharczyk cofounded Airbnb with Brian Chesky and Joe Gebbia and was responsible for coding the company's first website. He played a major role in Airbnb's rapid rise to prominence and success, overseeing the creation of its data science, engineering, and performance marketing teams. In 2017, Blecharczyk became Airbnb's chief strategy officer, a position he still holds, as well as chairman of Airbnb China (also known as Aibiying).

DANIEL EK
(b. 1983)

Born in Sweden, Daniel Ek was a website developer in his teens, leaving university early to concentrate on his growing business. In 2006, he sold his online advertising business, Advertigo, to the Swedish marketing company TradeDoubler. That year, Ek began a legal music streaming service, Spotify, with Martin Lorentzon, cofounder of TradeDoubler. Spotify then launched in 2008, paying royalties to musicians and using advertising to make it free for

users. With Ek as CEO, the company rapidly grew, adding millions of songs to its catalogues, attracting many investors, and going public in 2018.

PAVEL DUROV
(b. 1984)

The son of a Russian academic, Pavel Durov was born in Leningrad (now St. Petersburg). After graduating from college in 2006, Durov founded VKontakte (later VK), a social media and networking website for Russian-speaking users. Working with his brother, Durov grew VK into one of the largest websites in Russia. In 2014, VK was purchased by Mail.ru, a Russian internet company, and Durov later stepped down as CEO. He now runs Telegram, a messaging service that he and his brother set up in 2013.

DAVID KARP
(b. 1986)

Born in New York, American David Karp began computer programming at a young age. He was a web developer for an internet forum, UrbanBaby, and, after its sale in 2006, started a software consultancy. Karp founded a blogging and social networking website called Tumblr, which was launched to the public in 2007. Within five years, it was hosting over 70 million blogs and had around 100 employees. In 2013, Yahoo! purchased Tumblr for $1.1 billion. Karp was the company CEO until 2017.

MICHELLE PHAN
(b. 1987)

Originally from Boston, Michelle Phan grew up in Florida and in 2005 began a personal blog about makeup. She made and published online tutorials,

then set up a YouTube channel in 2007. Her videos have been viewed over one billion times. In 2011, Phan cofounded MyGlam (later ipsy), a subscription service delivering monthly cosmetic samples. She also worked with L'Oreal to create her own line of makeup.

PHIWA NKAMBULE
(b. 1992)

Born in Swaziland (now Eswatini), Phiwa Nkambule started fixing computers in his teens. He moved to South Africa in 2007 and left college in 2014 to found Cybatar, a software company involved in fuel delivery. The year after, Nkambule cofounded Riovic, which uses online solutions to help customers find insurance, lowering the price of premiums through crowdfunding. This enabled many South Africans to buy car, household, or health insurance for the first time. Nkambule has also established an online platform to help students with debt from tuition fees.

CARL KRONIKA
(b. 2000)

In 2014, Carl Kronika, a Danish 14-year-old high school student founded a communications and web solutions agency, Copus. The company, which is based in Odense near Copenhagen, provides public relations services for start-ups, including web design, video production, and also social media campaigns. Copus initially won business by offering work for free to nonprofit organizations. Within a year of founding Copus, Kronika had taken on a partner five years his senior. The firm began to attract larger and more high-profile clients, including the Danish brewing company Carlsberg in 2017. Kronika continued to attend high school while holding the role of Copus's CEO.

INDEX

C

D

ACKNOWLEDGMENTS

Dorling Kindersley would like to thank the following; Dr Rachel Doern for content advice, Jess Cawthra for additional design assistance, Sonia Charbonnier, Andy Hilliard, and Gillian Reid for additional production assistance, and:

Proofreader: Debra Wolter
Indexer: Helen Peters
DTP Designer: Rakesh Kumar
Jackets Editorial Coordinator: Priyanka Sharma
Managing Jackets Editor: Saloni Singh

PICTURE CREDITS

The publisher would like to thank the following for their kind permission to reproduce their photographs:

(Key: a-above; b-below/bottom; c-center; f-far; l-left; r-right; t-top)

1 Alamy Stock Photo: Pictorial Press Ltd. **2-3 Getty Images:** David Paul Morris. **8-9 Alamy Stock Photo:** Interfoto. **10 Getty Images:** DEA / G. Roli / Contributor (Background). **Musei Comunali di Rimini:** Rimini, Museo della Città "Luigi Tonini". **12 Alamy Stock Photo:** World History Archive (clb). **Dreamstime.com:** Roman Egorov (Ribbons); Bernd Schmidt (c). **Getty Images:** DEA / A. Dagli Orti (Florins); Universal History Archive (Crowns); Heritage Images / Hulton Archive (crb). **Musei Comunali di Rimini:** Rimini, Museo della Città "Luigi Tonini" (tc). **13 123RF.com:** Vladimir Yudin / rrraven (tc). **Alamy Stock Photo:** Granger Historical Picture Archive (crb). **14 Alamy Stock Photo:** Classic Image. **15 Alamy Stock Photo:** Interfoto. **16-17 123RF.com:** Marek Uliasz. **17 Alamy Stock Photo:** Dpa Picture Alliance (tr). **19 Alamy Stock Photo:** Artexplorer. **20 Alamy Stock Photo:** GL Archive. **21 Alamy Stock Photo:** Pictorial Press Ltd. **22 Alamy Stock Photo:** Ian Dagnall. **24-25 Library of Congress, Washington, D.C.:** LC-USZC4-7217. **25 Dreamstime.com:** Teewara soontorn / Slalomp (crb). **26 Alamy Stock Photo:** The Artchives. **30 Getty Images:** Apic / Hulton Archive. **32 Alamy Stock Photo:** Science History Images. **33 Alamy Stock Photo:** The Print Collector. **34-35 Alamy Stock Photo:** Prisma Archivo. **35 Getty Images:** Bettmann (tr). **37 Alamy Stock Photo:** The Granger Collection. **38 Alamy Stock Photo:** Niday Picture Library. **39 Library of Congress, Washington, D.C.:** LC-USZC4-4160. **40-41 Alamy Stock Photo:** Unknown. **40 Library of Congress, Washington, D.C.:** LC-USZC4-4160 (tr). **41 Alamy Stock Photo:** Unknown (t). **Getty Images:** Bettmann (tc); Museum of the City of New York / Archive Photos (crb). **42 Library of Congress, Washington, D.C.:** LC-DIG-ppmsca-32620. **43 Library of Congress, Washington, D.C.:** LC-DIG-ppmsca-35586. **44 Alamy Stock Photo:** Granger Historical Picture Archive. **46 Alamy Stock Photo:** Granger Historical Picture Archive. **47 Getty Images:** Fotosearch / Stringer (br); Heritage Images / Hulton Archive (clb). **48 Getty Images:** Popperfoto. **49 Getty Images:** Hulton Deutsch / Corbis Historical. **50 Alamy Stock Photo:** Agefotostock. **51 Alamy Stock Photo:** Science History Images. **52 Getty Images:** Apic / Hulton Archive. **53 Library of Congress, Washington, D.C.:** LC-DIG-det-4a19413. **54-55 Alamy Stock Photo:** History and Art Collection. **54 Dreamstime.com:** Teewara soontorn / Slalomp (tr). **Library of Congress, Washington, D.C.:** LC-USZ62-68497 (cb). **58 Getty Images:** Heritage Images / Hulton Archive. **60 Courtesy Tata Central Archives**. **62 Getty Images:** Transcendental Graphics / Archive Photos. **62-63 Getty Images:** General Photographic Agency / Hulton Archive. **63 Getty Images:** Bettmann. **64 Alamy Stock Photo:** The History Collection (tc). **64-65 Alamy Stock Photo:** Imago History Collection. **67 Getty Images:** Bettmann. **68 Getty Images:** Heritage Images / Hulton Archive. **69 Alamy Stock Photo:** Hi-Story. **70 Getty Images:** Ullstein bild Dtl. (br). **Library of Congress, Washington, D.C.:** LC-DIG-ggbain-26953 (tc). **70-71 Dreamstime.com:** Swisshippo (cb). **71 Getty Images:** ND / Roger Viollet (c); Print Collector / Hulton Archive (crb). **72 Library of Congress, Washington, D.C.:** LC-DIG-ds-13079. **73 Library of Congress, Washington, D.C.:** LC-USZ62-105139. **74 Getty Images:** Bettmann (tc); Welgos / Stringer / Archive Photos (cla); Vintage Images / Archive Photos (clb); Schenectady Museum Association / Corbis Historical (tr). **Library of Congress, Washington, D.C.:** LC-USZ62-98067 (cl). **74-75 Dreamstime.com:** Maryna Kriuchenko (Railroad). **Getty Images:** Hulton Archive / Stringer (Telegraph poles). **75 Getty Images:** Bettmann (tl); Hulton Archive (tc); Science & Society Picture Library / SSPL (fcrb, crb). **76 Getty Images:** Bettmann. **77 Getty Images:** Hulton Archive / Stringer / Archive Photos. **78-79 Getty Images:** Underwood Archives / Contributor / Archive Photos (cb). **Library of Congress, Washington, D.C.:** LC-DIG-det-4a27964. **78 Alamy Stock Photo:** Martin Bennett (cb/Tractor). **Getty Images:** Fotosearch / Stringer / Archive Photos (clb, fclb); Underwood Archives / Contributor / Archive Photos (cb). **Library of Congress, Washington, D.C.:** LC-DIG-hec-28787 (tc). **79 123RF.com:** Kittisak Taramas (tr). **Dreamstime.com:** Roman Belogorodov (br). **Getty Images:** Bettmann (tc); Underwood Archives / Contributor / Archive Photos (bc, fbr). **80 Getty Images:** Bettmann. **82 Alamy Stock Photo:** GL Archive. **83 Alamy Stock Photo:** Science History Images. **84 Alamy Stock Photo:** The History Collection. **85 Getty Images:** adoc-photos / Corbis Historical. **88 Getty Images:** Bill Ray / The LIFE Picture Collection. **90 Library of Congress, Washington, D.C.:** LC-USZ62-25665. **91 Library of Congress, Washington, D.C.:** LC-DIG-ggbain-35656. **92-93 Library of Congress, Washington, D.C.:** LC-DIG-npcc-30671. **92 Getty Images:** Bettmann (tc). **93 Dreamstime.com:** Teewara soontorn / Slalomp (br); **Getty Images:** Francis Miller / Contributor / The LIFE Picture Collection (bc). **94-95 Alamy Stock Photo:** Pictorial Press Ltd. **94 Getty Images:** Lipnitzki / Contributor / Roger Viollet. **96-97 Alamy Stock Photo:** Hugh Threlfall (Chanel pin). **Dreamstime.com:** Molotok007. **96 123RF.com:** Chris Mouyiaris (bc/Coachman). **Dreamstime.com:** Valentyna Chukhlyebova (br); Isselee (bc, bc/Horse). **Getty Images:** Mark Von Holden / Stringer / WireImage (tc). **97 Getty Images:** Lipnitzki / Contributor / Roger Viollet. **99 Getty Images:** Lipnitzki / Contributor / Roger Viollet. **100 Getty Images:** John Kobal Foundation / Moviepix. **101 Getty Images:** John Springer Collection / Corbis Historical. **102 Alamy Stock Photo:** Everett Collection Inc (ca). **Dreamstime.com:** Irochka (c). **Getty Images:** Bettmann (b); Universal History Archive / Universal Images Group (cra). **102-103 Dreamstime.com:** Gl0ck33 (Filmstrip). **Getty Images:** LMPC (c). **103 Library of Congress, Washington, D.C.:** LC-DIG-ds-13079 (tr). **104 Panasonic**. **105 Getty Images:** Bill Ray / The LIFE Picture Collection. **106 123RF.com:** Saranya2908 (l). **Panasonic:** (cl). **107 123RF.com:** Nikola Roglic (ca). **Getty Images:** The Asahi Shimbun (r). **Panasonic:** (cb). **108 Getty Images:** Ullstein bild Dtl. (cb). **109 Getty Images:** Bill Ray / The LIFE Picture Collection. **111 Getty Images:** Mondadori Portfolio. **112 Getty Images:** Bettmann (bl). **Library of Congress, Washington, D.C.:** LC-DIG-highsm-12949 (br). **113 Getty Images:** Bettmann. **115 Getty Images:** Bloomberg (Background); Dinodia Photos / Hulton Archive. **116-117 Alamy Stock Photo:** Andrew Oxley. **116 Getty Images:** Bettmann (cb). **117 Alamy Stock Photo:** Uwe Deffner (tr). **Getty Images:** Howard Sochurek / The LIFE Picture Collection. **Magnum Photos:** (cla). **120 Getty Images:** Steve Dykes / Getty Images Sport. **122 Alamy Stock Photo:** Everett Collection Inc / CSU Archives. **124 123RF.com:** Kittisak Taramas (clb). **124-125 Getty Images:** Terry Fincher / Hulton Archive. **125 Alamy Stock Photo:** Granger Historical Picture Archive (cr). **127 Getty Images:** Ron Galella / Ron Galella Collection. **129 Alamy Stock Photo:** Archive PL. **130-131 Alamy Stock Photo:** The History Collection. **131 Getty Images:** Thomas D. McAvoy / The LIFE Picture Collection. **132 Getty Images:** Mondadori Portfolio (tc). **132-133 Getty Images:** Mondadori Portfolio. **134 Getty Images:** Graham Bezant / Toronto Star. **136 Alamy Stock Photo:** Agefotostock (crb). **Getty Images:** R. Gates / Staff / Archive Photos (br). **137 Getty Images:** Luke Frazza / AFP. **138-139 Alamy Stock Photo:** Ilene MacDonald (b). **Dreamstime.com:** Beata Becla / Acik (c/fruits). **138 123RF.com:** nito500 (Yogurt). **Dreamstime.com:** Yvdavyd (Bagels). **140-141 Getty Images:** Jack Garofalo / Paris Match Archive. **142 Getty Images:** Jack Garofalo / Paris Match Archive (cr). **Rex by Shutterstock:** Neal Ulevich / AP (c). **142-143 Getty Images:** Science & Society Picture Library / SSPL. **143 Dreamstime.com:** Julynx (cra). **Getty Images:** Clodagh Kilcoyne / Getty Images News (crb). **144 Getty Images:** The Washington Post. **145 Getty Images:** Henry Groskinsky / The LIFE Picture Collection. **146 Alamy Stock Photo:** Tom Bible. **147 Getty Images:** Daniel Acker / Bloomberg. **148-149 Rex by Shutterstock:** Ibl. **149 Getty Images:** Jonathan Nackstrand / Stringer / AFP (Background). **150 Alamy Stock Photo:** Roger Tillberg (cr). **Dreamstime.com:** Ifeelstock (tr); Kettaphoto (br). **Getty Images:** Casper Hedberg / Bloomberg (ftr); Don Werner / The Enthusiast Network (c). **151 Alamy Stock Photo:** ALDI SÜD / Dpa Picture Alliance (cra). **152 Getty Images:** Sven Nackstrand / Staff / AFP. **153 Alamy Stock Photo:** Marka. **154 Alamy Stock Photo:** Independent Photo Agency Srl. **155 Getty Images:** Jean-Claude Deutsch / Paris Match Archive. **156 Getty Images:** Steve Dykes / Getty Images Sport. **157 Dreamstime.com:** Ruslan Gilmanshin. **158-159 123RF.com:** Kchung (Shoe box, Shoe box lid); Sihasak Prachum (Stadium). **158 Alamy Stock Photo:** Alexey Panferov (cb, cr); xMarshall (ca/Onitsuka Tiger shoes). **Dreamstime.com:** Sergey Kohl (c/Car). **Getty Images:** Rich Clarkson / Sports Illustrated Classic (fcr); Patrick McMullan (tc); Focus on Sport (crb). **159 Alamy Stock Photo:** xMarshall (clb). **Dreamstime.com:** Pojoslaw (cb). **162 Getty Images:** Steve Granitz / WireImage. **164 Getty Images:** Andrew Harrer / Bloomberg. **165 Getty Images:** Adam Dean / Bloomberg. **167 Getty Images:** Christian Liewig / Corbis Historical. **168 Dreamstime.com:** Ilyach (cl); Teewara soontorn / Slalomp (fclb). **Getty Images:** John van Hasselt / Sygma (crb); Noah Seelam / Stringer / AFP (cb, br). **168-169 123RF.com:** Kolesnikov90 (Palm trees). **Dorling Kindersley:** Amit Pashricha / Avinash Pasricha / (Path). **169 Getty Images:** Chip HIRES / Gamma-Rapho (cb); Viviane Moos / Corbis Historical (clb); Farjana K. Godhuly / Stringer / Afp (crb); Michael Loccisano (tr). **170 Alamy Stock Photo:** Christopher Pillitz. **171 Alamy Stock Photo:** David Pearson. **172 123RF.com:** Martin Spurny (Recycle sign). **Dreamstime.com:** 7xpert (c). **Getty Images:** Georges Gobet / AFP (cla); Edward Wong / South China Morning Post (bc). **173 Dreamstime.com:** Teewara soontorn / Slalomp (cr). **Rex by Shutterstock:** Times Newspapers (crb). **174 123RF.com:** Martin Spurny. **175 Getty Images:** Staff / Mirrorpix. **176 Alamy Stock Photo:** Photo 12. **177 Getty Images:** Terry O'Neill / Iconic Images. **179 Getty Images:** Dickson Lee / South China Morning Post. **180 Alamy Stock Photo:** Angus Lamond. **Dreamstime.com:** Jeremy Swinborne (l). **182 Alamy Stock Photo:** Adrian Sherratt. **184 Alamy Stock Photo:** Razorpix (fcr). **Dorling Kindersley:** Museum of Design in Plastics, Bournemouth Arts University, UK (cr). **Getty Images:** Michael Nagle / Bloomberg (l). **184-185 Dreamstime.com:** Zoya Fedorova. **185 Alamy Stock Photo:** Frankie Angel (c); Hugh Threlfall (cla, tc); Alistair Heap (crb). **Getty Images:** Alex Tai / SOPA Images / LightRocket (cr). **186-187 Getty Images:** Chalkie Davies / Premium Archive. **187 Getty Images:** Fairfax Media Archives (Background). **188 Alamy Stock Photo:** James Jagger (cra); Jan Palmer (cb). **Getty Images:** Simon Dawson / Bloomberg (cla); Chris Ratcliffe / Bloomberg (tc); Chris Jackson (cr); Fairfax Media Archives (crb). **188-189 Dreamstime.com:** creativecommonsstockphotos; Sdbower (Turntable). **Getty Images:** Oli Scarff / Getty Images News (c/Train). **189 Getty Images:** David Paul Morris / Bloomberg (cl). **191 Getty Images:** John Downing / Hulton Archive. **192 Alamy Stock Photo:** Wenn Rights Ltd. **194 Getty Images:** George Osodi / Bloomberg. **195 Getty Images:** Bandeep Singh / The India Today Group. **196 Getty Images:** Daniel Acker / Bloomberg. **198 Dreamstime.com:** Teewara soontorn / Slalomp (cra). **Getty Images:** Jeff Haynes / AFP (clb, ca, cr); Stephen Hilger / Bloomberg (c). **199 Getty Images:** Jeff Haynes / AFP (cl); Neil Rasmus / Patrick McMullan (tr). **200-201 Getty Images:** Steve Granitz / WireImage. **202 Dreamstime.com:** Akkaranant (cla/TV). **Getty Images:** Jamie McCarthy / WireImage (cla, ca). **202-203 Dreamstime.com:** Monkey Business Images. **203 Getty Images:** Jim Spellman (tr). **205 Getty Images:** Andrew Chin. **206 Alamy Stock Photo:** Imaginechina Limited. **207 Alamy Stock Photo:** Imaginechina Limited. **210 Getty Images:** Chesnot. **212-213 Getty Images:** Elsa. **213 Alamy Stock Photo:** Craig Joiner Photography (Background). **214 123RF.com:** Agnieszka Murphy (cl). **Dreamstime.com:** Scott Winer / Rewniwimagery (c). **215 123RF.com:** Sergey Nivens (b). **Alamy Stock Photo:** Dpa Picture Alliance Archive (cla); IndiaPicture (tr). **216 Getty Images:** David Paul Morris. **218 Getty Images:** Phillip Faraone (tc). **218-219 Getty Images:** Apic / Hulton Archive. **219 Getty Images:** Ty Wright / Bloomberg (cl). **221 Getty Images:** Justin Sullivan. **223 Getty Images:** Ron Galella, Ltd. / Ron Galella Collection. **224 Getty Images:** Wei Leng Tay / Bloomberg. **227 Getty Images:** Jim Bennett. **228 Dreamstime.com:** Julynx (clb). **Getty Images:** G Fiume (tc). **231 Alamy Stock Photo:** Imaginechina Limited. **232 Getty Images:** Tibrina Hobson. **234 Getty Images:** Visual China Group. **235 Getty Images:** Fabrice Coffrini / AFP. **236 Dreamstime.com:** 7xpert (cra). **Getty Images:** Wang HE (cb). **236-237 Getty Images:** China Photos. **237 Getty Images:** David M. Benett (tr). **238 Getty Images:** STR / AFP. **240 Getty Images:** Emmanuel Dunand / AFP; Matthew Horwood (Background). **241 Getty Images:** Saul Loeb / AFP. **242 Alamy Stock Photo:** WorldFoto. **243 Getty Images:** Marlene Awaad / Bloomberg. **245 Getty Images:** David Paul Morris / Bloomberg. **246 Alamy Stock Photo:** Imaginechina Limited. **247 Getty Images:** KK Ottesen / The Washington Post. **248 Getty Images:** Noah Berger / Bloomberg. **250 Getty Images:** Digital First Media Group / Bay Area News (tl). **251 Getty Images:** Brian Ach (fcrb); David Paul Morris / Bloomberg (crb). **252 Getty Images:** JB Reed / Bloomberg. **254-255 Getty Images:** James D. Wilson / Liaison Agency / Hulton Archive. **255 Getty Images:** Norm Betts / Bloomberg (tr). **256 Getty Images**. **258 Alamy Stock Photo:** Imaginechina Limited (br). **Getty Images:** Bertrand Rindoff Petroff / French Select (tc). **258-259 Alamy Stock Photo:** Imaginechina Limited (Background). **259 Alamy Stock Photo:** Imaginechina Limited (cb). **Getty Images:** Glenn Chapman / AFP (crb); Gilles Sabrie / Bloomberg (clb); Giulia Marchi / Bloomberg (fcrb). **260 Getty Images:** Drew Angerer. **261 Neuroelectrics:** Daniel Loewe. **262 Getty Images:** Ollie Millington / WireImage. **264 Alamy Stock Photo:** Newscom (tc). **264-265 123RF.com:** Olaf Herschbach (b). **Getty Images:** Ollie Millington / WireImage. **265 Dreamstime.com:** Maksym Yemelyanov (c/Speakers). **266 Alamy Stock Photo:** Allen Creative / Steve Allen. **267 Alamy Stock Photo:** Alex Mateo. **268 Alamy Stock Photo:** Konstantin Shaklein (cl, t). **Getty Images:** Nicholas Kamm / AFP (cb). **270 Getty Images:** Samir Hussein. **271 Getty Images:** Paul Morigi. **272 Getty Images:** Rune Hellestad / Corbis Entertainment (cb). **273 Getty Images:** Joe Kohen / WireImage. **274-275 Getty Images:** Visual China Group. **276-277 Alamy Stock Photo:** Imaginechina Limited. **276 Dreamstime.com:** Mohamed Ahmed Soliman (cr). **Getty Images:** Sean Dempsey / WPA Pool (tc). **277 123RF.com:** Vasilis Ververidis (b). **Alamy Stock Photo:** Imaginechina Limited (ca). **Dreamstime.com:** Ilia Burdun (crb); Teewara soontorn / Slalomp (fcr). **Getty Images:** Rafael Henrique / SOPA Images / LightRocket (cr); Anthony Kwan / Bloomberg (cla). **279 Getty Images:** Qilai Shen / Bloomberg. **281 © KeepCup**. **282 Dreamstime.com:** Dan Bar (Cups). **Getty Images:** Marc Grimwade / WireImage (tc). **283 123RF.com:** Kittisak Taramas (tr). © KeepCup: (cl). **284-285 Getty Images:** James Leynse / Corbis Historical. **286 Alamy Stock Photo:** Gordon Shoosmith (cl). **Getty Images:** Kim Kulish / Corbis Historical (tc). **288 Alamy Stock Photo:** CoinUp (b); Trevor Collens (tc). **290 Alamy Stock Photo:** John Davidson Photos. **292-293 Dreamstime.com:** Scanrail. **292 Getty Images:** Stephen Yang / Bloomberg (cb). **293 123RF.com:** Alhovik (tl/Masks); Jakub Krechowicz / sqback (tl). **Alamy Stock Photo:** M4OS Photos (ca). **Dreamstime.com:** Draghicich (c); MI12nan (crb). **294-295 Getty Images:** Kiyoshi Ota / Bloomberg. **295 Getty Images:** Stefano Montesi / Corbis News (br). **296 Getty Images:** Kevin Mazur. **297 Getty Images:** Larry Busacca / PW18. **298 Dreamstime.com:** Teewara soontorn / Slalomp (bl). **Getty Images:** Jamie McCarthy (tc). **300-301 Getty Images:** Chesnot. **300 Getty Images:** Rick Friedman / Corbis News. **302 Getty Images:** Glenn Chapman / AFP. **303 123RF.com:** Kittisak Taramas (br). **Alamy Stock Photo:** Tobias Hase / Dpa Picture Alliance (tr). **305 Getty Images:** Emmanuel Dunand / AFP. **306 Alamy Stock Photo:** Jeff Gilbert

All other images © Dorling Kindersley
For further information see: www.dkimages.com